TALK
TO THE
ELEPHANT

DESIGN LEARNING FOR BEHAVIOR CHANGE

JULIE DIRKSEN

New Riders

VOICES THAT MATTER™

TALK TO THE ELEPHANT
Design Learning for Behavior Change

Julie Dirksen

New Riders

Find us on the Web at voicesthatmatter.com.
New Riders is an imprint of Peachpit, a division of Pearson Education.
To report errors, please send a note to errata@peachpit.com.

Executive Editor: Laura Norman
Project Editor: Charlotte Kughen
Proofreader: Sarah Kearns
Technical Editor: Paul Chadwick
Compositor: Bronkella Publishing LLC
Indexer: Johnna Vanhoose Dinse
Graphics: tj graham art
Cover Design: Chuti Prasertsith
Interior Design: Danielle Foster

ISBN-13: 978-0-13-807368-8
ISBN-10: 0-13-807368-6

1 2023

CREDITS

PEARSON'S COMMITMENT TO DIVERSITY, EQUITY, AND INCLUSION

Pearson is dedicated to creating bias-free content that reflects the diversity of all learners. We embrace the many dimensions of diversity, including but not limited to race, ethnicity, gender, socioeconomic status, ability, age, sexual orientation, and religious or political beliefs.

Education is a powerful force for equity and change in our world. It has the potential to deliver opportunities that improve lives and enable economic mobility. As we work with authors to create content for every product and service, we acknowledge our responsibility to demonstrate inclusivity and incorporate diverse scholarship so that everyone can achieve their potential through learning. As the world's leading learning company, we have a duty to help drive change and live up to our purpose to help more people create a better life for themselves and to create a better world.

Our ambition is to purposefully contribute to a world where:

- Everyone has an equitable and lifelong opportunity to succeed through learning.
- Our educational products and services are inclusive and represent the rich diversity of learners.
- Our educational content accurately reflects the histories and experiences of the learners we serve.
- Our educational content prompts deeper discussions with learners and motivates them to expand their own learning (and worldview).

While we work hard to present unbiased content, we want to hear from you about any concerns or needs with this Pearson product so that we can investigate and address them.

- Please contact us with concerns about any potential bias at https://www.pearson.com/report-bias.html.

ACKNOWLEDGMENTS

For supporting this book and holding the ship steady as we speak: Laura Norman at Pearson/Peachpit and Charlotte Kughen at The Wordsmithery LLC. I'm sorry I've been giving you gray hair, Charlotte, but thank you so much for all you are doing. Thanks also to the talented team of folks who pulled all the individual graphic and design pieces together to turn them into this book.

For technical editing and invaluable insight: Paul Chadwick from UCL Centre for Behaviour Change. Your input has been invaluable (mistakes are my own), and I so appreciate you agreeing to take this on.

For collaboration, insight, and education: Dustin DiTommaso, the smartest person I know on digital behavior-change interventions, and my favorite workshop collaborator. This book wouldn't exist in this form without all I've learned from you (including your knowledge of the best places to get cocktails in most cities).

For helping wrangle myriad details and being excellent friends and colleagues: Ann Woods and Brian Dusablon.

For providing the models and workshops that did the most to inform this book and my practice: Susan Michie, Lou Atkins, and Robert West and the folks from UCL Centre for Behaviour Change.

For inspiration and making time for interviews: Katrina Mitchell from Picture Impact, Manya Dotson from JHPIEGO, Australia Alexis Cooper and Shelly Chard from Sports Integrity Australia (double thanks, ladies, for your patience and help with technical errors), Dustin (again) and Paul (again), Brian Kaleida from Simcoach Games, Sebastian Bailey from MindGym, Michelle Segar from the University of Michigan, Christian Hunt from Human Risk, Roberta Dombrowski from Learn Mindfully, John Cutler of The Beautiful Mess, and Matt Wallaert from BeSci.io.

For reviewing chapters or advising on case examples or contributing generally: Matt Richter, Mark Lassoff, Jeff Dalto, Susi Miller, Sarah Mercier, and Jim Billings. I'm grateful to know so many smart and kind people.

Also thanks to the Learning Guild folks: Jane Bozarth, David Kelly, and Mark Britz, and also Justin Brusino and the other great people at ATD.

To the Wednesday maker night crew: Heidi Harris Mathews, Tracy Parish, Kristen Hayden Safdie, Judy Katz, and Jane (again) for being indefatigable supporters and sounding boards. You got me through lockdown and more.

Thanks and love to my professional peoples for all the help and advice and community: Bianca Woods, Becca Wilson, Jennifer Solberg, Steve Howard, Sarah (again), Wendy Wickham, Koreen Olbrish Pagano, Trina Rimmer, Maria Andersen, Kevin Thorn, Edmond Manning, Megan Torrance, Diane Elkins, Karl Kapp, Zsolt Olah, Jason Bickle, Ellen Wagner, Connie Malamed, and Emma Weber. And thanks to Tom Kuhlmann—if not for your support for the first book, there might not have been a second book.

To my evidence-to-practice compatriots: Clark Quinn, Will Thalheimer, Jane (again), Patti Shank, and Mirjam Neelen. And to my mentors always—Kathy Sierra and Michael Allen. Also, thanks to Simon Rosser at the University of MN and the other folks on the MINTS project, and the folks at Preventive Medicine LLC for starting me on this road.

To my parents, Roger and Regina, for letting me take over their pool lanai to write on, and for being amazing and supportive always. To Jonathan Dirksen for transcription support and being patient with me, and to Eric and Tess for the love and support.

And to all my best women who I couldn't do without—Lisa Boyd, Kathleen Sullivan, Lori Baker, Michele McKenzie, Tesia Kosmalski, Samantha Bailey, Mags Hanley, Ashley James, and Rebecca Davis. Love to you all.

CONTENTS

PREFACE

So, if you are viewing the preview pages for this book on a website or while you're standing in a bookstore right now, you might be asking yourself if this book is useful for you. That is a fair question.

This book is intended for people who create learning experiences. Specifically, this is for people who are designing or creating or implementing learning experiences that are intended to change behavior.

This could be for just about anything. For example, these experiences could include

- A training program on safety procedures for food service workers
- A tutorial on a financial services website about how customers can save for retirement
- A class to help middle school teachers learn ways to support positive communication traits in their students
- A study skills online course for college students
- A community education class for seniors on maintaining strength and flexibility as they age

You might be noticing that this list is mostly about learning experiences for adults, and you'd be absolutely correct about that. I've been creating learning materials for about 30 years, and pretty much all of the projects I've worked on have been for adult audiences, either in workplace settings or higher education.

Although a lot of what I will discuss in this book could also be relevant for school-age kids, that's not my area of expertise, so I won't comment on how to translate any of this material for those age groups.

WHO IS THIS BOOK NOT SO MUCH FOR?

So, maybe knowing who the book is for has left you wondering who the book is not for. The contents may be helpful for other audiences, but it's *not* really directed at

- **People who are trying to change their own behavior.** I'm sure that many of the strategies discussed in this book are relevant to people who are trying to make changes in their own lives, but that won't be the focus.
- **People who are treating audiences with diagnosed conditions relating to mental or behavioral health.** For example, this book is not intended for therapists working with clients in a mental health setting. Again, some of the strategies may be useful, but this is not my area of expertise, and most of the solutions and strategies discussed have been designed for a general audience.
- **People who are working with kids.** As already mentioned, people who are creating educational materials for school-age children may find some useful ideas but would definitely need to filter it through their own expertise with the age group they work with.

IS THIS BOOK FOR BEHAVIORAL DESIGNERS?

As I'm writing this book, the field of behavioral design is rapidly expanding in organizations. Roles like "behavioral designer" and "behavioral strategist" are popping up in many organizations and consultancies (okay, at the moment, it's mostly consultancies). While I don't have any particular insight into how the field will evolve, I think it's reasonable to suppose that training and instruction will continue to play a role in many behavior-change initiatives. This book is not intended to teach behavioral designers how to do instructional design, but it will have many options they may want to consider when part of their intervention relies on the creation of effective learning materials.

WHAT IS THIS BOOK TRYING TO DO?

Billions of dollars are spent every year on workplace training, and most of it is in service of training the participants to do something differently when they leave the training environment and go back to the workplace.

It's not clear how much of this training is effective in supporting those behavior changes, but I don't think it's controversial to say that we could do better. Over the last dozen years, there has been an abundance of new research happening in the behavioral sciences, but not much of it has made its way into learning and development or higher education.

Additionally, training and education are often part of interventions designed by behavioral scientists, and integrating instructional design with behavioral design can help make those learning experiences more effective.

In this book, I share tools and strategies to help people create learning that supports behavior change. Here's a brief overview of what you'll find in each chapter:

- **Chapter 1, "Talking to the Elephant":** I explain why the book is titled *Talk to the Elephant* and how we need to think about learning design differently when we are trying to help people with complex behavior-change challenges.
- **Chapter 2, "Taking a Systems View":** Often behavior-change efforts require a very narrow focus on the behavior, but too narrow a focus can cause us to miss more systemic causes. In this chapter, I share examples of how to consider both the specific behavior and the broader systems that influence that behavior.
- **Chapter 3, "Moving Along the Change Path":** Change is a process, not an event, and this chapter covers the stages of change and how you can support learners at different points in the change process.
- **Chapter 4, "Communicating Value":** Most learning and development professionals are given the advice that they need to communicate WIFFM (What's In It For Me), but often how we communicate value fails to achieve the desired outcomes. This chapter looks at how the elephant perceives value and how to craft messages to help the learners buy in to a behavior change.
- **Chapter 5, "Understanding Motivation":** This chapter covers some of the most useful models of motivation and how to frame learning experiences to support intrinsic motivation, autonomy, and agency.
- **Chapter 6, "Analyzing Behaviors":** I share how to frame, prioritize, and select behaviors and how to use the Behaviour Change Wheel and COM-B model to analyze a behavior.

- **Chapter 7, "Determining if It's a Training Problem":** Often learning and development people are presented with problems to solve that aren't really training problems. In this chapter, I go through some of the most common issues that often get handed to us as training problems and examine what we can and cannot do for each.
- **Chapter 8, "Mapping to Solutions":** This chapter looks at how you take the COM-B analysis of the behavior and start to map your analysis to different types of behavior-change interventions.
- **Chapter 9, "Using Persuasion and Motivation Techniques":** This chapter looks at examples of behavior-change techniques that are related to persuasion and motivation.
- **Chapter 10, "Using Planning, Practice & Feedback":** This chapter looks at examples of behavior-change techniques that are related to planning, practice, and feedback.
- **Chapter 11, "Using Environmental and Social Support":** This chapter looks at examples of behavior-change techniques that are related to environmental and social support.
- **Chapter 12, "Values and Identity":** This chapter looks at examples of behavior-change techniques that are related to values, identity, and ownership.
- **Chapter 13, "Designing Responsibly":** This chapter looks at the ethical issues involved in behavioral design and at ways to ensure that you are designing as responsibly as possible.
- **Chapter 14, "Putting It All Together: A Case Example":** This chapter walks through an example of using all the tools I've discussed so far and applying it to a particular behavior-change challenge.
- **Chapter 15, "Real-World Examples":** To conclude the book, we hear from people who are doing behavioral learning design and examine different examples of the behavioral design process.

HOW DOES THIS MATCH UP WITH MY PREVIOUS BOOK?

First of all, if you are reading this book because you also read my book *Design for How People Learn*, then THANK YOU. I'm very happy to know that the first book was useful enough to bring you back.

This book is an expansion and elaboration on the motivation chapter and some other points in *Design for How People Learn*. It's a deeper dive on the topics, and my rough estimate is that 10 to 20 percent of the material will sound familiar to readers of the previous book, but if that's not your experience, please let me know. All the words are new, but many of the principles have not changed between the two books, and I can't assume a reader of this book has also read the other book, so there will be some necessary repetition.

WHO AM I TO WRITE THIS BOOK?

When people ask me what I do, I usually say, "I'm an instructional designer." Most of the time (like, 99 percent), this provokes a slightly puzzled head tilt and a hesitant, "Okay....?" (Other instructional designers know what I'm describing.) My degree is in "Instructional Systems Technology," and I've worked for almost 30 years on the design of learning materials and experiences for adults. I also spent about half my time in graduate school studying human-computer interaction (or what we now more commonly call UX (User Experience) design).

I became interested in behavioral design in the early 2000s because I felt like there was a gap in my toolbox, but I've spent the last dozen or so years educating myself on the principles and models of behavioral design via books, media, research papers, practical application, and formal workshops.

Many of the books on behavioral design come from academic researchers, and it's great that so many of them are able to translate their work for more general con-sumption. It can be difficult, though, to take even the best written books on behav-ioral science and connect those to practical guidance in an applied domain. I'm not a researcher; I'm very much a practitioner who tries to translate research into practical application. I try to approach all of these topics with humility and strongly encourage you to test any recommendations or solutions with your audience in your context. Just because something worked in one context doesn't mean it will work for you, but these concepts and models do give you a place to start.

Thanks for considering this book, and best of luck.

Julie

Materials and resources to support this book can be found at usablelearning.com/elephant

TALKING TO THE ELEPHANT

(IN WHICH WE MEET THE ELEPHANT AND PUZZLE SOME VERY HUMAN CONUNDRUMS)

What do you do when people know *what* to do, but still aren't *doing* it?

I'm an instructional designer. That means I design learning experiences that help people learn and remember what to do. But what do you do when learning and remembering aren't enough? What do you do when your learning strategies toolbox doesn't help solve the actual problem?

Here's an example: A dozen or so years ago, I worked on a project related to AIDS/HIV prevention. By that point, the public health community had known for more than two decades that condom usage was a key strategy to prevent disease transmission, and they'd gotten the word out. People had heard that message. So why was transmission still happening?

The people in our audience knew what they were supposed to do, but they still weren't consistently doing it.

If people knew the answer (use condoms) and they still weren't doing it, then it wasn't really a knowledge problem. And if it's not a knowledge problem, then telling people the same thing louder and more emphatically probably isn't the solution.

The learning experiences people have in school as they're growing up focus more on learning and remembering because our educational systems focus on giving students the foundational skills necessary to move on to more complex skills for life or work. As people get older, educational experiences shift their focus from foundational skills and become more about application in a life or work context. By the time you are in a training class at your job, the focus has almost entirely moved away from *knowing*, and is instead focused on *doing*.

So if a learning experience creates knowing but doesn't support doing, then maybe we need to consider other ways to design learning experiences.

SO WHY?

So why might people not do something when they know they should? And what other tools do we need in the toolbox beyond helping people learn and remember the material?

Those will be the main questions that I tackle in this book:

- How do you diagnose and understand the reasons why a behavior is or isn't happening?
- How do you design learning experiences that support and motivate behavior change?

I also share ways to identify when learning really isn't the solution at all.

AREN'T PEOPLE JUST STUBBORN/CLUELESS/LAZY?

So, are the reasons people don't do things because they are stubborn or clueless or lazy?

No.

Next question.

Okay, so maybe I should expand on that a little. There are several problems with the stubborn/clueless/lazy idea, and I discuss them throughout this book, but the first and most practical problem is that *it doesn't help you design for that audience.*

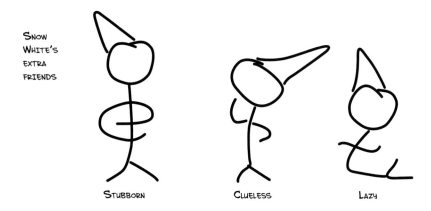

People have a tendency to attribute other people's behavior to their innate character, whereas they explain their own actions as being due to circumstances. For example, I can believe a person was rude online because they are fundamentally a rude person, but if I was rude in turn, it was only because that person provoked me by posting something stupendously idiotic.

People's innate characteristics probably do influence their behaviors, but so do many other factors, and trying to change innate characteristics is not the best use of time or resources when you are trying to help people with behavior change.

If you are disdainful of your audience and their circumstances, you are unlikely to be able to design helpful solutions for them.

HOW DOES LEARNING FIT IN?

Learning is a crucial tool for behavior change, but learning often isn't the only thing needed to help people with behavior change. For example, I bet you already know that flossing your teeth is a good way to prevent tooth decay and gum disease. Does that knowledge mean that you are perfectly consistent about regular flossing? Maybe you are (and good for you!), but maybe you are like most of us who, despite the best intentions, are not quite *that* consistent in our flossing habits.

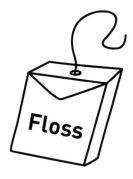

So, again, if the problem isn't knowledge (people know flossing is a good idea) or a likely a problem of skill (many people who know how to floss effectively may still not do it regularly) or even of motivation (people can *want* to floss regularly while still not managing it), is it likely that more education about flossing will change the behavior?

Well, it depends. If that education is comprised of telling people louder and more emphatically that FLOSSING IS A GOOD IDEA, then that strategy probably won't help. If louder-and-more-emphatically was an effective way to change behavior, most smokers would have quit smoking, we'd all exercise every day, and I'd have no problem maintaining an ergonomically correct posture while I write this book.

That's not to suggest that education has no role to play in promoting good dental hygiene. Of course it does. It's just not *all* that is needed, and some types of educational experiences are going to be more effective than others, which I discuss in later chapters.

WHAT ELSE MATTERS?

In the case of daily flossing, many other factors besides education could influence whether the behavior happens for me:

- Do I have access to floss? Is it handy and easy to find, or is the only floss I have one of those little freebies from the dentist that is somewhere in the back of the drawer in the bathroom?
- Do I have a dedicated time to floss? Do I have a daily ritual, or do I only think of it when I have something annoying jammed between my back molars?
- Do I have some kind of reminder? I don't have a reminder set, but there are several ways I could put a daily prompt on my phone or computer.
- Do I associate flossing with an already-existing habit? For example, when I've tried to improve my habits for taking vitamins, I put the vitamins next to the coffee container because coffee-making is a very reliable existing habit.

- Do I see other people flossing? Generally, I don't see other people flossing, so that doesn't help me reinforce the habit.
- Do I like the feeling of flossing, or do I find it uncomfortable? Generally, I find the feeling of flossing satisfying, so that helps because I don't avoid it the way I might something uncomfortable.

These are just a few of the many factors that could influence whether I floss on a regular basis. People who have not been taught about flossing almost certainly will not floss regularly, but being taught about flossing is only one part of the equation.

MEET THE ELEPHANT

So, what's the deal with the title of this book?

In my first book, I made use of a metaphor from Jonathan Haidt, a social psychologist. In his book *The Happiness Hypothesis*, he talks about the brain being like a rider and an elephant:

> *The rider is ... conscious, controlled thought. The elephant, in contrast, is everything else. The elephant includes the gut feelings, visceral reactions, emotions, and intuitions that comprise much of the automatic system. (Haidt, 2006)*

Basically, he's talking about the idea that there are two separate parts of your brain that are in control—the conscious verbal thinking brain and the automatic, emotional, visceral brain.

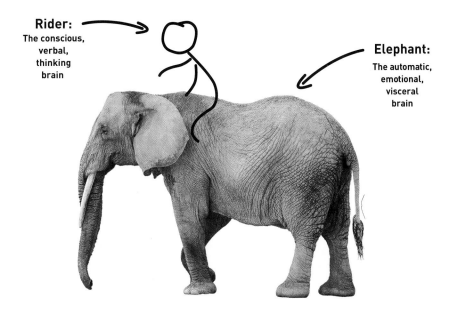

Rider:
The conscious, verbal, thinking brain

Elephant:
The automatic, emotional, visceral brain

THE ELEPHANT

Basically, there are parts of our brains and systems of cognition that focus on things like sensing and perceiving present conditions in the world, navigating in space, doing things automatically, and reacting emotionally. In this metaphor, these things get grouped together as the elephant.

Elephant:
The automatic,
emotional,
visceral
brain

THE RIDER

The rider part of your brain is the part of your brain that you have internal conversations with. It's also the part of your brain that does math problems, thinks through logical answers, is careful and deliberate, and plans for hypothetical future events.

Rider:
The conscious,
verbal,
thinking
brain

Many of the models of decision-making that use this kind of dual-process theory have this idea that our brains have more than one system influencing our choices and behaviors. (The System 1 and System 2 that Daniel Kahneman describes in his book *Thinking Fast and Slow* or Joseph LeDoux's concept of low road and high road cognition are two examples.) I happen to like Haidt's elephant/rider metaphor because I think it's visual and easy to remember, but I am wrapping several different psychology theories and models into the idea of the elephant and rider as used in this book.

WHO ARE YOU TALKING TO?

When we are designing learning experiences, we have a tendency to talk to the rider. Learning experiences that are primarily about the transfer of information are aimed at the rider. For example, if you've ever made a presentation slide that is mostly bullet points, you are really talking only to the rider and ignoring the elephant.

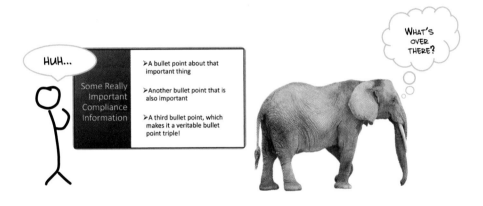

The rider and the elephant pay attention to very different things:

Things the rider pays attention to:

Information
Facts
Procedures
Rules
Logical arguments

Things the elephant pays attention to:

Personal experiences
Things you can touch, taste, feel, etc.
Stories
Emotions

TALK TO THE ELEPHANT

At the beginning of this chapter, I talked about the problem that can happen when someone knows what to do but still isn't doing it. This frequently happens when the rider and the elephant disagree about the importance of something.

For example, let's talk about safety glasses.

We frequently see training curriculum about the importance of wearing appropriate safety equipment to prevent injury in settings like factories, construction sites, laboratories, yard work, and so on. Eye-related injuries happen every day in different workplaces and home scenarios, and wearing proper eye protection can mitigate or prevent those injuries. But who understands that—the elephant or the rider?

I was using a spray foam product to seal some cracks in my garage last year. The illustration shows more or less that interchange between my elephant and rider.

Not great, right? Intellectually, I knew that I shouldn't use the pressurized chemical that can cause eye injuries without appropriate safety gear, but my personal experience was that I'd gotten away with similar courses of action in the past, and I didn't really want to deal with the hassle of driving to the hardware store. I had some old sunglasses, and, well ... you get the picture.

Fortunately, it did occur to me that with about three clicks on my phone, I could have safety glasses shipped to my house, and my safety glass wearing has improved tremendously since then.

The elephant has a different way of seeing the world than the rider and focuses on different things. Let's look at a few examples.

VISCERAL EXPERIENCE

The elephant cares much more about visceral or personal experience and rates that much more highly than intellectual knowledge.

EMOTIONS AND FEELINGS

The elephant is going to be much more persuaded by emotions and feelings. Advertisers are very aware of this. The next example is an accurate reflection of how my elephant feels about bungee jumping.

HABITS AND IMPULSES

The elephant is all about habits and automatic actions, like reflexes and impulses. This is part of how the elephant can keep us safe, but it can be a problem when you need to interrupt a habit with a different behavior.

PRESENT BIAS

The elephant is very focused on what is happening right now and values immediate rewards over longer-term rewards that require extra effort or delay over time.

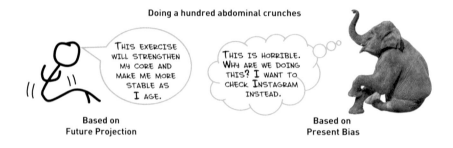

IMPORTANT: THE ELEPHANT ISN'T STUPID

I need to make one important point: The elephant isn't stupid. Or lazy. Or necessarily wrong. The elephant evolved over millennia to do things like optimize effort and reward, keep us from dying early, and do things efficiently. The elephant is marvelous and amazing in many contexts. The challenge is that sometimes the elephant doesn't have the whole picture. It can't project out into the future and consider consequences, and it can fight us on effort we know to be necessary. (The elephant is an accomplished procrastinator.) All of the elephant's behaviors come from a functional place, though some of those behaviors aren't always functional in a new context.

For example, an attraction to high-calorically dense foods was a survival mechanism for most of human history. Overeating sweet or fattening foods helped our ancestors survive in hunter/gatherer societies. But when the elephant gets moved to a new context where there is very little food scarcity (for example, your average convenience store), the impulses and habits that may have been useful in the past may not be ideal going forward. This doesn't make the elephant's impulses bad, but it can create challenges.

When the rider and the elephant disagree, the rider can typically drag the elephant along for a while, but this is exhausting and usually fails quickly. It's a much better idea to see if there's a message that appeals to BOTH the rider and the elephant.

TALK TO THE RIDER AND THE ELEPHANT

Far too often, learning design has focused on talking to the rider and largely ignored the elephant. As learning designers, we can do better. We need to ensure that we are talking to both the rider and the elephant.

To do this, we need to ensure that we actually understand what is going on with the elephant. This is harder than it might appear. If we skip over the step of really understanding what the elephant perceives and how the elephant feels, we are often solving the wrong problem. We need to make sure we are talking to the people we are designing for and really understand their needs and challenges.

My former boss Michael Allen (a renowned expert in learning technology) once told me a story about trying to encourage his 90-something father to go to the gym to work on his strength and stability. Dad was very reluctant, and it took a lot of effort to figure out why.

It turned out that it wasn't the obvious explanations of not wanting to make the effort or not being persuaded that it would be valuable. The problem was that Dad thought he had to wear shorts to the gym, and he didn't like wearing shorts, particularly not in a public place.

Once he was assured that he could wear long pants, he was happy to try it out. What I'm saying is *we can't assume we know what's going on with people's elephants.*

In the rest of this book, we will look at formats and frameworks that help us understand what could be going on with peoples' elephants and riders, and how we can match that up to strategies in our learning designs. We will also see a series of interviews and case examples on how this has been done in different contexts.

ABOUT THE EXAMPLES IN THIS BOOK

Before we get started, I want to mention something about the examples I use in this book. I very much believe that understanding these approaches and techniques requires examples and have tried to include as many application examples as possible.

At the end of the book, there will be interviews about actual case examples, but through the first part of the book, I use common training challenges (related to topics like safety, compliance, financials, healthcare, and so on). In some cases, these are related to projects I've worked on as an instructional designer (though specific details are changed and fictionalized).

It's important to note that *I am not an expert in any of these subject areas*. I've tried to do my diligent best to run examples by people who are experts or use academic literature to verify details, but I'm sure I still got some things wrong, and I apologize here for those errors. Also, things change, and the best practices in a few years may be very different. This is true about the material in the case examples and about the behavioral design methods in this book. The field of behavioral design is still fairly new and will no doubt continue to grow, so the content of this book should be considered a starting place.

I've done my best to use respectful language and terminology about the people and challenges described in this book, but language changes quickly, so I apologize for any problems and welcome feedback about how to do better.

So let's get started!

KEY POINTS

- You can't just tell the elephant to change, no matter how loud and emphatic you are.
- The elephant pays attention to things like personal experiences and things it can touch, taste, feel, and so on. It responds to stories and emotions.
- You can't guess what the elephant cares about. You have to actually have conversations with the audience you are serving to understand what they want and need.

RESOURCES

Haidt, Jonathan. *The Happiness Hypothesis: Finding Modern Truth in Ancient Wisdom* (New York: Basic Books, 2006), 17.

LeDoux, J.E. *The Emotional Brain* (New York: Simon and Schuster, 1996).

Petty, Richard E., Cacioppo, John T. "The Elaboration Likelihood Model of Persuasion," *Advances in Experimental Social Psychology* 19 (1986): 124–129.

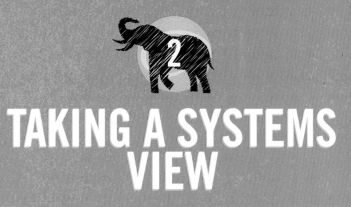

TAKING A SYSTEMS VIEW

(IN WHICH THE ELEPHANT IS JUST PART OF A WHOLE ECOSYSTEM)

"WE NEED TRAINING"

When a system fails, "training" is almost always promised as part of the solution. Here are some examples:

- In 2018, Starbucks Coffee Company—in response to complaints about discriminatory actions from Starbucks employees—closed approximately 8,000 Starbucks locations for a day and had roughly 175,000 employees participate in "racial-bias education geared toward preventing discrimination in our stores."
- Police officers spend thousands of hours every year in "Use of Force" classes aimed at teaching them how to not use unnecessary or excessive force.
- Billions of dollars are spent every year on things like "leadership" training.

It's not difficult to see that for each of these, training is likely only a small fraction of what is needed to truly make significant change.

LEARNING AS PART OF A SYSTEM

There's a quote that I'm a bit obsessed with (attribution is a bit murky, but a likely originator is Paul Batalden based on ideas from W. Edwards Deming, a well-known engineer and management consultant):

Every system is perfectly designed to get the results it gets.

Whenever we are dealing with a problem, challenge, or difficulty, it's always worth asking these questions:

- What is it about the system that is causing an outcome?
- And how is the system influencing the behavior of the people in that system?

When we attribute outcomes to people's attitudes or capability (for example, "They're just lazy"), we miss the crucial point that there's usually a reason for someone's behavior, and if we don't ask what that reason could be, we are missing vital data that could help change the situation. A behavior can be "wrong" according to standard operating procedures and still be right in the sense that there is some functional reason in the environment or system for that person's behavior.

For example, a store clerk might guess the price of an item rather than holding up a large line of customers while they go through the official process of getting the price checked. Some stores recognize that a very strict adherence to a procedure like price checking can compromise bigger goals like good customer experience, so they deliberately give clerks latitude about using judgment for small-stakes items in service of that better customer experience.

IRRATIONALITY AND BIAS EXIST IN SYSTEMS

Much has been made of irrationality and bias when it comes to behavior change. There are impressive infographics that show all the cognitive biases. Several books have been written about the quirks of human irrationality. These are often interesting and entertaining, and there are important things we can learn from them, but they aren't always useful. Looking at these biases as interesting phenomena ignores the fact that they're related to the context and environment in which they occur.

Daniel Kahneman (the winner of the Nobel Prize for his contributions to behavioral economics), in his seminal text *Thinking, Fast and Slow,* explains a riddle that they used to test what he describes as people's "Lazy System 2":

A bat and ball cost $1.10.

The bat costs one dollar more than the ball.

How much does the ball cost?

Many people answer 10 cents. The actual answer is 5 cents, with the bat costing $1.05 (one dollar more than the ball). In his book, Kahneman describes how System 2 "allocates attention to effortful mental activities that demand it, including complex computations," but goes on to explain that "The distinctive mark of this easy puzzle is that it evokes an answer that is intuitive, appealing, and wrong." This is

Kahneman's "Lazy System 2." By not paying appropriate attention, many people get this answer wrong.

So let's look at how this question appears to the elephant:

- **It's clearly historical.** Baseballs and bats cost much more now, and this is presented as a puzzle. It's not a real, immediate problem with any real stakes to it, and so the signal to the elephant is *it kind of doesn't matter*.
- **It's an odd format.** If I wanted to know the price of an item, I would never ask it in this format, nor would I expect anyone to ever give me this piece of information for two unsimilar items (item one costs much more than item two). For example, if I was splitting a check with someone, I might compare the price of two similar items (for example, two glasses of wine), but I would never tell anybody, "My entrée cost $28 more than your dessert." The deliberately confusing format tricks the elephant.
- **It's close to a format we are used to.** A much more common conversation might be "Q: How much was the ball?" "Answer: Well, it was a $1.10, and the bat was $1.00, so...." You've probably had versions of that conversation many times in your life. You may never have had a question in the format of the example from Kahneman's book.
- **It's trivial.** The difference between the right answer (the ball is 5 cents) and the intuitive answer (10 cents) is trivial for most people, so this is something where the consequences of getting it wrong just don't matter very much, so it makes sense that people would not allocate a lot of effort to figuring it out. This is also a cue to the elephant that the answer isn't particularly important.

So this example has several cues to the elephant that a quick guess will be sufficient here, and whether you consider that laziness or efficiency depends on your perspective.

There's probably no shortage of people who would point out (with some ire) to me that it's *still wrong*. And they would be correct about that, and I'm not suggesting that it doesn't matter that people get it wrong. But if we ask ourselves the reasons that they got it wrong—it's a weird format no normal person would ever use, and all the cues are telling our brains that this is a problem not worth a lot of attention, with low stakes if you get it wrong—we know a lot more about how to recognize situations where people need to heighten their attention or risk error, and how to help people avoid those errors.

SYSTEMS THINKING

So how do we take into account all the other variables that exist in the environment and consider them as we discuss a behavior? We are going to zoom in to focus on very specific behaviors in later chapters of this book because that sharp focus helps us analyze and diagnose, but a too-narrow focus can also cause us to miss other causes and solutions.

Donella Meadows, author of the classic book *Thinking in Systems: A Primer*, describes a system as "A set of things—people, cells, molecules, or whatever—interconnected in such a way that they produce their own pattern of behavior over time." Trying to understand the complexity of a whole system can be overwhelming, but being able to both focus on individual behaviors and keep in mind the overall system is a necessary balancing act for any serious behavior change effort.

For example, we know that plastics cause many ecological issues, so you could have a narrow focus on the behavior "People need to recycle consistently and correctly." But it's worth asking if that narrow behavior will make a big enough change. Maybe people recycling more frequently and accurately will change things significantly, but we probably need to look at the bigger system and consider variables like the cost and availability of recycling facilities, the market for recycled plastics, the incentives for manufacturers to use less plastic, and so on.

One tool we can use to consider how a system works is system mapping. There's no single way to do this kind of mapping, and I'm only going to use the simplest examples here. Peter Senge's *The Fifth Discipline* and Donella Meadows's *Thinking in Systems* are both excellent books if you'd like to explore this further.

Peter Senge explains that the building blocks are reinforcing processes, balancing processes, and delays. Let's look at a reinforcing process. If you've been in the world of learning and development or higher education for any time, you are probably very familiar with the "end of class survey."

The illustration shows how this should probably work. Evaluation data should be used to improve classes, which will then improve the evaluation scores.

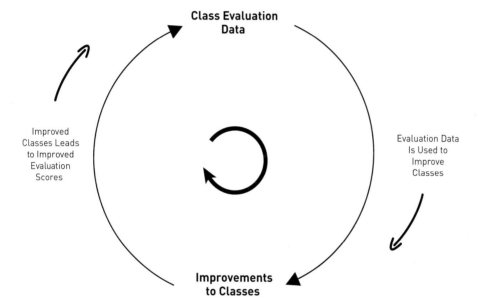

Class Evaluation Data

Improved Classes Leads to Improved Evaluation Scores

Evaluation Data Is Used to Improve Classes

Improvements to Classes

Eventually the system will balance out when the evaluation data and the class quality can't get any higher. Everybody wins!

That's how it theoretically *should* work. It often doesn't go quite like that. I've seen organizations where it goes something like this:

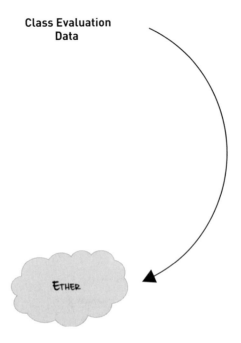

**Class Evaluation
Data**

Yep, the evaluation data is collected, but then doesn't go anywhere, except into the metaphorical ether.

If a system is supposed to work a particular way, and it's not, then it's worth asking "why not?"

You can tug on each of these threads and, for example, ask why the data isn't actionable or who should be responsible for paying attention to the data.

Let's say that you are managing the training function, and you decide the team will evaluate all the evaluation data and allocate resources to improve the classes, which hopefully improves business results. That sounds pretty good! But, of course, other things are involved, like resource allocation to new projects, stakeholder support, and so forth. If you think about how these all interact, it can get complicated quickly:

If we try to figure out how these things interact, we might find that the assignment of resources to improve existing classes doesn't come with an overall increase in team resources, so they have to be pulled from somewhere. That means fewer resources for new training projects, which makes some stakeholders unhappy and leads to a decrease in business results from new projects. And the unhappy stakeholders decrease their funding support, so now you can't fill the open staff position you were counting on to support the improvements.

Thinking through these relationships can help you identify key places in the system where you can intervene and adjust to make beneficial changes.

A system view can help show where there isn't enough reinforcement, where there are unintended effects, or where difficulty seeing feedback can be causing problems.

UNINTENDED CONSEQUENCES

Any behavior change intervention can have unintended consequences. For example, the *intended* consequences for most compliance training efforts are outcomes like employees not doing things that are illegal or problematic, or legal defensibility if the company is sued.

But if we create compliance training that isn't relevant to the audience, and the message is that you just need to tick the completion box, then we may not like the unintended consequences of forcing compliance training where it's not relevant or useful.

I talked to Christian Hunt, author of *Humanizing Rules: Bringing Behavioural Science to Ethics and Compliance*, and he described it this way:

> It used to frustrate me in banking when my assistant had to do training on obscure regulations that made no sense to her whatsoever. It was not relevant to her job. And so she would sit there and go, "Oh, it's another one of those things from the people who brought you the tedious trade course." So even when it was relevant, she would sit there and go, "Here's more useless stuff from those idiots that don't understand me, I'm going to ignore it." **We are teaching people to ignore our training**.

> I think the key bit with all of this is that we're dealing with human beings that are sentient. And so they will react to what they see us doing. Attempts to assess whether our training has been effective needs to bear in mind that the test itself sends a signal to employees. If you teach them something you say is important, but then if the assessment is dumb—you tell them to just regurgitate what they've just been told or give them an "everybody knows this" kind of test—that's not a genuine test of whether they know it, and they'll recognize that. And so in trying to test the effectiveness, we often actually make the situation worse and we undermine the subject matter in the tests.

WHERE DOES FEEDBACK BECOME VISIBLE?

Often, in a behavior-change project, we decide that a set of behaviors will produce the desired outcomes. At that point, it's worth asking, "Where do the consequences of a behavior becomes visible?"

Here are some example behaviors:

- Salespeople should increase their sales of the turbowidget (desired result: increased turbowidget sales).
- Hospital healthcare providers should wash their hands according to governmental guidelines (desired result: decreased patient infections).
- Jan needs to buy extra milk while her brother and nieces are visiting (desired result: there will be enough milk for breakfast and other meals).
- Managers need to ensure that salary offers to new hires are fair and equitable (desired result: staff will be paid appropriately for their qualifications and responsibilities).

Results of behaviors can becomes visible at very different levels. I usually use the distinction of individual, group, and system levels.

INDIVIDUAL-LEVEL CONSEQUENCES

Jan's behavior will be visible at the individual level. She'll be able to see whether they have enough milk or she needs to buy more. The behavior and consequences will be pretty easy to see at the individual level:

The same thing is probably true with the sales example. Most organizations track sales results at the individual level, so we can see how a particular salesperson did, as shown in the illustration.

So buying milk and selling Turbowidgets both have a visible outcome at the individual level.

GROUP-LEVEL CONSEQUENCES

Sometimes, evaluating the outcome can require comparison across a group. For example, selling 180% sounds great, but if everybody does exactly the same, then it's less impressive. But if most other people on a sales team sell around 100% of goal, then 180% is going to be exceptional.

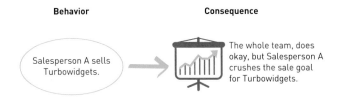

In most healthcare facilities, the consequence of handwashing is very difficult to measure at the individual level. It would be extremely unlikely that a patient only has contact with a single healthcare provider in a hospital setting. Impact would really only be visible at a group level.

Since it's pretty much impossible to see the consequence at the individual level, the consequence has to be examined at the group level, but that might not be enough data for comparison either.

If a manager is hiring a new employee, that manager might have all sorts of reasons for the salary offer being 15% less than the person currently doing the job. The new person might have less experience or different qualifications, or the current employee might have been in the job for several years and received merit increases over the years.

A manager might be able to judge the fairness of a salary offer against several other people in the department doing the same work with similar qualifications, or they might not have anyone else in that same role.

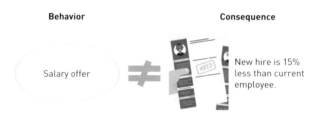

So, sales goals, handwashing, and salary offers need comparison or aggregate data to be relevant. We need to have some basis for comparison to know if the rate of sales or patient infections are good numbers, and a single salary offer can't be judged equitable without comparing it to similar offers.

SYSTEM-LEVEL CONSEQUENCES

Sometimes consequence can be judged only at the level of whole systems. A hospital might not know whether its infection rates are excessive without being able to benchmark against similar hospitals or national averages. Behavior changes that focus on changing the individual will be easiest when the results or consequences are visible at the individual level.

When you are being asked to design learning for a behavior change where individual learners can't see any feedback because there are no systems in place to measure at the group or system level, it's important to recognize that this will be a difficult and uphill battle, and you should make stakeholders aware that training alone will probably not be enough to support change.

For example, it can be very difficult to judge the fairness of a job offer without more data than most hiring managers have access to.

THE EXAMPLE OF PAY EQUITY

The company Salesforce.com set out to look at salary disparities. In an article in *Wired* magazine, Salesforce.com CEO Marc Benioff and two members of the senior executive team, Cindy Robbins and Leyla Seka, raised the issue of gender pay equity and proposed an audit of compensation for all employees. Benioff described how they had been working on equity initiatives for a few years at that point, so he didn't expect the audit to show much disparity.

It wasn't simple to look at the data. They "assembled a cross-functional team and developed a methodology with outside experts that analyzed the entire employee population to determine whether there were unexplained differences in pay." Benioff was chagrined to discover that there were significant disparities and that 6% of Salesforce.com employees needed their salaries adjusted, at a cost of approximately $3 million. They found that the next year, they had to perform a similar adjustment (mostly due to acquiring companies who brought their own salary disparities to the organization). The company discovered this would be an ongoing effort and publishes an annual update on their website regarding goals and progress.

Benioff describes how this is not the product of deliberate bad actors in the system. No bad person is scheming to pay people less based on race or gender. He describes pay inequity as "a stubborn, slippery problem in business." He also explains that the reasons to fix it aren't about reputation or even doing the right thing, but that diversity and equity are good for business, according to research from McKinsey & Company and others.

The point of this example isn't to promote pay equity (though I'm a fan), but to show how a focus on individual behavior would be inadequate here. I've worked on many diversity training projects over the years, and the training has had learning objectives like

> Managers will be able to describe the importance of fair and equitable treatment.

Or even

> Managers will be able to identify the characteristics of a fair and unbiased salary offer.

But in the Salesforce.com example, they were unable to see the problem clearly without a system in place to measure and correct for the issue. After the initial audit, they "devised a new set of job codes and standards and applied them to each newly integrated company." With those measures in place, it might be possible to address the problem at an individual level, as disparities against those standards would be visible on an individual basis.

TUNING A SYSTEM

Behavior change initiatives are often treated as a campaign, a class, or an event, but in the Salesforce.com example, they found that one correction was not enough. Instead, they have built up ongoing systems and publicly release their outcomes every year on their website.

We tend to view training classes as a Start > Learn > Finish process. You now know the thing you needed to learn and move on to the next thing or go out and use your knowledge.

Behavior change efforts may not always work like that. It may be an ongoing effort to reinforce and adjust. The metaphor may not be a journey, but more of a garden that needs tending as it grows or a thermostat that needs adjusting over time.

If that's too vague, we can use the example of cybersecurity. The behavior is that learners should create strong, unique passwords. There's a class that's really fun and engaging, and people come up with the hardest passwords they can imagine, and everybody leaves ready to do the right thing. That lasts for maybe six weeks or so, and then the behavior of weaker, reused passwords starts to creep back in.

I don't want to get into solutions here, but there are many kinds of behaviors that may never be a one-and-done training solution.

HOW THIS IMPACTS BEHAVIOR-CHANGE PROJECTS

If you are being asked, as a learning designer, to design a class or resources to help address individual behaviors in a system where results are not visible at an individual level, it probably won't be enough. It doesn't mean that you shouldn't try or that it can't be part of the solution, but it may be useful to have that discussion with stakeholders so the expectations are set appropriately.

- Teaching healthcare providers how to talk to patients about exercise won't help if providers aren't given the time to have those conversations.
- Teaching people the right method for handwashing will be of limited usefulness if the environment lacks clean water and adequate supplies.
- Teaching people to sort their recycling won't make a dent in plastic going to landfills if there's no market for recycled goods.

Please understand that I do not mean this in a pessimistic way! As we proceed in this book, I'm going to speak optimistically about our ability as learning designers to impact or influence behavior. I wouldn't be writing this book if I wasn't optimistic about this topic. That said, I want to be as clear as possible about the limitations of a tight behavioral focus, how solutions may often need to be part of a broader system approach, and how learning designers should also be part of those broader systems discussions.

HOW THIS IMPACTS LEARNING DESIGN

I started this chapter talking about how training often gets invoked to help solve large systemic problems. Let's take a look at a small example of making biased judgments.

You've probably heard the message that it's wrong to judge people based on their appearance. "Don't judge a book by its cover" and all that. *Sesame Street* made sure my four-year-old self knew that judging people based on how they looked was bad. And it's not difficult to look at the news and see examples where judging by appearance leads to awful consequences. Making people aware of unconscious bias is a large part of many training initiatives.

But imagine you live in an apartment building, and a delivery person contacts you over the intercom to let you know that you have to sign for a package you ordered. You walk into the lobby and see these three people:

I don't think you would be guilty of any problematic bias or irrationality if you walked up to the person in the uniform holding a delivery box.

The point isn't that "judging by appearance" is okay. The point is that *sometimes it's okay and sometimes it's not*, and the hard part is *knowing the difference.*

So the learning objective isn't helping learners understand that "this bias exists." The learning objective is helping learners "recognize in which environments and circumstances I need to use extra vigilance to make sure I'm not making unfair assumptions."

The first is an interesting psychological phenomenon that you tell the rider about, and the second is a skill or habit you probably need to practice consistently to help the rider and elephant both develop.

This is an important distinction for learning design, because *the learning design will look very different*. If you are describing an interesting phenomenon, you might only need a single slide in the presentation deck, but helping people develop a skill or habit requires learning activities with practice, a feedback mechanism, and reinforcement over time.

Describing a phenomenon		**Helping people develop a skill**

Slide: Common Biases

VS.

Practice Activity

Sorting Activity

Planning and Goal Setting Activities

Role Play

Plan

Learning where and when you need to heighten your vigilance is a product of the environment you are in, the influences that shaped your learned behavior, and the cues you have acclimated to.

The behavior, like the elephant, never exists in a vacuum. The elephant is always operating in the social and physical environment it exists in. We need to consider these things if we want to design effective learning experiences.

Elephant   Environment

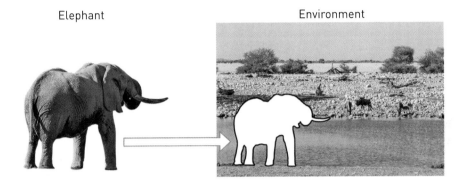

KEY POINTS

- Training is often called upon to provide solutions to difficult problems, but there are often bigger system issues at play, and an intervention that only focuses on training is often not enough.
- Every system is perfectly designed to get the result it gets, so always ask, "What is causing this behavior to happen or not happen right now?"
- If a behavior is being blamed on attitude or capability, it's important to dig deeper and see if there's anything in the system or environment that is causing that behavior to happen.
- Mapping a system, and considering what forces are encouraging the change and what forces are restraining the change, can help you identify the best places to intervene in that system.
- A tight focus on individual behavior can help you design for behavior change, but you do need to periodically zoom out and consider the whole system to ensure that the individual behavior supports the outcome.
- Always ask where the feedback or consequences of the behavior will become visible. If it's visible at the individual level, it will be easier to provide feedback to individual learners. If the feedback only becomes visible at the group or system level, then there will need to be mechanisms in place to measure and assess group- or system-level impact.

RESOURCES

Hunt, Christian. *Humanizing Rules: Bringing Behavioural Science to Ethics and Compliance* (Hoboken, NJ: Wiley, 2023).

Kahneman, Daniel. *Thinking, Fast and Slow* (New York: Farrar, Straus and Giroux, 2011), 20 and 43.

Langley, Monica and Marc Benioff, "How Salesforce Closed the Pay Gap Between Men and Women," Wired.com, October 15, 2019, https://www.wired.com/story/how-salesforce-closed-pay-gap-between-men-women/.

Meadows, Donella H. *Thinking in Systems: A Primer* (White River Junction, VT: Chelsea Green Publishing, 2008), 1.

Parker, Kim. "When negotiating starting salaries, most U.S. women and men don't ask for higher pay," Pew Research Center website, April 5, 2023, https://www.pewresearch.org/fact-tank/2023/04/05/when-negotiating-starting-salaries-most-us-women-and-men-dont-ask-for-higher-pay/.

Senge, Peter M. *The Fifth Discipline: The Art and Practice of the Learning Organization* (New York: Currency Doubleday, 2006).

Starbucks Coffee Company. "Starbucks to Close All Stores Nationwide for Racial-Bias Education on May 29." Starbucks press release, April 17, 2018. On the Starbucks website. https://stories.starbucks.com/press/2018/starbucks-to-close-stores-nationwide-for-racial-bias-education-may-29/, accessed May 22, 2023.

3

MOVING ALONG THE CHANGE PATH

(IN WHICH THE ELEPHANT MEANDERS DOWN THE CHANGE PATH AT ITS OWN PACE)

Change is complex because people are complex, and we live in a complex world. Consequently, we can conclude that there are no simple answers to designing to support behavior change. One thing that I think we can say with some confidence (in the overwhelming majority of cases) is

> Change is a process, not an event.

There are certainly stories about lightning strike moments for people who have done things like suddenly deciding to put down the cigarette pack and never smoke again or opting to become a vegetarian or swearing off phone use while driving after having a scary near-miss while texting in traffic. These examples aren't a great model for design. You can't really arrange for people to be struck by lightning (figuratively or literally).

It's a good thing that people aren't usually so easily changed, and those examples I offered are not really lightning strikes. In all of those cases, we can assume that, at a minimum, the person had already been exposed to information about the behavior and had been primed to consider the change.

HOW THE CHANGE PROCESS IMPACTS LEARNING DESIGN

I discuss solutions for learning design in more detail at the end of this chapter and later in the book, but the idea that change is a process has a few obvious implications for learning. For our purposes, let's use a very simple change process. Meet Joe, who is slightly interested in flossing more regularly. Let's assume his change journey looks like this:

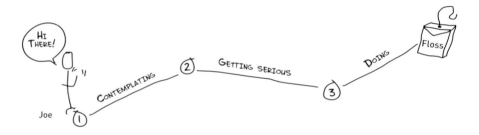

For now, let's assume that Joe's change process for flossing follows this path:

Step 1: Joe contemplates flossing more because of a conversation with his dentist about gum disease. He thinks about what he's currently doing and what would need to change for him to floss more regularly.

Step 2: Joe gets serious about the whole flossing thing and starts to make a plan. He can never find the good dental floss at home, only the cruddy unwaxed travel size, so he plans to get a few packages of the good kind when he's at the store. He'll leave it with the toothpaste, so he'll always be able to find some.

Step 3: Joe attempts flossing daily. He's a little hit or miss, but he's definitely flossing most days. He figures out that work travel interrupts his flossing habit, so he makes sure to get some travel size packages of good floss. After a few months, he's still flossing most days, so he counts this as a win.

Joe did pretty well on his own, but let's say the national dental foundation wants you to make a text-message learning experience that dentists can supply to their patients. To keep things simple, let's assume that the people in the audience are pretty similar to Joe (though it's rarely that easy).

There are a few different approaches you can take, though these aren't discrete options. You can mix and match these strategies.

APPROACH 1: DESIGN FOR THE WHOLE PROCESS

The first approach is that you design an experience that guides people through this whole process. For example, you could create a text with a short video each week for three weeks:

- Week 1 you could focus on messages about the importance of flossing and the consequences of gum disease.
- Week 2 you could focus on helping people plan their flossing habit and identify what type of floss works best for them.
- Week 3 could be messages of encouragement and advice about troubleshooting any difficulties they might be having.

The benefit of this method is that it takes them through the whole process and spreads it over time so participants can get used to each part. The downside is that everyone might not be on the same timeline. Some people might be ready to skip past the week 1 material and get right to the preparation part. Someone might be on vacation and ignoring their phone on week 2, and then they might feel like they are getting material that isn't relevant to them on week 3.

With something like a digital text-message course, it could be possible for people to gate their own experience. You could have them opt in for the next step when they are ready. Some people might go through the steps in three days; other people might take three months.

It's harder for synchronous experiences, like in-person classes or virtual online classes. For example, if you are creating a four-week virtual class on time management with weekly video conference meetings, you can't adjust the content of each class for the pace of each attendee.

APPROACH 2: MEET PEOPLE WHERE THEY ARE

Another approach is to try to meet people where they are. For example, you could message the audience and let them decide if they just want to learn about the behavior, if they're ready to make a plan, or if they need help or support with the plan they're already implementing. They control what resources or support they get.

It's more difficult to adapt to individuals the audience in when everybody is in a classroom or a virtual session, but you can make the activities or homework assignments flexible to try to engage the learners where they are:

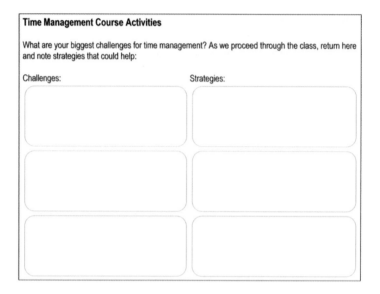

APPROACH 3: LEAVE TOOLS ALONG THE WAY

The last main option is to craft a path and leave tools along the way. This requires learners to be fairly self-directed. For example, you could have a website with lessons and tools and support for each stage in the process, so it's there for the learner when they need it.

These approaches aren't mutually exclusive. It's likely that some combination of approaches may make the most sense, particularly because it's pretty much impossible to have a whole audience that is exactly at the same point at the same time.

STAGES OF CHANGE

It's useful to consider how someone moves through a change and how what they need probably changes as they go. There's no one single way anyone makes a change, but it's fairly likely that people will do each of the following:

- **Consider a change:** Someone is thinking about making a change.
- **Planning:** Someone is intending to take action soon.
- **Making the change:** Someone is taking specific overt actions to change.
- **Maintaining the change:** Someone is working to solidify the behavior and prevent relapse into old habits.

Not every change requires maintaining. For example, if the change is buying life insurance or making a will, the person might not have to expend any additional effort after they make that change.

You'll see these stages as part of many change models—for example, the Transtheoretical Model of Change by Prochaska and DiClemente—so let's look at how they could play out.

Meet Henry. He's a database administrator for a tech company and a diehard Taylor Swift fan. The current bane of his existence is his bottomless email inbox. He has no problem managing databases, but he'll tell you that whatever he is doing to manage the flood of unread emails in his inbox just isn't working.

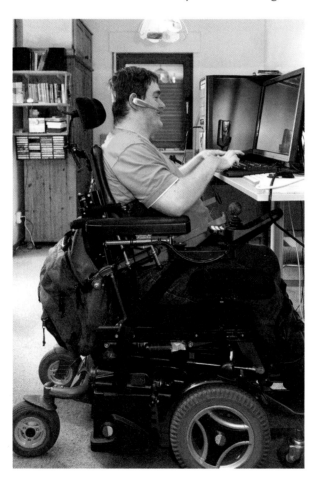

Stage	What Happened
Considering	Henry knows there's a problem, but he doesn't really have any intention to resolve it or even any idea what behavior would help. One day, he's scrolling his social media feed looking for new Taylor Swift dance challenges, and he sees a suggested video that promises to help you defeat your inbox.
	He clicks the video, which describes an inbox management method called SuperNBox that promises to make you an inbox superhero. Based on that click, his social media feed suggests 26 more videos on the topic. Henry watches several and likes the sound of the method.
Planning	Henry decides he's definitely going to do it, so he starts to figure out the logistics. He finds a preparation checklist online, installs some browser extensions to help, and makes a plan to get started. He also enrolls in a two-hour online class that teaches the method and walks you through your own inbox.
Making the change	He takes the class and starts the method, and it's working pretty well for him. To get started, he archived approximately a thousand unread messages, but he figures he can get them back if he needs them.
Maintaining	A few weeks into the method, it's working okay, but he's noticing that he's not superhero-ing his inbox quite as often. He convinced his work buddy, Mai, to try SuperNBox at the same time, so they make a bet. If one of them can catch the other person with more than 100 unread emails, that person has to buy beverages at Taylor Swift–themed karaoke.
	Six months in, Henry has learned some extra tips from videos posted by other SuperNBoxers and realizes that he follows the method without really thinking about it. He and Mai close out the debt by going to celebratory karaoke.

The main point of this example is to consider what support and materials would be helpful to Henry at each stage in the process. Specific instruction on the method (the most common type of learning intervention) is most helpful at the preparation and action phases.

Stage	What Helped Henry
Considering	A video that shows up at the right time with the right message
	Introductory videos that explain the method in broad strokes and have persuasive messaging about the benefits of the method
Planning	A "getting started" checklist
	Technology support (browser extensions)
	An online class

Making the change	Guidance during the online class for clearing his inbox
	Reference materials to support performance
Maintaining	Troubleshooting tips
	A commitment agreement with his colleague Mai
	Expert videos on how to refine the method

A different version of this story could have the effort failing because Henry couldn't find what he needed at the right time. Detailed instructions might be overwhelming during contemplation, and a lack of support mechanisms might have resulted in Henry starting strong but failing to keep it up.

CHANGE LADDER

One tool that has been useful for me is a change ladder. The particular version I use is based on a few different Risk Assessment Ladders used by researchers (Perski et al., 2021; Gould, 2016) in attempts to target messaging to the specific challenges faced by individuals engaging in behavior-change efforts. I find it a helpful way to consider the path that someone might go through toward behavior change and to use as part of audience research. It's more detailed and specific than the stages of change.

When it comes to someone changing a behavior, it's possible that person

1. Doesn't know about it (the behavior)
2. Knows about it but doesn't really get it (doesn't understand why it's important)
3. Gets it but doesn't really believe it (they aren't convinced)
4. Believes it but has other priorities
5. Prioritizes the behavior but doesn't know how to change it
6. Prioritizes it but thinks it's too hard
7. Prioritizes it but isn't confident
8. Is ready but needs help to start
9. Has started but isn't consistent
10. Has been consistent but is struggling to maintain

There are other versions of this kind of list, and it's definitely not a path that everyone follows, but it is a good set of potential points where people can get stuck.

I find this helpful for my own practice because it's easy to assume you know where people are getting stuck, and that can lead to giving them unhelpful solutions. For example, if someone is stuck because regardless of how much they prioritize the behavior, they are convinced that it's just too difficult to change given their current circumstances, then telling them louder and more emphatically that IT'S REALLY, REALLY IMPORTANT isn't going to help them. At all.

Let's take a look at an example of how this might go, and what learning materials can support people along the way.

MEET JANE

Jane is a project manager for a professional association that organizes conference and events for association members.

Everyone in the organization recognizes that they are going to have a few busy weeks around the biggest events during the year, and most people in the organization make sure to take some extra time off afterward to offset that workload. However, Jane's boss, Carla, notices that Jane is not really taking a break after one of their big events. In fact, she's the last person in the office most nights. Carla decides she should discuss this with Jane:

CARLA: Hey—it seems like you've had a lot of late nights lately. Is there too much on your plate?

JANE: Oh, well, no, but there's just a lot to keep up with. IT reached out, and they need some help with testing the new registration interface. And Malcolm is out, so I've been keeping his stuff moving. And I agreed to be on the branding committee. And to help review applicants for the intern program. And planning Carlita's retirement party. And I'm helping organize the local project management meetup.

CARLA: Wow. Um...okay.

JANE: Is there a problem? I'm staying on top of my regular responsibilities.

CARLA: There's no problem. You are doing a great job, but it sounds like you are committing to a lot of extra things. Do you really have time for all of that?

JANE: Well, I guess I have to. What choice is there?

CARLA: Actually, saying "no" sometimes is an option! Do you have any way to prioritize those extra projects to make sure you are picking the ones most meaningful to you—that you actually have time for?

JANE: Um, no, I guess I don't. I'm not even sure what that would look like.

CARLA: I'll pull a few resources for you to look at. I think it might be helpful.

JANE'S PROGRESS

Jane modifies her behavior by using a process to evaluate extra work requests to determine which requests she should say no to. Let's see what helps Jane with this. Again, not every person will have every sticking point, but if Jane has them all, it might look like this:

Doesn't know about it (the behavior)

What Happens	What Helped
Jane told Carla that "she doesn't even know what that would look like," so Carla pulls together an email of some resources for Jane, including a video and some blog posts and articles about how to align priorities to values.	Informational and educational resources
Jane looks through the resources.	

Knows about it but doesn't really get it (doesn't understand why it's important)

What Happens	What Helped
Jane chats with some of her project management colleagues in an online networking group and talks about how her boss brought this up, but Jane really thinks it's not a problem.	Social modeling
	Persuasive messages
A couple of the members are surprised that Jane doesn't already have a way to do this, and they swear they can't imagine not having a method prioritizing what they work on.	
One of the members sends Jane a link to a TED talk that makes an impassioned case for that behavior.	

Gets it but doesn't really believe it (they aren't convinced)

What Happens	What Helped
Jane is having lunch with Amira, her best friend from college, who also has a project management background. Jane describes the whole thing to her friend but concludes that it's a lot of fuss.	Appeal to identity
	Invocation of values
	Trusted social contact
Amira asks, "Would you respect a project manager who ran projects that way? I know you would never run a project that way; you value your team, and you protect the people on your projects. Why wouldn't you do that for yourself?"	

Believes it but has other priorities

What Happens	What Helped
After the conversation with her college friend, Jane is convinced but feels overwhelmed by all the things that she's already committed to. She doesn't feel like she's got the bandwidth to invest in it.	Allocating of resources to enable the behavior
She talks to Carla about how she's ready to get started. Carla helps her move some work responsibilities to other team members and approves a time for Jane to take a half-day class in the topic.	

Prioritizes the behavior but doesn't know how to change it

What Happens	What Helped
Jane takes the half-day workshop on a specific method for prioritizing. She really likes the method but feels like the workshop ends just as she's getting it. She wishes she had more opportunities to practice.	Formal instruction

Prioritizes it but thinks it's too hard

What Happens	What Helped
Jane is ready to sit down and get started, but it dawned on her during the workshop that she really needs to offload some of her current commitments as part of the process. She really doesn't want to let anyone down or make anyone angry, but she needs to do it. After a week of procrastinating, she tells Amira about the problem, and her friend helps her brainstorm and think through strategies for handling her current workload.	Social support Practical troubleshooting

Prioritizes it but isn't confident

What Happens	What Helped
After successfully handing off some of her existing tasks, Jane is ready to use the method to evaluate some new requests for her time. She realizes that she doesn't remember some details from the workshop, and she's not sure how to handle some things. She has some job aids from the workshop she can work though, but because she really cares about process, she wants to feel confident she's doing it right. She talks to her networking group, and one of the other members who currently uses the process offers to walk her through some examples over a virtual call. After practicing with help, Jane feels much more confident.	Coaching Job aids Skills practice

Is ready but needs help to start

What Happens	What Helped
Jane feels more confident and is ready to go. To help get started, she and Erin, another person from her workshop, have agreed to go through the process together to support each other.	Accountability partner

Has started but isn't consistent

What Happens	What Helped
When Jane sits down and focuses on using the process, it works pretty well. In particular, she uses it when she goes through her email. It works less well when requests come through a different way, like a coworker asking in person or a request in a meeting of the local meetup chapter. She figures out that she can ask people to send her the task or request in an email, and that helps her stick to the process.	Habit troubleshooting

Has been consistent but is struggling to maintain

What Happens	What Helped
Jane has been using the method for about six months when her boss, Carla, asks her how it's going.	Recommitment
	Social accountability
Jane tells her "It was great the first few months. I was following all the guidelines. But I've noticed a few things sneaking in. You know—something sounds like a little request, but when you get going, it turns into a much bigger time suck that you anticipated. I never let people on my projects lowball their time estimates, but I still seem to rationalize that 'it won't take that long' for my own time."	
Carla asks Jane if she wants her to help her with accountability about running all requests through the process, and they decide that Carla will help double-check Jane's numbers to help her keep herself on track with her time estimates.	

There were a few places in Jane's process where formal instruction was the right answer, but there were just as many places where social support, accountability, practice, or troubleshooting were the helpful answers.

Some of these elements are outside of the domain of the learning designer. You can't build trusted peer relationships just by putting a group of strangers in a virtual meeting breakout room. But you can create spaces for social learning to happen, and you can design materials that see people through the process.

THE LEARNING JOURNEY

When creating materials for a learning experience, these are the categories I typically consider:

Prelearning	Learning Activities	Practice / Visceral Experience	Feedback, Coaching, & Mentoring	Job Aid, Resources, and Just-in-Time Learning	Refreshing	Developing Further

SCENARIO: DOCUMENTING CODE

Let's take a look at each of these using a scenario.

Mai (Henry's work buddy and fellow Taylor Swift fan) teaches classes in JavaScript (a computer coding language) at the local community college, and it's going pretty well. She teaches Intro to JavaScript and runs a web development bootcamp for students where they use JavaScript to build web apps.

The one thing that isn't working well is that she can't seem to convince her students that it's really important to document their code, which is when the developer leaves notes in the computer code about what a particular bit of code is doing. The notes make the code easier to read and understand if the developer goes back to it later or if someone else needs to read and modify it. Mai's students are writing dozens or hundreds of lines of code but forgetting to put any notes in to remember later what each bit of code does.

Prelearning

Prelearning is anything that you might do to prepare learners for a learning experience. For example, you could have prelearning materials to do the following:

- **Priming:** What can you do to help learners get into the right frame of mind for the learning experience? It could be an article, a video, or a question for them to consider.
- **Qualifying:** Is this person ready to take this class? Qualifying could be a prerequisite, an assessment, or a set of questions the learner could ask themselves.

- **Stoking interest and excitement:** Is the learner excited about this learning experience? You could help ramp up interest through a promo video, testimonials from previous participants, teaser messages, or anything else that could get learners excited.
- **Identifying personal content/relevance:** Does the learner see how the material is relevant for them? This could be a request to identify problems or projects that the learner will work on in the class or questions that help them identify how the material will help them.

> Mai realizes that one of the reasons that her students aren't better about documenting code is that they've never had the experience of trying to wade through mountains of old code and figure out what's going on. As a prelearning activity for the next bootcamp, she gives them 10 mini problems, and they have to find the bug. They have to do at least three of the problems, but they can choose which ones and get extra credit for any they solve beyond the three required problems. Half the examples have well-documented code and half are poorly or not documented. She doesn't tell them that's what she is doing, but she collects up the results.

One challenge with prelearning activities is that it can be very difficult to get everyone in a class to participate. In the ideal world, everyone would complete prework, which would enable you to make the most of actual class time, but it rarely works out that way. A better plan is to have prelearning activities that enhance the experience for people who participate but aren't actually required.

Learning

There are too many options for learning to list all the types of activities. I focus on learning strategies to support behavior later in the book, but here a few quick strategies to consider:

- **Active learning:** Having the learners participate in the process helps make it feel easier and more relevant for them.
- **Eliciting from the audience:** If there's anything you can get your audience to tell you rather than you telling them, try to do so. It promotes buy-in and creates a more active experience for your learners.
- **Using examples:** For anything that is complex or subtle, examples are crucial—and the more the better.

> When Mai starts the first bootcamp session, she shows her students the results from the prelearning activity. The majority of the completed challenges were from the well-documented code examples. She then has the group critique the

poorly documented challenges and create a list of all the ways the well-documented examples differed from the poorly documented examples. In groups, the students then have to fix documentation in the poor examples.

Practice/Visceral Experience

For any learning objective, I always ask, "Is It reasonable to think they can be proficient without practice?" For example, someone can probably be proficient at filling out a timesheet without practicing, but it's less likely they'll be skilled at playing golf without practice.

Practice can occur during the learning experience, after the learning experience, or both. The first time someone does something, it can feel awkward and wrong, but additional practice will almost always help learners with comfort and confidence. Here are some strategies you should consider when designing practice activities:

- **Cycles of expertise:** Instead of having a single example that learners work through, try to introduce them to the content or process in a simple conceptual example that they try; then move on to a few increasingly complex real examples, including their own problems or challenges.
- **Leveling up:** Ensure that initial challenges are appropriate both in challenge and ability. Something too easy is boring for learners. Too hard, and it's frustrating. Try to have the next challenge be something where they have to stretch to reach it without being something that's totally out of reach.
- **Real-world missions:** Try to identify ways that learners can take the practice back to their real-world environment and practice in a way that they have accountability and feedback.

    Mai continues to have mini challenges for students throughout the bootcamp where they identify or fix documentation. She also carves out time at the end of the bootcamp session that is dedicated to just fixing or adding documentation.

Feedback, Coaching, and Mentoring

Practice is important for skill development, but so is feedback. Practicing an action doesn't necessarily make it perfect, but it does encode those actions in automatic memory, so feedback is crucial. A good feedback mechanism can help with the following:

- **Adjusting performance:** In physical skills like sports, it's a given that feedback is necessary to improve. Feedback is just as important for improving cognitive skills, but people sometimes forget this principle.

- **Accountability:** Having some accountability can make a world of difference in being able to execute and maintain behaviors.
- **Increasing independence:** People who are very new to a skill often need scaffolding in the form of supports or guardrails for correct performance. Gradual removal of scaffolding can be part of getting learners to proficiency.

Instead of reviewing and providing feedback to students individually, Mai implements code reviews as part of the intro class and the bootcamp, and part of the review is to critique the documentation. She also creates materials for students to peer-review each other's code.

Job Aid, Resources, and Just-in-Time Learning

This category is essentially about whatever will help learners when they are actually trying to do the thing. What materials or support will they need? Here are some examples:

- **Job aids or performance support:** Job aids are explanatory aids that can help walk a learner through performing. According to Dave Ferguson, an experienced instruction designer, job aids can be training wheels or guardrails (Ferguson 2009). Training wheels are job aids you use until you get to proficiency, whereas guardrails are job aids that help people keep on the track (for example, a job aid that contains the legal disclaimer language that needs to be read to customers on a call).
- **Troubleshooting help:** What resources will help people troubleshoot problems? It could be a decision tree, a series of resources for different problems, or a check-in with a coach or mentor to get help adjusting a plan to work better going forward.
- **Checklists:** Atul Gawande's book *The Checklist Manifesto* is full of good examples of how to support performance with checklists. These can be good tools for learners to do self-assessment as well.
- **Reference materials:** This includes all the references and resources you would provide to learners, such as a series of just-in-time videos, a wiki, or a support manual. You can use whatever will be a good resource for learners.

Mai provides a library of documentation examples and encourages students to add to it. She also has a collection of shortcut strategies they can use.

Refreshing

If a behavior is infrequently used, it's likely that it will need to be refreshed. Refreshing serves two main purposes:

- **Cognitive spacing:** One of the best-established findings in educational psychology is the idea that people's memories decay over time if not used, but periodically stimulating a memory causes it to decay more slowly. So a periodic refresh (for example, an email, an article, a video, a question) can help people retain knowledge over time, even if it's infrequently used.
- **Prompting the behavior:** People can come out of training with many good intentions about a new behavior, but it can fall off over time. Periodic prompts can help refresh people's resolve to engage in the behavior.

Mai has her students come up with their own mini challenges and then sends them out weekly over the course of the bootcamp. She also sends some of the challenges to bootcamp alumni, so previous students can also refresh their knowledge.

Developing Further

Developing further is just what it sounds like: what resources are available if someone wants to take it to the next level? A lot of training material focuses on introductory content rather than materials to help people go from beginner to intermediate. Provide tools for those people who don't want to stop at the first level:

- **Next level:** It's always worth asking what would help people move to the next level if they are motivated to learn more. One way to do that is to ask expert performers what experiences helped them improve their skills and use that information to design opportunities and experiences for intermediate learners.
- **Curated resources:** Often, developing further is about curating resources because as people move along the skill curve, what they need becomes more individual. It becomes less about a fully structured learning experience and more about providing people with what they need.
- **Social:** Often, social learning solutions (participating in discussions, networking groups, events, and social media) can be good to help people level up their skills.

Mai points students to additional resources to help them improve their practice and arranges for some of her bootcamp graduates to be teaching assistants for new students. ■

KEY POINTS

These are a few of the key takeaways for this chapter:

- Understanding the process that learners go through makes it more possible to meet them where they are and to create materials that support them throughout the process.
- Rushing learners who aren't ready yet is likely to produce frustration or resistance.
- If you give learners choices that are clear and easy to understand, they will be more able to select what they need at that point.

RESOURCES

Ferguson, Dave. "Job aids: training wheels and guard rails." *Dave's Whiteboard* (blog), March 31, 2009, http://www.daveswhiteboard.com/archives/1939.

Gawande, Atul. *The Checklist Manifesto: How to Get Things Right*. Metropolitan Books; 1st edition (December 15, 2009).

Gould, Gillian Sandra, Kerrianne Watt, Robert West, Yvonne Cadet-James, and Alan R. Clough. "Can smoking initiation contexts predict how adult Aboriginal smokers assess their smoking risks? A cross-sectional study using the 'Smoking Risk Assessment Target'." *BMJ Open 6*, no. 7 (2016): e010722.

Perski, Olga, Claire Stevens, Robert West, and Lion Shahab. "Pilot randomised controlled trial of the Risk Acceptance Ladder (RAL) as a tool for targeting health communications." *PLOS ONE 16*, no. 11 (2021): e0259949.

Prochaska, James O., John C. Norcross, and Carlo C. DiClemente. *Changing for Good: A Revolutionary Six-Stage Program for Overcoming Bad Habits and Moving Your Life Positively Forward* (New York: William Morrow and Co. Inc., 1994).

COMMUNICATING VALUE

(IN WHICH THE ELEPHANT COMPARES IMMEDIATE KETTLE BELLS TO DELAYED DISSERTATIONS)

WHAT'S IT WORTH?

One of the crucial parts of most behavior-change interventions is communicating the value of the change. The learning and development industry struggles with this.

Despite the ubiquitous advice to communicate WIIFM (What's In It For Me?—more on this later), the description of the value is almost always directed to the rider but not the elephant.

⟨VALUE...⟩

Discussing Value   Looking for Snacks

Chapter 3 talks about the problem of competing priorities. Basically, there are many, many behaviors that everyone agrees would be good to do, but in order for them to actually happen, they need to be better to do than the 37 other things we could do with that same amount of time.

37 Other Things

For example, let's say I'm leveraging some carefully guarded time I have staked out for myself. I have an hour where I don't need to do work, do chores, or take care of family. This time is all mine. I want to use it in a way that brings me the most overall benefit and meets my values and goals.

A few options could include

- Making healthy food
- Doing something creative
- Reading an enlightening book
- Taking a walk outside
- Spending time in nature
- Doing yoga

- Spending time with friends
- Helping with a cause I believe in
- Scrolling around in a streaming service to decide what to watch and finally settling for an episode of TV that I've actually already seen

If you've never resorted to that last option, good for you. I'm pretty sure I'm not the only person who has done that, though. And I'm not sneering at taking time to relax or to consume media. Both of those things can add a lot to our lives. But to understand how to communicate the value of a behavior, we need to take a closer look at how that value is calculated. A behavior needs not only to be valuable but deemed *more valuable* than the 37 other things.

VALUE – EFFORT

The next illustration shows the most basic equation for assessing and communicating value.

It's pretty simple: Does the value I get outweigh the effort to do something? Some other variables can also factor into this equation. If the math doesn't add up, the behavior probably won't happen.

Let's look at some common tasks and see how each does in terms of this equation. First, we look at some scenarios of value:

Timesheet

Filling out a timesheet

Value: You get paid and can subsequently afford rent, food, and other necessities of life. (**VALUE = HIGH**)

Taxes

Filing your taxes

Value: You don't get fined by the tax revenue people, and you aren't subject to legal proceedings for non-payment of taxes. (**VALUE = VERY HIGH**)

Salad

Making a salad for dinner

Value: You've been wanting to eat more fruits and vegetables, so this is a good way to accomplish that, and you do actually like eating a tasty, well-prepared salad. (**VALUE = PRETTY GOOD**)

Okay, so let's consider the same scenarios for effort:

Timesheet

Filling out a timesheet

Effort: The company updated the payroll system, so you need to find the instructions for how you log in to update your timesheet. And of course they couldn't actually make it easy by putting a Timesheet button on the main page. And the last time you logged in, it rejected your password, and you had to do one of those visual not-a-robot things where you clicked the square that contained images of stoplights. And you spent way too long figuring out whether that included the wire the stoplight was hanging from, and what did you do with that sticky note where you jotted your hours anyway? (**EFFORT = WAY HIGHER THAN IT SHOULD BE**)

Taxes

Filing your taxes

Effort: It wouldn't be so bad because you actually find filling out the SimpliTax online app to be kind of satisfying, but you still need to go through the shoebox of receipts and match them up to your work trips. And you still have a month until the tax deadline, and you just can't make yourself, especially because that *Game of Thrones* reboot starts tonight. (**EFFORT = NOT SO BAD AFTER YOU GET THROUGH THAT SHOEBOX**)

Salad

Making a salad for dinner

Effort: This wouldn't be too bad because you know yourself well enough to know that you need to buy the prewashed lettuce, but it's been sitting in the refrigerator for a week and some of the lettuce is starting to look a little slimy, so you'll need to pick through it. And it seems like the salad dressing is mostly empty, so you'd have to figure out how to stretch it out. Or you could just make the frozen pizza instead. It's the kind of pizza that has a few green peppers, mushrooms, and olives, so those are still vegetables, right? (**EFFORT = I'LL DO BETTER NEXT TIME**)

So, while the value of all these activities is substantial, the effort means that at the very least, the action is going to be delayed until the urgency is higher or the effort is lower. Also, none of these topics are particularly exciting, and that's kind of the point. We're often creating learning experiences for things that are necessary and important but not all that exciting.

WIIFM — WHAT'S IN IT FOR ME?

Anyone who has worked in learning and development has heard the advice that you need to include the WIIFM for the audience (What's In It For Me?—pronounced *whiff-em*), and they are absolutely right. But it's also more complicated than that.

Let's look at four different objectives for some workplace training materials and the WIIFM for each one.

Behavior 1	Behavior 2	Behavior 3
Healthcare staff need to safely dispose of vaccination needles or other sharps.	Salespeople need to use consultative selling to build client relationships (rather than product-based selling).	Managers need to effectively use the new performance evaluation system, which will be used for quarterly or monthly performance reviews (rather than annual reviews).

If we ask the question of why these behaviors are valuable, it's fairly easily to see the argument for each behavior:

Behavior	Value
Healthcare staff need to safely dispose of vaccination needles or other sharps.	Helps prevent injury or infection for health care workers and cleaning staff.
Salespeople need to use consultative selling to build client relationships (rather than product-based selling).	Potential benefits include improved client relationships, cross-selling based on client needs, and more durable and trusting client relationships that could translate into higher sales overall.
Managers need to effectively use the new performance evaluation system, which will be used for quarterly or monthly performance reviews (rather than annual reviews).	If this works as designed, the effort of doing each performance review could be less if managers are updating an ongoing review rather than writing a new one from scratch. Employees would be less likely to be surprised by an unexpected issue. Employees could get more timely feedback that improves their performance and improves their relationship with their manager.

These are all pretty valuable, right? We will discuss intrinsic or extrinsic rewards more in Chapter 5, "Understanding Motivation," but these are all benefits that are directly germane to the job role of the person performing the behavior, which should help make them powerful motivators.

Imagine you are a manager who gets an email from human resources:

EMAIL

Subject: SYSWORKSHOP 2876B - Mandatory Performance Evaluation System Training

Which of the following do you think would be your most likely reaction?

a. Great! This is an amazing opportunity to improve my managerial abilities and build a stronger, more successful team!
b. Oh goodness, I really don't have time for that right now. Can't they just send me a job aid?
c. Sigh. Another new system? Haven't we been here before?
d. Some other reaction.

If you picked option A, that's marvelous. The world needs good managers, so I hope that's part of your career path.

I think the other options are a little more common, based on similar projects I've been involved with over the years. And that's not because the participants in those training efforts weren't good managers who sincerely cared about the well-being of their teams. It's because they are *busy,* and they have had experiences in the past with organizational systems and initiatives that took a lot of time but didn't really add up to much benefit.

And how would the elephant look at that subject line?

EMAIL

Subject: SYSWORKSHOP 2876B -
Mandatory Performance Evaluation
System Training

CALCULATING VALUE

So if we ask how the elephant perceives value, it can't just be an abstract good thing. It needs to have some other characteristics if it's going to motivate action and raise itself above the other 37 things someone could be doing with that time and effort.

To understand how to communicate value, it's worth asking the following questions:

- How SIGNIFICANT is the reward/consequence?
- How IMMEDIATE is the reward/consequence?
- How TANGIBLE is the reward/consequence?
- How LIKELY is the reward/consequence?

VALUE — SIGNIFICANT

If someone asked you, "Is a $25 gift card a good reward?" the first question you'd probably respond with is "A reward for what?"

If it's a reward for answering a five-question survey about your customer experience at a local retailer, it might be a pretty good reward. If it's an acknowledgment for months of intense work on a project for your company that has involved overtime, extra effort, and sacrifices of personal time, then it's not really such a great gesture, and it may actually be demotivating.

There's a trope in the training world that "if someone can do it if you give them a million dollars, then it's not a training problem." The implication is that if they know how to do it and could do it with a big enough incentive, then the problem is management, motivation, or something else unrelated to training.

This is probably true enough, but "significant" can mean very different things in context.

For example, I've worked on several healthcare-related projects over the years, and one of the challenges has been getting healthcare workers to user test the solutions (an essential part of any design process).

On some of the projects, we were able to source nurses through a temporary staffing agency. We needed an hour of their time to go through the course and test the solution, but usually the minimum shift was four hours, so we would pay for four hours while only requiring an hour or so of their time. They were often a bit bemused by the process but were fine with the situation. Four hours of pay at their regular rate was an acceptable reward for the behavior.

When we had a project that had physicians as the target audience, getting test subjects was much more difficult. There are user testing agencies that will do this kind of recruiting now, but we didn't have access to those on some of these earlier projects.

The actual dollar amount that would be needed to pay doctors was often prohibitive for the project budgets. Four hours of their time at their usual salary wasn't as compelling to doctors as it had been to nurses for a variety of reasons. Even if that amount was in budget for us, doctors were paid more overall, so extra money wasn't as compelling, and they often had to guard their free time because of long work hours.

So when we needed doctors for user testing, we often relied on the doctors who were working on the project with us to recruit physician friends and colleagues for user testing. We typically offered these people no money at all. They were doing it as a favor to a trusted friend or colleague, and bringing money into the equation would likely have only made it awkward.

For the nurses, four hours' wage was "significant" enough, but for doctors, zero dollars was okay if there was also a social connectedness element. Presumably there was a dollar amount (if we had had an unlimited budget) that we could have found that would have made a paid reward motivating for the doctors, but it likely would have been much more than four hours' standard wage.

So "significant" isn't the only factor that influences the calculation of value for a reward or consequence, and there are other factors to consider. Let's take a look at a few of them.

Behavior	Benefit
Healthcare staff need to safely dispose of vaccination needles or other sharps.	Helps prevent injury or infection for healthcare workers and cleaning staff.
Salespeople need to use consultative selling to build client relationships (rather than product-based selling).	Potential benefits include improved client relationships, cross-selling based on client needs, and more durable and trusting client relationships that could translate into higher sales overall.
Managers need to effectively use the new performance evaluation system, which will be used for quarterly or monthly performance reviews (rather than annual reviews).	If this works as designed, the effort of doing each performance review could be less if managers are updating an ongoing review rather than writing a new one from scratch. Employees would be less likely to be surprised by an unexpected issue. Employees could get more timely feedback that improves their performance and improves their relationship with their manager.

So, however likely it is that the new training initiative will produce a desired reward or avoid a negative consequence, it often does not *feel* likely to learners, which is going to make them less likely to judge the behavior as valuable.

VALUE – IMMEDIACY

When you receive a reward or consequence may be as or more important than how big the reward or consequence is. Let's look at the behaviors from the beginning of the chapter in terms of the timing of the rewards or consequences:

Timesheet

Filling out a timesheet

Reward/Consequence	Timing
You get paid.	One or maybe a few weeks, typically
You get the satisfaction of crossing a pesky task off the to-do list.	Immediate
You avoid getting nagged or chastised for being late on the timesheet.	A few days, typically

Taxes

Filing your taxes

Reward/Consequence	Timing
You have met your obligation to the tax agency and can stop thinking about taxes for the year.	Immediate
You get a refund (if you are getting one).	A few weeks or more
You avoid getting fined or audited for tax payment noncompliance.	It depends on how close to the deadline you are—it could be minutes or months.

Salad

Making a salad for dinner

Reward/Consequence	Timing
If you like salad, you get to eat something you enjoy.	Pretty immediate
You get a health benefit from increasing your vegetable intake.	Days to weeks before you'll likely notice the benefit of dietary changes

Each of these items have variable timeframes for the rewards (or avoidance of consequences), from "immediate" to "weeks or months." This is going to influence where you rank them in your priorities compared to the 37 other things you could do with the same time or effort.

DELAYED REWARDS

It's logical that an immediate reward will be the most compelling, but what happens when the reward or consequence gets pushed into the future? There's a phenomenon in behavioral economics that helps us understand this. (I've written about this before, but it's a crucial point, so I'm going to reiterate it here.)

What is your answer to these questions?

1. If someone is handing out free money, would you rather have $10 or $11?
2. If someone is handing out free money, would you rather have $10 today or $11 tomorrow?
3. If someone is handing out free money, would you rather have $10 today or $11 in a year?

There's a term behavioral economics called hyperbolic discounting. Basically, the valuation of a reward or consequence is the greatest if it happens immediately, and then it falls off at a steep curve. The valuation flattens out after a certain amount of time, so in my example, the value of the eleventh dollar would probably not be all that different if it was offered at 11 months or 12 months.

I've asked groups of people Question 1 dozens of times, and almost everyone opts for the $11 option. That's a pretty logical choice (it's not a trick question).

Question 2 gets a more mixed answer. It's usually roughly a 50/50 or 60/40 split between people who want the more immediate $10 or the slightly delayed $11.

And for Question 3, everyone opts for the $10 now, except for an occasional outliner (who usually want to talk to me about interest rates). If you opt for the $10 today, you are in the overwhelming majority of people.

So everybody wanted the extra dollar if they could have it immediately, roughly half would wait a day for it, and almost no one wanted to wait a whole year for it. If we graph who wants the extra dollar, we see something like this:

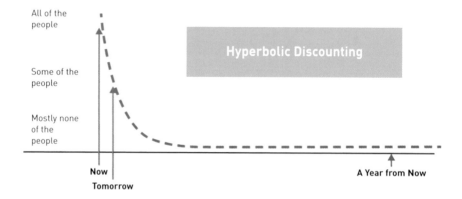

As soon as we move the reward into the future, people start to value it a bit less. In experiments, it falls off fairly quickly, then flattens out over time.

Behaviors with delayed rewards or consequences tend to be difficult behaviors for us as humans. For example, smoking provides immediate satisfaction for a smoker (by stopping the craving), but the potentially life-threatening consequences of smoking can be delayed for years or even decades.

I don't want to oversimplify the issues around smoking cessation (it's a complex challenge with chemical and biological components), but one part of the equation may be delayed consequences.

Smoking cessation messages have recognized that health consequences in a distant future may seem less compelling for people who are trying to quit, and health communications have started to also feature more salient and immediate health benefits for smokers, such as in this communication from the Centers for Disease Control:

When you quit smoking:

In Minutes	In One Day	In Several Days	In 1-12 Months	In 1-6 Years	In 5-10 Years
your heart rate drops	Nicotine levels in the blood drop to zero	Carbon monoxide in the blood drops to level of a non-smoker	Shortness of breath and coughing decrease	Risk of heart attack drops sharply and added risk of coronary heart disease drops by half	Added risk of cancers of the mouth and throat, drops by half and risk of stroke decreases

Source: The Health Consequences of Smoking: What It Means to You – a 2004 summary of *Surgeon General's Report on the Health Consequences of Smoking*.

When it comes to motivation for activities like exercise, there is research to suggest that immediate rewards are viewed as a more compelling reason to exercise (Segar, 2011). For example, my possible reasons to take the dog for an afternoon walk could be

To clear my head between meetings, and make sure I don't end the work day all stiff and sore

To improve my cardiovascular fitness

Arguably, improving cardiovascular fitness could be a *bigger* (*more significant*) goal than clearing my head, but it could be weeks or months before I notice myself feeling better or seeing some physiological change. That's a long time to keep the elephant going.

But the first goal has much more *immediate* rewards: I feel more clear-headed and less stiff pretty much as soon as I do the activity. Also, Bella the Schnauzer usually launches into a frenzy of joy, and I often get to socialize with my friend Rebecca while she walks her dog. Altogether, I get more than enough rewards for the activity that it becomes a no-brainer. Instead of feeling like I *have* to exercise, I feel like I *get* to take a walk. Because the benefits are immediate, the effort feels negligible.

Bella, waiting for her walk

One research inquiry into how different types of goals impacted participants' exercise (Segar et al., 2011) found that a focus on more immediate *"quality of life"* goals were deemed better reasons to exercise by participants than a more distant goal like *"healthy aging."*

If we go back to our behaviors of filling out a timesheet, filing your taxes, and making a salad for dinner, they are a little thin on immediate rewards. The timesheet and the taxes only have the satisfaction of task completion. The salad, if you like salad and it's delicious salad, is the only one likely to have intrinsic immediate payoff, which means these tasks may get delayed. Obviously, your context matters (for example, are you getting a tax refund, and do you need that money sooner rather than later?).

The satisfaction of completing a task probably varies by person. My friends who are get-it-done folks seem to derive more satisfaction than I do from crossing tasks off their lists. Undone tasks seem to bother them, so crossing them off is a big win. I like crossing off tasks and have been known to do that thing where you write down a task you've already done just to have the satisfaction of crossing it off, but I don't have their discomfort with undone tasks until the deadline starts to loom.

How does immediacy impact learners?

If we go back to our learner behaviors, we need to ask how quickly will they see the value of those behaviors.

Behavior	Value	Timeframe
Healthcare staff need to safely dispose of vaccination needles or other sharps.	Helps prevent injury or infection for health care workers and cleaning staff.	Immediately for healthcare workers, but the benefit isn't a positive outcome. Instead, it's a lack of negative outcomes (injuries or infections). The sense of reward may depend on how informed learners are about previous levels of injury or infection.
Salespeople need to use consultative selling to build client relationships (rather than product-based selling).	Potential benefits include improved client relationships, cross-selling based on client needs, and more durable and trusting client relationships that could translate into higher sales overall.	The benefit of increased sales will likely not be immediate because it will take a while for salespeople to adapt to the new methods. In fact, the immediate impact could even be a dip in sales while they change their methods.

Managers need to effectively use the new performance evaluation system, which will be used for quarterly or monthly performance reviews (rather than annual reviews).	If this works as designed, the effort of doing each performance review could be less if managers are updating an ongoing review rather than writing a new one from scratch. Employees would be less likely to be surprised by an unexpected issue. Employees could get more timely feedback that improves their performance and improves their relationship with their manager.	Benefits will likely take months to become apparent, and may be difficult to connect to the new system.

For all of these behaviors, it might be a bit difficult for learners to pin down exactly when they might experience a reward or consequence, and it's unlikely that any of the rewards or consequences would be immediate.

Instead of WIIFM, Maybe Consider WCIDWT

While WIIFM is easier to pronounce, I actually like WCIDWT (not sure how you'd pronounce that—*Wa-sid-wit* maybe?). And by that acronym, I mean What Can I Do With That?

I often ask workshop groups these questions, too:

1. On a scale of 0 to 10, what is your current level of interest in watching a five-minute video on printer repair?

   The answer is usually mostly 0, with a few people higher (presumably due to an intrinsic interest in printer repair?).

2. Imagine you need to print an extremely important document that really needs to go out in today's mail and your printer is broken. Now on a scale of 0 to 10, what is your current level of interest in watching a five-minute video on printer repair?

   This question gets answers in the range of eight, nine, or ten.

3. Now imagine that you are working with a few of your fellow participants, and I just put a broken printer in front of you. Your job as a team is to fix it. Now on a scale of 0 to 10, what is your current level of interest in watching a five-minute video on printer repair?

Think about your own answer to this last question. It's logical that a real-world need (the important document) would make the video more interesting, but even a simulated problem usually gets answers in the five to nine range. There's no real-world consequence for not fixing the printer, but even a classroom activity where they need to apply the video increases the interest level of the audiences.

So how do we use this for learning design?

The intrinsic reward for learning something is getting to use what you've learned. Some learning is about the pleasure of knowing or understanding, but in most adult contexts, the purpose of training is to be able to apply a procedure, skill, or judgment.

If we look at some common learning experiences, the getting-to-use reward might be quite delayed:

Learning Experience	Time to Application
An annual compliance class for financial planners on identifying red flag indicators of money laundering.	A planner could go months or years without seeing money laundering red flags, or they could see something the next day.
Elearning for all new faculty joining a university on the ethical guidelines for using human subjects in research studies.	Some new faculty may be planning to start research immediately, but many may not need this information for months or more.
A video for staff on emergency evacuation procedures for a sports arena.	This is also difficult to predict. The timing of potential application goes all the way from "immediately" to "never."

One answer is to move the point of learning closer to the point of use. For example, instead of requiring new faculty to take the ethics course when they join the university, it could be delayed until the point that a particular faculty member gets involved with a research study. The content will be more relevant to them, and their learning experience will be fresh when they begin to apply it.

But since the money laundering or evacuation examples could happen at any time, it's difficult to move the point of learning close to the point of use because we just don't know when they will need it, and you don't really want people watching videos when they should be evacuating the building.

IMMEDIATE USE

Immediate use is first giving the learners a problem to solve and *then* giving them the information to solve it. This is not a new idea. Howard Barrows used this in the 1960s when he pioneered problem-based learning in medical education, and it's what elearning guru Michael Allen would refer to as "Test Then Tell" learning.

Basically, you give people a problem to solve and only then give them the information they need to solve it. For example, you might give learners a problem to solve, and then have them use the job aids and resources from their workplace to figure out the answer or the next course of action.

Example: Emergency Evacuation Training

VALUE – TANGIBLE

The next question to ask about the rewards or consequences is "Do they feel real or tangible to the learners?"

For example, the consequence of not getting paid because you didn't fill out your timesheet is pretty tangible and easy for people to picture, and we all have a general idea that not filing your taxes leads to "something bad" even if we might be a bit vague on exactly what will happen (unless you've already been through it and know from personal experience).

But the positive benefits of eating a salad are a bit harder to picture. If you like salad, then the benefit of getting to eat something you enjoy is plenty concrete, but if you are eating the salad more because you want the health benefit of increasing your intake of fruits and vegetables, then it starts to be a little more abstract. What exactly does improved vegetable intake get you? Everyone probably has an impression about this. If you know a lot about nutrition, you might have a concrete sense of the benefits, but if you are part of the general population with no special knowledge of nutrition, it may be a little vague.

So, the more that the benefit is tangible to people, the more likely it is to *feel* real to them.

In his book, *Louder Than Words*, Benjamin Bergen (a cognitive scientist with a specialty in cognitive linguistics) describes how people are able understand ideas and abstract concepts faster if they're framed in a way they can picture in their minds. He discusses this as the likely cause for abstract terms like "the rates climbed" or "she grasped the idea" to be expressed with physical actions or directional movement.

So I think it's worth asking if rewards or consequences are tangible or abstract for the audience. In an effort to make our discussion of this topic more concrete, let's use the scale I just invented called the "Kettle Bell to Doctoral Dissertation Scale."

If I want to explain the concept of "heavy," I could say, "A kettle bell is heavy," or I could say that a doctoral dissertation entitled "Kant & Wittgenstein: Noumenal and Empirical Human Nature" is heavy and mean it entirely in an abstract, conceptual way (although it admittedly might also be physically heavy when printed out).

So when we say something is pretty concrete, we mean it's something a learner could see, touch, taste, feel, or picture in their mind in a visual way (more kettle bell), and when we say abstract, we mean something that is conceptual and not easily visualized by learners (more dissertation).

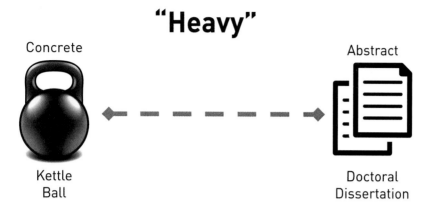

"Heavy"

Concrete — Kettle Ball

Abstract — Doctoral Dissertation

Your rider understands conceptual and abstract, but guess what the elephant responds to?

HUH, WHAT'S THIS?

Let's look at some research studies where experimenters have tried to investigate this question.

THE VIRTUAL CHAINSAW

In a research study (Ahn et al., 2014) conducted at the Virtual Human Interaction Laboratory at Stanford University, researchers looked at the question of whether people felt like they had control of their impact on the environment. To study this, they created two conditions. In one condition, a group of people, after being educated about the impact of paper usage on deforestation, read about trees being cut down (a more abstract experience, where participants do not take action). In the second condition, after the same education about paper usage and deforestation, participants would go into a virtual reality environment and cut down trees with a virtual chainsaw. The sights, sounds, and physical (haptic) feedback made the experience much more visceral and real than the reading condition with the first group.

Image credit: Stanford Virtual Human Interaction Lab.

So after doing the reading or going through the virtual reality experience, participants were asked if they would change their paper usage based on the experience, and both groups said they would in roughly equal measures. This is a question about future actions (how you will use paper in the future), so this question is really directed at the rider, which is the decision-making entity that projects into the future.

However, experimenters would then "accidentally" spill a glass of water and ask participants for help cleaning up the spill. They would then count the number of paper napkins the participant used.

Participants in the more-kettle-bell virtual reality condition used *significantly fewer* paper napkins than the people in the abstract dissertation-y reading condition.

People who had a direct physical experience of consequences (which engaged their elephant) used less paper in the present. I don't want to overgeneralize from this single experiment, but giving learners a more visceral experience of rewards or consequences is a potential strategy to try if your learners don't seem to feel the impact of potential consequences.

SMOKERS AND COWBOYS

Another area of research that has looked at this tangibility effect is smoking cessation. As I discuss in the immediacy section, the beneficial impact of quitting smoking is not something you can immediately detect. If you quit, you don't immediately find it easier to walk up a flight of stairs. Many of the benefits are related to long-term health consequences, some of which might be hard to visualize. (If someone isn't in healthcare, does that person have a visualization for what "emphysema" looks like? I know I don't. I know it's bad, but no visual image comes to mind.)

So the health rewards for quitting smoking have historically been more in the dissertation camp than kettle bell camp, and if you can visualize what the benefits of quitting look like, it's probably because the public health communicators have worked extremely hard to put those images into your mind.

One of the most memorable television ads from the mid-2000s was the singing cowboy, which was created by Truth Initiative, a nonprofit public health initiative trying to end tobacco use and nicotine addiction.

The Singing Cowboy was released in 2006 and showed a pair of cowboys (a riff on the Marlboro Man—the iconic cowboy image used to sell Marlboro cigarettes for more than 40 years) sitting around a campfire in the middle of traffic in Manhattan. One of the cowboys sings a song about how smoking doesn't always kill you but has many other horrifying health effects. The hook of the ad is that the singer has had a laryngectomy (removal of the larynx) due to smoking-related cancer and is singing with the aid of an electrolarynx, which he holds to his neck. The expressions of passers-by suggest that is an eye-opening thing to witness.

So, if we go back and look at some of our behaviors for learners, are they more kettle bell/concrete, or do they seem to be more dissertation/abstract?

Behavior	Benefit	Concrete or Abstract?
Healthcare staff need to safely dispose of vaccination needles or other sharps.	Helps prevent injury or infection for healthcare workers and cleaning staff.	This one is mercifully concrete. It's quite easy to picture the consequences to be avoided. Assessment: Five Kettle Bells!
Salespeople need to use consultative selling to build client relationships (rather than product-based selling).	Potential benefits include improved client relationships, cross-selling based on client needs, and more durable and trusting client relationships that could translate into higher sales overall.	Maybe salespeople have experience doing some of this already so they can draw on it, but it's still a bit abstract. Assessment: Two Dissertations:
Managers need to effectively use the new performance evaluation system, which will be used for quarterly or monthly performance reviews (rather than annual reviews).	If this works as designed, the effort of doing each performance review could be less if managers are updating an ongoing review rather than writing a new one from scratch. Employees would be less likely to be surprised by an unexpected issue. Employees could get more timely feedback that improves their performance and improves their relationship with their manager.	This one is veeeery fuzzy. Although managers can probably picture good conversations with their employees, it's going to be very difficult for learners to connect the dots here. Assessment: Five Dissertations

VALUE — LIKELY

There is a wide body of content in the world documenting just how bad humans are at understanding probability. A few favorites on the "People Bad at Understanding Probability" bibliography are

- *Thinking Fast and Slow* by Daniel Kahneman
- *Thinking in Bets* by Annie Duke

Being bad at understanding probability impacts a person's ability to assess rewards or consequences where the outcome is uncertain. For example, if you don't file your taxes, the probability is pretty high that there will be a consequence for that. It's not 100%, but it's also probably not a good idea to bet on the tax authority *just not noticing*.

But often people act based on how likely something *feels* rather than how likely something actually is. There's a trope that the most dangerous part of a commercial airline flight is the drive to the airport. It's difficult to get an apples-to-apples comparison of the safety of driving versus flying, but by any metric, commercial air travel is extremely safe. The likelihood of dying in commercial airline crash is extremely low.

But people who have flight phobias have heard that math many times, and for many of them it just doesn't matter. Their logical rider can read the statistics all day long, but their elephant is still going to exercise veto power and refuse to get on an airplane.

I dislike the framing of this fear as irrational. It might not be a statistically justifiable position, but I believe framing it as the person being illogical isn't helpful.

I have typically flown a lot for work and am not a fearful flyer, but it turns out that while my rider knows that I'm in a metal tube in the air, my elephant is convinced that it's just a crowded uncomfortable room with a solid foundation underneath my feet. I was deplaning on the tarmac a few years ago and happened to get a good look at just how small the luggage area under that particular plane was, which messed with my "solid foundation" perception. My elephant immediately took charge and was all, "STOP LOOKING AT THAT. NOPE, NOPE, NOPE. DON'T WANT TO KNOW."

So perceived risk often outweighs actual risk, and perceived risk can be affected by many variables, such as media coverage, information sources, and personal experience.

WE LEARN FROM EXPERIENCE

In a book about learning design for behavior change, it should be fairly uncontroversial to say, "We learn from experience." I think everyone would agree with that statement.

But it might be worth asking exactly *what* we learn from some experiences.

For example, my friend Samantha joined her community gym several years ago. As part of the membership, she received two free personal training sessions.

She'd been a member of other gyms, and so was expecting someone who would give her an intro to the facilities and suggest some workout strategies, but her personal trainer for the first session was THE DRILL SARGEANT OF PERSONAL TRAINERS.

(Not the actual trainer but someone of equivalent intensity).

The trainer had my friend doing lunges across the gym and calisthenics and weights and all the things. My friend was so sore the next day, she could barely move.

So, what did she learn from that experience? Or more specifically, what did her elephant learn?

THE GYM IS THE PALACE OF PAIN.

Yep, her elephant wasn't all that enthusiastic about the gym after that. Fortunately, her rider knew intellectually that gym membership was a good thing and that it would be beneficial to go back. She never did use the second free personal training session, though.

LIKELIHOOD VERSUS PERSONAL EXPERIENCE

So when our personal experience contradicts the probability, which one wins?

In one study, drivers who had longer driving experience were less likely to use their phones (texting/browsing) while driving, but drivers who reported using their phones while driving were more likely to do so again in the future (Oviedo–Trespalacios et al., 2018). It's likely that their experience using their phones while driving in the past gave them confidence to continue doing so.

Annual screening mammograms are source of debate in the medical community (Bilodeau, 2020). It's not entirely clear if the results justify the effort and expense and discomfort. I'm not going to pretend I'm qualified to judge that science, but my decisions are always going to be colored by the fact that a close family member had a rare and aggressive form of breast cancer detected by annual screening. Aside from the change to my own risk profile, I'm going to be influenced by my personal experience that mammogram screening led to a positive outcome for her.

In her book, *Thinking in Bets*, Annie Duke describes the phenomena of *resulting*. She describes this as "the tendency to equate the quality of a decision with the quality of its outcome." Duke is an expert in decision-making, with a background in cognitive psychology, who was also a professional poker player for decades. So for example, if you have a poker hand that should pay off 70% of the time, you should bet on that hand. If it doesn't work, then the logical assumption is that you fell into the 30% outcome that particular time.

Resulting occurs when you next encounter that same hand. You should bet on that hand because 70% is a pretty good probability. If you don't bet on the hand because "last time it didn't work," then you are *resulting*.

WHAT EXPERIENCE ARE THEY BRINGING TO CLASS?

So how does the learners' previous experience affect what we do in the design of learning environments? For example, if you are teaching a class on exercise and fitness, you may have people in your audience who have had very real experiences of exercise being unpleasant, painful, or humiliating (don't get me started on how grade school physical education is structured). How can you ensure that your learning design helps people address those experiences or encourages them to reframe them in a productive way?

What could be the personal experience of the learners for the topics we've been looking at in this chapter? From my own experience, I've seen many situations like the following examples:

Behavior 1: Healthcare staff need to safely dispose of vaccination needles or other sharps.

Benefit: Helps prevent injury or infection for healthcare workers and cleaning staff.

Marcus:

"I get that needlestick injuries are a bad thing, but in my experience they are quite rare, and I just don't think we need to change anything right now while we are so overwhelmed."

Behavior 2: Salespeople need to use consultative selling to build client relationships (rather than product-based selling).

Benefit: Potential benefits include improved client relationships, cross-selling based on client needs, and more durable and trusting client relationships that could translate into higher sales overall.

Eliana:

"I've been in sales for 25 years, and I've seen these programs come and go. But, by all means, take time I could be spending with clients to tell me how 'this great new sales method' works."

Behavior 3: Managers need to effectively use the new performance evaluation system, which will be used for quarterly or monthly performance reviews (rather than annual reviews).

Benefit: If this works as designed, the effort of doing each performance review could be less if managers are updating an ongoing review rather than writing a new one from scratch. Employees would be less likely to be surprised by an unexpected issue. Employees could get more timely feedback that improves their performance and improves their relationship with their manager.

Yasmina:

"Performance appraisals are such a grind, and now you want me to do it MORE often? My team knows it's just about justifying their annual raise, and we are all just too busy to add more bureaucracy into the system."

So however likely it is in actuality that the new training initiative will produce a desired reward or avoid a negative consequence, learners often *feel* as if it's not likely, which is going make them less inclined to judge the behavior as valuable.

SO HOW DOES THIS IMPACT TRAINING?

We discuss solutions later in the book, but for now I can address one example of an abstract, delayed, unlikely reward so we can think about how we can make it feel more concrete, immediate, and certain.

We will come back to some of the other examples later, but for now, let's take this one on:

> Behavior 3: Managers need to effectively use the new performance evaluation system, which will be used for quarterly or monthly performance reviews (rather than annual reviews).

We know that there's already some skepticism in that audience, so how excited do you think learners will be to get this email?

To: Workshop Participant

From: The Training Department

Subject: SYSWORKSHOP 2876B - Mandatory Performance Evaluation System Training

Some time in the next month, you need to attend a 2-hour training workshop orientation on the new PerformStar System, which will implement monthly or quarterly appraisals.

The workshop will cover entering performance appraisals into the system and updating existing appraisals.

At the end of the workshop, participants will be able to:

- List the five key benefits of the new system.
- Create a new performance appraisal.
- Import data from the existing system.
- Describe an ongoing plan to keep appraisals updated.

Click here to select a workshop time.

That was the email that the elephant was completely uninterested in. Let's see how this strikes our audience member. Do you think she'll see the value of this?

Two hours? What can possibly take two hours? And I don't have any reviews due for at least two months, so do I really need to do this now?

I think we should take that as a no, she doesn't see the value right now. Instead, she's pretty focused on the effort and the fact she isn't going to have an immediate use for the system.

FIX THE EMAIL

To improve the email, we want to make it feel more significant (bigger) to learners, more tangible, more immediate, and more likely.

Here are some options for improving how we communicate the value of this initiative:

- Use a compelling subject line.
- Have a visual that helps the recipient pay attention and process the message, allowing the learner to picture what the change can look like.
- State the problem being solved by the change.
- Present the benefit in a way that is tangible and immediate—how will this help them?
- Use social proof in the form of testimonials from trusted role models or a story about use.
- Address perceived barriers and explain how the effort will be made as easy as possible.
- Provide a compelling call to action.
- Get feedback.

The following sections cover each one of these.

USE A COMPELLING SUBJECT LINE

I'm not a fan of linkbait or the ridiculous flood of political or fundraising emails that fill my inbox, but I acknowledge that the writers of those subject lines know a thing or two about getting people to click. Some of the better strategies include

- Making it extremely easy to read. People are dealing with overwhelm in their inboxes, so make sure they can understand what the email is about at a glance.

- Focusing on what the recipient will be able to do and how it solves a problem for them.

So let's take our email's subject line and make it better—more tangible and immediate:

Original SYSWRKSHOP 2876B - Mandatory Performance Evaluation System Training

Revised Workshop: Use PerformStar to Stay Connected with Your Team (Even When Everyone Is Busy)

I might think that's a better subject line, but actually it doesn't matter what I think about it. Is the audience going to respond to it better than the original?

The next thing to do is to test that subject line with some people from your audience. You can ask them what they think it means and see if it sounds interesting and useful to them. You might show them three different subject lines and have them pick the one that sounds best or most interesting to them.

This might sound like a lot of work for a simple email, but this message is the first point of contact for everyone. If they start with a positive impression, then everything afterward will likely work better. If nothing else, removing the jargon-y number codes and the word "mandatory" are improvements. (It may be mandatory, but when did that word ever signal that something good was coming?)

HAVE A VISUAL THAT HELPS THE RECIPIENT PAY ATTENTION AND PROCESS THE MESSAGE

Marketers will always be better than instructional designers at taglines and visual designs, but ask yourself if there is a way to give learners a concrete visual that lets them visualize what the value is going to be. Try to avoid overly cliched stock images, and hire a graphic designer if you can.

Original (no visual)

Revised *PerformStar*

Less of this... Performance Evaluation F... ...and more of this!

STATE THE PROBLEM BEING SOLVED BY THE CHANGE

Any behavior-change messaging should always focus on how the change will solve a tangible problem for the learner. You can try explaining what problem is being solved and what the benefit is to someone who doesn't know anything about the topic, and you use those words to craft a non-jargony version for your audience.

Original   Some time in the next month, you need to attend a 2-hour training workshop orientation on the new PerformStar System, which will implement monthly or quarterly appraisals.

Original   The workshop will cover entering performance appraisals into the system and updating existing appraisals.

Revised   Performance appraisals are meant to be one of the crucial ways you connect with your team to help them be the best they can be, but the current performance appraisal system isn't helping you do that.

Revised   We've heard what you've told us about an annual system being too little too late and not helping you build your team. We've found a better tool to support you and your team.

PRESENT THE BENEFIT IN A WAY THAT IS TANGIBLE AND IMMEDIATE

One of the common pieces of wisdom in instructional design is that you need to tell learners the learning objectives that often show up at the beginning of the course or in the description. The problem with this practice is that learning objectives are often written in stiff formal language, which is pretty much like alerting your learners by saying, "This content is boring." Try instead to think about how you'd explain the benefit of the class to someone if you were just talking to them and use that conversational tone to communicate the goals and objectives to learners.

Original   At the end of the workshop, participants will be able to
- List the five key benefits of the new system
- Create a new performance appraisal
- Import data from the existing system
- Describe an ongoing plan to keep appraisals updated

Revised   In this workshop, we'll cover the basics of how you can use PerformStar to help team communication and feedback right away, whether you are starting a new appraisal or transferring or updating an existing one.

USE SOCIAL PROOF IN THE FORM OF TESTIMONIALS

If you were browsing online to buy this or another book, you might have looked at the following parts of the book information:

- The book description written by the author or editor
- Quotes from well-known people endorsing the book
- The score and reviews from readers

If those don't match up—say, for example, that the reader reviews say the book doesn't match the description and that it's not very good—who are you more likely to believe: the readers or the author/editor who wrote the book description? If you are like most people I've asked this question, the answer is that reader reviews are the most trusted source.

Original   (no testimonials)

Revised   Hear from your colleagues about how it's working for them:

Janet

Peter

Ellis

Ideally, the testimonials you offer are based on results from a pilot test that allowed a small group of employees to try things out and provide feedback.

Testimonials are a staple of marketing, but I haven't seen them used all that much in training applications. I discuss social proof and connectedness in other chapters, but keep this strategy in mind.

ADDRESS PERCEIVED BARRIERS/EASE OF USE

If you know what objections your learners are likely to have, you can address those directly.

Original   (no discussion of ease of use)

Revised   We have tested this solution with a pilot group to identify the easiest ways to make importing existing appraisals a smooth and hassle-free process. We look forward to your feedback about how to make it even easier going forward.

PROVIDE A COMPELLING CALL TO ACTION

Try to tie the action to the actual goal and not some bureaucratic step in the process.

Original   Click here to select a workshop time.

Revised   What are your goals for better performance and coaching? Click here to share your thoughts and get signed up for the workshop.

GET FEEDBACK

This last one is the most important of all. It really doesn't matter what *you* think of the effort. What matters is how it lands with your audience, and you can't guess at that. The only way to really know is to test it out and get feedback.

Original   Review by the training team and the stakeholder.

Revised   Test with six to eight members of the target audience who identified that the workshop sounded interesting and helpful, and ask if any of the language was boring, confusing, or seemed phony.

KEY POINTS

- People are always going to ask themselves what the value is minus the effort to realize that value, and even valuable rewards have to compete with many other priorities.
- Value isn't just how big or significant the reward or consequence is, but also how immediate, tangible, and likely it is.
- A smaller reward someone gets immediately may be more compelling than a bigger reward down the road.
- In addition to WIIFM (What's In It For Me?), also ask WCIDWT (What Can I Do With That?).
- Tangible rewards or consequences have the most impact. A reward or consequence feeling tangible and real may be more important that how likely it is.

- People learn from experience, so consider what prior experiences learners are bringing with them and how you can ensure that their first attempts at a new behavior are positive experiences.
- Use strategies to make the value more immediate, tangible, and real for learners.

RESOURCES

Ahn, Sun Joo Grace, Jeremy N. Bailenson, and Dooyeon Park. "Short- and Long-Term Effects of Embodied Experiences in Immersive Virtual Environments on Environmental Locus of Control and Behavior." *Computers in Human Behavior* 39 (2014): 235–245.

Bergen, Benjamin K. *Louder Than Words: The New Science of How the Mind Makes Meaning* (New York: Basic Books, 2012).

Bilodeau, Kelly. "Is It Time to Give Up Your Annual Mammogram?" *Harvard Health Publishing* (blog), May 1, 2020, https://www.health.harvard.edu/blog/is-it-time-to-give-up-your-annual-mammogram-2020050119682.

CDC (Centers for Disease Control). "Health Benefits of Quitting Smoking Over Time," accessed January 2, 2023, https://www.cdc.gov/tobacco/quit_smoking/how_to_quit/benefits/index.htm.

CDC. "2004 Surgeon General's Report: Consumer Summary," accessed January 2, 2023, https://www.cdc.gov/tobacco/data_statistics/sgr/2004/consumer_summary/index.htm. (Note this is an archived resource that may not reflect the most current scientific findings.)

Duke, Annie. *Thinking in Bets: Making Smarter Decisions When You Don't Have All the Facts* (New York: Penguin, 2019).

Fandom Public Information Film Wiki, s.v. "Truth - Singing Cowboy," accessed January 3, 2023, https://pif.fandom.com/wiki/Truth_-_Singing_Cowboy.

Gandhi, Rikin, Rajesh Veeraraghavan, Kentaro Toyama, and Vanaja Ramprasad. "Digital Green: Participatory Video for Agricultural Extension," *2007 International Conference on Information and Communication Technologies and Development*, Bangalore, India, 2007, 1–10, 10.1109/ICTD.2007.4937388.

Harwin, Kerry and Rikin Gandhi. "Digital Green: A Rural Video-Based Social Network for Farmer Training," *Innovations: Technology, Governance, Globalization* 9, no. 3–4 (2014): 53–61. https://direct.mit.edu/itgg/article/9/3-4/53/9789/Digital-Green-A-Rural-Video-Based-Social-Network.

Kahneman, Daniel. *Thinking, Fast and Slow* (New York: Farrar, Straus and Giroux, 2011).

Moore, Cathy. "Elearning Scenario Example: Have Learners Use the Job Aid," *Action@Work* (blog), accessed 1/3/2023, https://blog.cathy-moore.com/2011/10/how-to-create-a-memorable-mini-scenario/.

Noar, Seth M., Marissa G. Hall, Diane B. Francis, Kurt M. Ribisl, Jessica K. Pepper, and Noel T. Brewer. "Pictorial Cigarette Pack Warnings: A Meta-Analysis of Experimental Studies," *Tobacco Control* 25, no. 3 (2016): 341–354.

Oviedo–Trespalacios, Oscar, Md. Mazharul Haque, Mark King, and Simon Washington. "Should I Text or Call Here? A Situation–Based Analysis of Drivers' Perceived Likelihood of Engaging in Mobile Phone Multitasking," *Risk Analysis* 38, no. 10 (2018): 2144–2160.

Paek, Hye-Jin and Thomas Hove. "Risk Perceptions and Risk Characteristics." In *Oxford Research Encyclopedia of Communication.* 2017.

Segar, Michelle L., Jacquelynne S. Eccles, and Caroline R. Richardson. "Rebranding Exercise: Closing the Gap Between Values and Behavior." *International Journal of Behavioral Nutrition and Physical Activity* 8, no. 1 (2011): 1–14.

Segar, Michelle. *No Sweat: How the Simple Science of Motivation Can Bring You a Lifetime of Fitness* (New York: Amacom, 2015).

Sood, Suemedha. "What Is the Safest Mode of Travel?" BBC Travel (blog), January 27, 2012, https://www.bbc.com/travel/article/20120127-travelwise-what-is-the-safest-mode-of-travel.

Valente, Lisa. "10 Health Benefits of Eating Vegetables, According to a Dietitian," *EatingWell* (blog), June 1, 2021, https://www.eatingwell.com/article/7902170/10-health-benefits-of-eating-vegetables-according-to-a-dietitian/.

Wikipedia, s.v. "Problem-Based Learning," last modified November 30, 2022, https://en.wikipedia.org/wiki/Problem-based_learning.

5
UNDERSTANDING MOTIVATION

(IN WHICH THE ELEPHANT CHANGES A LIGHTBULB)

I like lightbulb jokes. Turns out jokes are easier to remember if you stick to one joke genre. A favorite lightbulb joke is this one:

QUESTION: How many therapists does it take to change a lightbulb?

ANSWER: Just one, but the lightbulb has to really want to change.

It's an oldie, but it speaks to the fact that motivation is a crucial element for behavior change.

Also, when we're talking about learning and motivation, there are two different ways to think about it:

- **Motivation to learn:** What is the motivation of participants to pay attention and participate in the learning experiences?
- **Motivation to do:** What is the motivation of participants to actually do the actions or behaviors they are learning about?

In this chapter, I refer somewhat to motivation to learn, but I focus primarily on motivation to do. (The two are interrelated.)

THEY'RE JUST LAZY

As I mentioned in Chapter 1, I've heard the following kinds of things about the learners in projects I've worked on:

- We can't get learners to pay attention.
- We want our learners to be more self-directed.
- They aren't motivated.
- They're just lazy.

Really? They're just lazy? How did they manage to hire a whole bunch of lazy people? If that's the case, I'd look at their hiring practices, not their training programs.

I don't really believe the "lazy people" explanation. First of all, I don't know that many lazy people. I'm sure some exist, but most people I know are so busy they can't see straight. And second, "lazy" isn't a helpful guide for design, for many reasons.

In Chapter 4, I talk about the 37-competing-priorities situation: *Sometimes people just have more important things to do.*

And have you talked to them about it? Because you should view the assumptions you're making about why they aren't doing something with extreme skepticism until you've talked to them about it.

IT'S NOT ABOUT MOTIVATING PEOPLE

When I was working on this chapter, I got assistance from my colleague Matt Richter, who had to remind me that it's not about motivating people.

Wait. That doesn't sound right. How can the motivation chapter *not* be about motivating people?

In a 2012 talk, motivation theorist and research Edward Deci explained it this way (Deci, 2012):

> "Don't ask how you motivate other people. That's the wrong way to think about it. Instead, ask 'How can you create the conditions within which other people will **motivate themselves**?'"

We discuss more about how to do this later in this chapter and in Chapters 9 through 12, but it's useful to remember that you don't get to decide what people care about, so it's much better to focus on creating environments that support them.

PERSISTENCE OF MOTIVATION

When we look at motivation, we also need to consider the persistence of that motivation. Are you seeing the behavior because you are standing there looking right at the person, or will the behavior persist after your attention goes elsewhere? Will the person start with initial enthusiasm that will quickly fizzle when the 37 other things show up?

INTRINSIC AND EXTRINSIC MOTIVATION

Because most of the work I do is designing learning experiences for workplace environments, the most simple explanation for why someone should be motivated is the fact that *it's their job*.

If you are a student in a university, then it's essentially your job to learn and engage, so theoretically a motivating learning experience shouldn't be necessary.

But if we get to the point where we are saying, "They should be motivated because it's their jobs!" it's a bit like when a disagreement between a child and parent gets to the "Because I said so!" stage. Technically true, but not the most helpful position for either entity.

So I'm going to take as given the idea that "it's their job" is not the best motivation to rely on and look at some of the other factors that might influence motivation. People always make choices and have the ability to accept or reject behavior changes in many ways.

EXTRINSIC MOTIVATION

Extrinsic motivation is anything that comes from outside the person being motivated. It could be money, rewards, grades, certificates, fruit baskets, being featured on an influencer's social media account, a cookie, kudos, a ride in the batmobile, or—you know—a gift card.

Extrinsic motivation could also be due to the avoidance of negative consequences like getting written up, a bad grade, getting fired, getting stuck doing the dishes, public shaming, having your social media account suspended, or getting arrested.

INTRINSIC MOTIVATION

Intrinsic motivation is anything that comes from someone's internal motivation. Someone could study animation because they really love Japanese anime and want to make something cool, or they could learn French because they love things that are French and really want to be able to visit Paris, or they could become a human rights lawyer because they are fascinated by legal arguments and want to help people.

Sometimes things can start for extrinsic reasons and become more intrinsic over time. For example, someone could take a class about plant-based cooking because they think it will help them reduce a genetic risk for cancer, but then they come to really enjoy it because they like figuring how to make vegan cuisine that's delicious and satisfying.

Notice how the list of intrinsic motivators is different than the list of extrinsic motivators? Each item contains the word "because" and the reason is that person cares about that thing.

Extrinsic motivators also form a continuum. For example, someone could dread a bad grade for fully external reasons—they need a certain grade point for a job, for graduate school admissions, or to qualify for a scholarship or program. But they could also dread a bad grade because they are deeply invested in their identity as a high-achieving student, they like that feeling of having a perfect academic record, and (even when there are no external consequences to the grade) it would make them feel bad about themselves and their accomplishments to get a poor grade. This involves fully extrinsic forces—external messages and opinions about grades—but also involves internal wants and values.

So one way to start thinking about motivation is to consider why someone would care, aside from the fully external factors.

Marcella is creating a curriculum around clean sports (anti-doping) for student athletes. So, Marcella, why should student athletes care about clean sports?

EXTERNAL "I think the external consequences are pretty obvious. They can get disqualified or banned for doping violations. If it's a team sport, the whole team could be affected."

WHY ELSE? "That's what we are really trying to get the kids to think about: What do they value? What kind of athlete do they want to be? What kind of team member do they want to be?"

Jerome is updating safety guidelines and training materials for agricultural workers working at heights. Hey Jerome, why should agricultural workers care about following safety guidelines for working at heights?

EXTERNAL "I guess if they get spotted being unsafe, they could get fired? Fines are usually levied on the employer, not the employee, but your boss would be pretty unhappy with you if they get fined."

WHY ELSE? "How about not dying? I think most people care about that. Or not winding up in a wheelchair or getting to see your kids grow up? That all sounds pretty important to me."

Deepa is creating a new campaign in her hospital about handwashing compliance for nonclinical staff. Deepa, why should nonclinical staff care about complying with handwashing guidelines?

EXTERNAL "Well, I guess they could get reprimanded by their manager, but honestly that's pretty rare for nonclinical staff."

WHY ELSE? "Well, nobody wants to get sick or be the reason somebody else gets sick. The difficulty is that it's really hard for people to know when that happens."

There's a place for all types of rewards or consequences, but when you are creating learning experiences, you don't usually have influence over the fully extrinsic rewards or consequences (although it may depend on your organization).

With intrinsic rewards, the challenge is that you as the designer don't get to decide what is intrinsic to someone else. You don't get to make something internally rewarding. What you can do, though, is figure out what people in your audience value and help them connect the dots between those values and the behaviors about which they are learning.

MOTIVATION THEORY

There are many different motivation models and frameworks—more than I can address in this chapter. I'm going to spend time with a particular model that I think is useful for learning design. The model is called Self-Determination Theory from psychologists Edward Deci and Richard Ryan. If you've read *Drive* by Daniel Pink, several of the ideas will sound familiar to you. We are going to look at how to incorporate it specifically into learning design.

Self-Determination Theory has many components to it, but it is founded on three basic psychological needs: autonomy, competence, and relatedness. Each of these needs provides a frame to look at how we design learning experiences.

AUTONOMY

Autonomy is what Deci and Ryan describe as "the need to self-regulate one's experiences and actions" (Deci and Ryan, 2018). Basically, people are motivated by feeling that they have some control over their own situation, that they are the actor rather than the acted-upon, and that their actions are in accordance with their values and goals.

Environments where people do not feel like they have any agency or control do not foster autonomy. You know what this looks like. We've all been in a business where no one seems engaged, nobody cares that things are a mess, and no one takes ownership of anything.

I'm not saying that lack of autonomy is the only reason that those businesses have issues, but it's almost certainly one of the ingredients.

So how does a learning experience foster autonomy? There are many ways, but the main way is to ensure that people have choice and control over what and how they do their jobs.

CAN EMPLOYEES DECIDE?

Eric Flamholtz, in his book *The Inner Game of Management*, talks about delegating work. He describes how, when a manager delegates a task, there are three possible outcomes:

- The employee achieves the outcome and does the task the way the manager would.
- The employee achieves the outcome but does not do the task the way the manager would.
- The employee does not achieve the outcome.

In the first outcome, there's probably no issue. The employee did what was wanted in the same manner as their manager. In the last example, the outcome wasn't reached, so something needs to be addressed.

But how about that middle option where the employee did it a different way? If the manager is cool with it, and everybody moves to the next priority, then that's an environment that likely supports employee autonomy, at least in this scenario.

However, I've also encountered quite a few people who just wouldn't be able to LET. IT. GO. They would have to exert control next time over how that employee did their job. These managers would not be fostering an autonomy-supportive environment.

I've often encountered the question about whether we should lock down navigation in elearning programs, and my answer is, "No, not unless there's a very good reason to lock it down." That answer can be extrapolated to many circumstances. Should I try to control things for this learner, employee, participant, whoever? No, unless there's a very good reason to do so. Otherwise, default to allowing them to decide.

It can even be reflected in the language that's used.

"YOU MUST" VERSUS "I CAN"

Highly regulated environments exist because someone is trying to eliminate error from the system. These are typically organizations where error can have fatal consequences, like commercial airlines, hospitals, and nuclear power plants. And we **want** those environments to have a very low error rate.

I was talking to a client who did medical supervisory visits in healthcare facilities, and she was telling me, "Nobody takes initiative. It's so frustrating!" I pointed out that a management style that was entirely about compliance might be stifling initiative, and the expression on her face while she processed that idea was a *sight*.

The two goals of "reduce error" and "support autonomy" don't automatically have to fight with each other. Here are some questions to ask while designing a learning experience that supports autonomy:

- Which behaviors *have* to be done according to the rules (such as for safety purposes)?
- If there is a purpose for the rules, is it clearly communicated, and are learners given the opportunity to connect that purpose to their own values or goals?
- Which behaviors can participants use their judgment about or modify for their own style?
- Are there any instances of "rules for the sake of having rules"?
- Is there anything in the class the learners can tell you rather than you telling them?

I went through a training slide deck on the U.S. Department of Labor site: "Asbestos Standards for the Construction Industry" (this was just as exciting as you might imagine). I counted how many times certain "control" words were used throughout the 80 slides:

- MUST: 53 times
- SHALL: 23 times
- CONTROL: 24 times
- STANDARD: 17 times
- COMPLY: 18 times
- MONITORING: 23 times

- REQUIRE: 36 times
- REGULATE: 27 times

Asbestos is dangerous stuff, and it absolutely makes sense that the Department of Labor is trying to reduce errors in how asbestos is handled.

But what if a client comes to you with this problem:

> "The guys who work with asbestos all the time take it very seriously, but some of the other workers will still pull stuff out during demolition without verifying it's safe. They know the rules, but I think they figure it's pretty infrequent exposure, and so as long as they toss on a mask, it's fine. The older ones are the worst—they joke that it hasn't killed them so far."

If that's the motivation challenge you are dealing with, how effective do you think it will be to sit them down and say "MUST" 53 times?

The experienced workers should be the most cautious, but that's not always the case. And, if someone feels they already know the material, does making them sit through it again help?

Experienced people may feel like their experience is being disrespected by being told repeatedly TO FOLLOW THE RULES.

And they'd be right to feel that way.

In my experience, nobody designing learning experiences knows more about the realities of the job than the people actually doing the job. That doesn't mean that experienced people can't have misconceptions or gaps in knowledge or skills. But it does mean that treating them like their experience doesn't matter is going to provoke irritation and resistance.

INVOLVE PEOPLE IN THE SOLUTION

One key way to foster autonomy and motivation is to involve people in determining the solution. One of my favorite examples of this is described in Atul Gawande's book *Better*. Gawande is a medical writer for the *New Yorker* magazine and a surgeon. In his book, he looks at ways that the medical profession is trying to improve its practice.

He describes a case study in his own Pittsburgh hospital about trying to improve handwashing performance. He admits that even he lapsed sometimes and describes how compliance/enforcement efforts were not producing better outcomes.

Eventually, they tried what Gawande describes as a "positive deviance approach" (more on this in the next chapter). They looked at what *was* working and had meetings with small groups of the staff to ask the question, "We want to know what *you* know about how to solve [the hospital infection problem]."

Gawande says that ideas poured forth, and everyone had ideas about how to improve processes and physical layouts to solve the problem. After a while, the ideas in groups began to repeat, but the organizers kept going so that everyone had a say and could contribute.

After one year of the project, the hospital's infection rates dropped to zero, despite not having budged for several years.

> **DON'T SAY:**   "Here's why this topic is important."
> **INSTEAD, ASK:** "Is this important? Why do you think so?"

COMPETENCE

Competence is feeling a sense of effectiveness or proficiency. Basically, people like to feel like they are good at things, particular their key roles (for example, work, family, hobbies).

Nobody loves to feel bad at something, and when someone feels like they're publicly bad at something, this can lead them to want to avoid involvement altogether.

RELATEDNESS

Relatedness is feeling socially connected to others, including feeling a sense of belonging or like a significant member of a social group. I discuss social connection and social proof later in the book, but people are often motivated by their sense of relatedness to others or by being part of a group or community.

For example, in a persuasive campaign, do the people in the images look like you or like people you know? Are the people represented part of groups that you identify with? Learners are more likely to be persuaded if they feel that the people modeling the behavior are similar to them.

It's one thing for an expert to tell you what to do, and it's much different when you see people who look like you who are sharing their authentic experience.

MOTIVATION AS A CONTINUUM

Deci and Ryan organize their range from amotivated to externally motivated to internally motivated on a continuum:

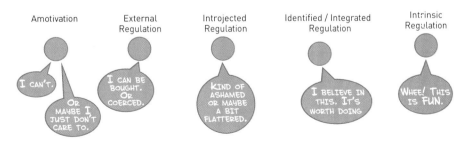

We are going to look at each of these five categories and discuss how using each perspective can change how we create learning materials. Part of what we are going to discuss is how to move focus from the left side of the continuum to use more motivation strategies from the right side, but all of these are tools in the toolbox.

Generally, we want to look at more internal motivators, but external motivators have their place, too. For example, money is usually considered a more external motivator, but most of us need money to pay for food and shelter and other necessities. If an employer stopped paying their workers, those workers would probably need to stop working there, no matter how worthwhile and meaningful they found the work.

AMOTIVATION

If someone is amotivated, it means they lack motivation. There could be different reasons for that. For example, the person may believe something isn't possible, or that it has a lack of interest, relevance, or value. Amotivated is our normal state for things we are not interested in. I, for example, am amotivated when it comes to most of the behaviors necessary to become a professional basketball player. This is for the best—there's no version of the future where that would work out well.

People can be amotivated due to an unmet competence need. Say, for example, that I take a new job that has a company retreat, and it turns out that my new coworkers have a historic basketball rivalry with another department. If it's suggested that I play, I'm going to be pretty amotivated. That's partially because I'm not all that interested in basketball, but also because I rate my ability to play basketball quite low. I don't have the perceived competence to be effective at playing basketball. If I thought I'd be good at it, it would be fine, but that's not how I would picture it going.

Perception is a key part of this. My motivation is going to be contingent on my *perceived* ability to play basketball rather than an objective assessment. The first time I went out with friends who were going rock climbing, I thought there was no way I would also be climbing; I was just along for the hike. It turns out, though, that I could rock climb on easier routes. I never got really good at it, but I enjoyed doing it on and off for years after that.

So that means that what a learner *believes* about their abilities is just as, or even more, important for motivation than their *actual* abilities.

Amotivation can also occur when someone could do something but just doesn't want to. For example, you could have a restaurant server who is *capable* of providing courteous customer service but *just doesn't want to.*

It's difficult to say if this is something a learning designer should tackle. For example, if someone is amotivated because they don't understand the value of the behavior (as discussed in the previous chapter), then a learning designer might be able to influence the situation by increasing the understanding. If communication of value doesn't make a dent in the amotivation, then it may be time to ask, "Is this the right person for this job?"

I learned a saying from my colleague Dr. Jane Bozarth, who is director of research for the Learning Guild, that goes, "If you had unlimited time and resources, could you teach a turkey how to climb a tree? Maybe. But wouldn't it have been easier to hire a squirrel?" Someone who understands the value of something and is still amotivated may just not be a squirrel.

EXTERNAL REGULATION

If someone is doing something only because of outside influence, that's external regulation. It could be some kind of reward, like a grade or a certificate, or it could be the threat of negative consequences like punishment, fines, or getting fired.

As I mentioned at the beginning of this section, there's nothing inherently *wrong* with external regulation, but it shouldn't be the only tool in the toolbox, and it can be misapplied.

I have a few examples where external regulation didn't quite go as expected.

DRAWING FOR REWARDS

Alfie Kohn, an author and speaker about education issues, cites a study (Lepper et al., 1973) where kids were given rewards for drawing. In the first group, kids were told there would be reward (a certificate with a gold seal and a ribbon) for drawing. A second group received the certificate, but only after they had done the drawing (an unexpected reward), and a third group received no reward.

After the initial activity, when the reward was no longer presented as an option, kids in the unexpected or no reward condition were more interested in drawing than the kids who had been in the reward condition. This is referred to as the *over-justification effect*.

It kind of makes sense. Many kids like drawing intrinsically and will often do it without needing any rewards. Adding a reward to the mix doesn't seem like it adds much to their motivation and may just be a distraction.

Overjustification doesn't always occur, though. There are examples of reward schemes (such as reading programs) for kids that haven't negatively impacted their behavior, and rewarding early attempts can keep people going while they build skill, which then provides additional motivation.

But because overjustification sometimes occurs, we know that rewards don't *always* increase the behavior and that you want to test an external reward solution to make sure you get the desired outcome.

A reward might also lead to an increase in the amount of behavior but not the quality. For example, if you start paying kids a dollar for each picture they draw, you might get a lot of pictures from them, but the level of detail and attention might suffer because you've changed the game from "Draw cool pictures" to "Get more dollars."

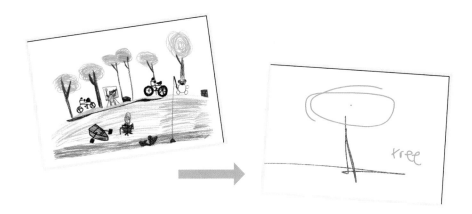

As Edward Deci (Deci, 2012) describes it:

> "When your motivation is controlled, you tend to take the shortest path to the desired outcomes."

GIFT CARDS FOR WELLNESS

Many employers have instituted wellness programs for employees to motivate healthier behaviors. Many of these programs involved doing healthy behaviors (for example, taking a walk over lunch), which would be rewarded with points or prizes. This is something that should be a win-win, right? Employees would be healthier, which in turn has the potential to improve employer outcomes by having healthier employees with fewer illness-related absences.

But the outcomes of these health programs are mixed. In one large randomized clinical trial (Song and Baiker, 2019), researchers found that although wellness programs increased the number of employees reporting exercise and weight management activities, there "were no significant differences in other self-reported health and behaviors; clinical markers of health; health care spending or utilization; or absenteeism, tenure, or job performance after 18 months."

The wildest anecdote I've seen about wellness programs is about the Kansas City employees who managed to defraud their employee wellness program of more than $300,000 in gift cards. One employee in particular collected $185,000 in gift cards by reporting health behaviors supposedly completed, including claims that a three-year-old child had completed four triathlons, three marathons, two duathlons, and three half marathons.

If the goal was to *be* healthier, the program didn't really work out so well. If the goal was to rack up lists of healthy behaviors, then they were absolutely winning (except for the whole fraud-punishable-by-law part).

MANDATORY LEARNING

Several years ago, I was asked to speak to a professional organization that was in the process of revamping their guidelines for professional development. At the time I was working with them, part of the requirement for maintaining your professional certification was 40 hours of continuing education each year.

Seems like a nice idea. You're a highly skilled professional who's spending a week every year growing your skillset or keeping up with advancements in your field—that all sounds great! It benefits you and your employer or clients for you to keep your skillset sharp.

But it's also a little arbitrary. Forty is a nice round number, and hours are a pretty easy thing to track, but again, they had problems with the fact that they had shifted the goal away from "increase your skills" or "keep up to date with new developments" and had made the goal "get to forty."

People at the event told me stories about people paying the babysitter extra to click the Next button on the elearning after the recorded narration stopped playing to get through several hours of tracked online learning.

One person told me a story about someone he'd seen in an 8-hour live workshop who sat in the back of the room and had two laptops open during the live class. This person was going through two 8-hour elearning courses while they attended the class, so at the end of the day, they would have 24 of the 40 hours completed. Given the fact that we now have learning available via multiple devices, phones, and tablets, someone could probably have courses going on three or four devices at the same time if they really wanted to.

Again, if the point of the game is "get to forty," then this person is *winning*.

External motivators are usually not set by the people creating the training materials, so the role in learning design is to communicate those rewards or consequences.

You'll recognize the tone of external regulation when you hear it:

And external regulation (with regulations, rules, or penalties) may be necessary, but if this is where the motivation stops, then that might not be enough.

For example, regulations and penalties are almost certainly part of the puzzle of how to keep performance-enhancing drugs out of athletics, but if the only message that student athletes hear is "don't take drugs because you could get caught," then there's the worry that the goal isn't "compete clean" but rather "don't get caught."

External regulation also can potentially provoke *reactance*, which is the negative reaction people can have to being constrained or forced to do something.

Using external rewards may not hurt anything, but it also may not achieve a useful result. For example, making the topic of handwashing "fun" probably won't change too many behaviors, but on the other hand, it might get people in the room to hear more useful messages.

INTROJECTED REGULATION

Despite being a dense term, the concept is pretty simple. Ryan and Deci (2000) describe it this way:

> "with introjected regulation ... consequences are administered by the individuals to themselves ... examples are contingent self-worth (pride) or threats of guilt and shame."

That doesn't sound great, but we feel guilt, shame, and pride for good reasons, and they are tools in the design toolbox. It is a move to the right on the continuum, so it does move us a little closer to internal motivations.

To explain what I mean about "moving to the right," let's look at the example of timesheets. Many, many organizations have struggled to get employees to fill out their timesheets on a regular and timely basis.

Here's the thing about timesheets: You are never going to have a lot of intrinsic motivation for timesheets. I don't think there are many people out there saying, "You know what I really enjoy? *Timesheets*!"

Some organizations have tried to have external penalties attached to timesheets, with mixed results. One difficulty is that the reward for filling out a timesheet (getting paid) is almost always delayed for employees until the next pay period, but the difficulty for the organization of not being able to complete accounting processes or bill customers is much more immediate.

I worked for a consulting company many years ago, and timesheets were always a struggle. Employees were supposed to have them completed each week by Tuesday at 10:00 a.m. And when I say it was a struggle, I mean it was a struggle FOR ME.

I frequently found myself on the naughty list of unfinished timesheets, and not because I wanted to be delinquent about it. It was a 37-things problem. At 9:00 a.m. on Tuesday morning, I could answer the client emails, check the blinking light of a voicemail, work on project deliverables, or handle the coworker question from the person standing right by my desk, or I could fill out my timesheet.

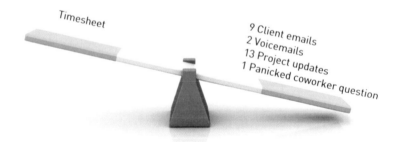

All of these things just felt more urgent and important than *paperwork*. My elephant just couldn't quite believe that the timesheet was the best use of a Tuesday morning, despite my rider knowing that timesheets were necessary for keeping the wheels on for the company.

So the company leadership decided to try an external penalty. If you didn't get your timesheet in on time for a three-month period, you would be docked $25 on any bonus payment for that quarter. Bonuses were typically not calculated until the quarter had been over for at least a month, and then weren't paid until one or two months after that.

So, based on the calculation of value that's covered in Chapter 4, how well do you think a $25 penalty (delayed up to four or five months) worked to influence people's behavior?

Yeah, not so much. So let's compare that to something more introjected:

> At the next company meeting, Debbie from accounting gets up to speak about timesheets. It's her job to chase everyone down when they are late. She describes how frustrating the process is and explains how many hours it adds to her already busy week because there are several processes she can't complete until she has all the timesheet data. Her voice actually cracks a bit when she talks about having to log in from a family event on a day off to get things submitted because of late timesheets.

> You know Debbie. She's a lovely, friendly person who has helped you out on a few expense report submissions. You've seen the pictures of her ridiculously cute kids at her desk, and you know how important her family is to her.

I don't know you about you, but my elephant is now *mortified*. It doesn't care that much about paperwork, but it cares a lot about not being a jerk coworker, especially to a nice person who has helped me in the past. Debbie's not trying to make me feel bad. I'm making me feel bad, and next Tuesday morning when my rider says it's time to fill out the timesheet, my elephant is chiming in with "YES! DON'T BE MEAN TO DEBBIE."

Another well-known study in the behavioral economics sphere is the one about picking up kids late from daycare. In a 1998 study, researchers found that imposing a small fine on parents who came late to pick up their kids from daycare actually caused the late behavior to increase. Basically, parents were able to trade money for feeling guilty about inconveniencing teachers, and several of them took that deal. In this case, they moved the motivation to the *left*, from introjected to external regulation.

So what does introjected regulation look like in a training context?

It could be a call to consider how your actions affect others, as shown in the next illustration:

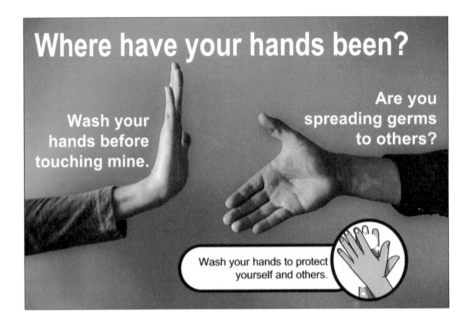

It could be a class activity where you consider the other people in your life who would be impacted by your safety choices.

Or it could be not wanting to look foolish in front of your peers:

To be clear, I'm not advocating that you should regularly use these kind of introjected regulation messages. I think they are often too heavy-handed, but these *are* tools in the toolbox and may have a place in a learning design.

IDENTIFIED/INTEGRATED REGULATION

Identified regulation is when you don't necessarily enjoy the activity but see it as important and worth doing. There are two categories on Deci and Ryan's continuum, but for our purposes, they are similar enough that we are going to treat them as a single category.

For example, when I started reading research studies to use the material in presentations, workshops, or books, I realized that my knowledge of statistics was a little rusty, and I needed to spend some time brushing up on research methods. I picked up some materials and signed up for a research methods massive open online course (MOOC). The purpose was less about an intrinsic interest in statistics and more about making sure I was being as responsible as I could about research translation.

Often this could be something that is worth doing because it supports other values or goals, like reminding kids of all the things they can do if they stay healthy through handwashing.

Identified regulation could be summarized as "because it's the right thing to do according to my values" or "because it helps me move toward other goals."

If you can, you want to help learners identify their own values and supporting behaviors rather than telling them what they should value or do. Values or reasons the learners contribute are more likely to be things they consider important.

In a training context, supporting learners might be about helping them see how the behavior is part of their own deeply held values or identities. For example, the following poster speaks to the identity of being a good father:

It might be prompting learners to define their own values or it might involve helping the learner to match up values and behaviors:

INTRINSIC MOTIVATION

Intrinsic motivation is when the behavior is enjoyable of its own accord. Someone does it because they like it. It may or may not be possible to identify intrinsic motivators for a particular job, and that's okay. As I mentioned in the timesheet example, I don't think you are ever going to find an intrinsically motivating timesheet (though if you do, please let me know).

You might be able to convince learners that they should enjoy handwashing. It could happen:

Handwashing…
A twenty second spa break in
your day

IT'S NOT JUST ONE

I don't want to give the impression that motivations always fall into a single category. Motivation for your learners may be a mix of many of these.

For example, if I look at the reasons why I might do a presentation at a conference, there are a lot of options:

- I like sharing my knowledge.
- It's a way to help people solve their own challenges.
- It helps me clarify my own thinking.
- It's how I market my services.
- It's fun to figure out how to explain something.
- It's how I connect with others in my field.

Many of these are closer to the internal end of the spectrum, but creating a presentation is a lot of work, so there also needs to be some external rewards (in this case, marketing) to make it worthwhile. But it's very fun for me to try to figure things out and craft good explanations, so it's also internally satisfying.

STRATEGIES TO FOSTER MOTIVATION

So as a learning designer, what do we do with all this information about the different ways people are motivated? One way I use this continuum is to identify where I think motivation currently falls on the continuum and consider if there's any way to support learners moving a bit more to the right.

For example, learners may be amotivated because they don't see the value of something, so I can focus on communicating the value. Or maybe the learners are doing a behavior only because it's required, but I can include an activity where we discuss how doing the behavior might support their values, and so on.

In the book, *Building Autonomous Learners* (Reeve, 2016), the author describes a number of ways that teachers can support autonomy, some of which include

- Take your learners' perspectives
- Focus on inner motivational resources like curiosity, relevance, and intrinsic goals
- Explain why and give rationales
- Use autonomy-supportive language
- Listen and acknowledge learners' views
- Adapt the pace and process to learners' needs

We are going to do a deeper dive into some of the strategies in Chapters 9 through 12, but a few key learning strategies to foster motivation include

- Letting them decide
- Providing goals and ways to level up
- Avoiding jargon
- Using strengths-based language
- Providing nonjudgmental feedback
- Associating the behavior with values

LETTING THEM DECIDE

As I talked about earlier, if there's any way to allow learners to have a choice about their learning experience and to involve them in the decision-making process around the behavior change, they'll be more likely to have durable, lasting motivation.

PROVIDING GOALS AND WAYS TO LEVEL UP

If you play video games, you are probably familiar with an intro level like the one in the illustration.

It's very easy, with big pointers telling you what to do. You're playing the game, but it's like bowling with the big inflatable bumpers in the gutters—the ball can't go off track, and you can't fail this level.

In game design, this is referred to as *onboarding*. Designers are trying to get the player into the game and comfortable enough to start playing without feeling frustrated or confused. If a new player of a game is immediately overwhelmed by the difficulty and complexity of the game, they'll abandon that game pretty quickly, so game designers ensure that players can learn the game while playing it. They're simultaneously learning the interface and building their confidence.

Then the game introduces levels with gradually increasing complexity or difficulty. If the game gets too hard too fast, players will get frustrated and go play something else.

When someone is trying out a new behavior, many training experiences have just one opportunity to practice. Depending on the behavior, it might be better to have a few opportunities to practice, with the trials going from quite easy (something they can definitely be successful at) to a little more challenging. Giving learners an opportunity to feel themselves getting better at something can promote their competence and motivation.

Part of this can be helping learners set reasonable and achievable goals, even when the whole behavior change might feel overwhelming.

AVOIDING JARGON

A certain amount of jargon is unavoidable in many fields, but it's always worth minimizing wordiness and trying for a friendly and conversational tone. One reason is that jargon can be a form of gatekeeping. If you don't speak all the technical-ese of a profession, it's a signal that you aren't part of the "in group."

If you're trying to foster motivation through a sense of competence, jargon and highly technical language are not your friends. One study (Moreno and Mayer, 2004) found that conversational, personalized messages (including "I" and "you") meant students remembered more and performed better on problem-solving transfer tests.

In this chapter, I can't avoid the term "introjected regulation" if I want to talk about Self-Determination Theory, but I can try to make all the other language around it as comprehensible as possible. I know smart folks are reading this book, and if something is hard to understand or doesn't make sense, then that's my failing, not yours. Avoiding unnecessary jargon makes content easier to understand and fosters learners' sense of competence. It's a win-win.

High-jargon version: "The company has recently implemented a self-appraisal system for its annual performance evaluations. All employees are required to attend a classroom learning event that is designed to help them learn about the new system and the tools they should use to conduct and submit the self-appraisals."

Low-jargon version (more like humans talk): "Our company just added a self-appraisal system to help with annual performance reviews. You will attend a class to learn how to use it."

USING STRENGTHS-BASED LANGUAGE

It's a small thing, but the language you use can matter. When you talk about behaviors, you can frame the actions as something the learner CAN DO instead of talking about what they MUST or SHOULD do.

Controlling language

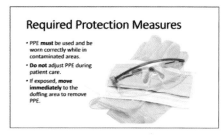

Strengths-based language

Instead of:

Use instead:

PROVIDING NONJUDGMENTAL FEEDBACK

I'm a sucker for makeover shows—any kind: clothes, home décor, baked goods, whatever. Years ago, I watched quite a few episodes of *What Not To Wear*, and it seemed like in about half the episodes, there would be some version of this conversation:

Woman (trying on skirt that doesn't fit): "Ugh, it doesn't fit. I hate my hips!"

Host (reassuring): "Your hips are your hips. There's nothing wrong with them. The skirt is what's wrong. We'll get a different one."

I've thought about this a lot when I consider how to create learning experiences that don't make people feel like they've failed or are less-than. To foster a sense of competency, learners should walk away from a learning experience feeling smarter and more capable.

One option for this is to focus on successes, rather than noting failures.
In a study (Eskreis-Winkler and Fishbach, 2019), researchers had subjects take tests where each question had two possible answers. In one condition, participants were told when they got a question right but received no response if they were incorrect. In the other condition, participants were told when they got a question wrong but got no feedback for right answers. On a follow-up test, participants learned

less from the failure feedback than from the success feedback. The researchers hypothesized that

> "Failure feedback undermined learning motivation because it was ego threatening: It caused participants to tune out and stop processing information."

Another option is to show consequences instead of saying "you're wrong." For example, if you're creating an elearning course for mobile phone salespeople about how to select the right product for a customer, you could show what happens instead of giving a feedback statement:

You offered the customer the MegAPhone XR27.

JUDGMENT FEEDBACK:	"Incorrect. A better choice would have been the AdaptAPhone 1286."
CONSEQUENCE FEEDBACK:	"The customer looks over the phone and hands it back to you. She says, 'Hmm…I'll think about it,' and goes off to wander over to home appliances. Want to try again?"

ASSOCIATING THE BEHAVIOR WITH VALUES

Learning experiences should have learners walking away from the experience feeling like they have capability, and that capability should be related to their values and goals.

Trying to change someone's value and goals is really difficult, and that's probably not your role. Your job is also not to trick or sugarcoat. But if you can help people connect behaviors with their values, that can be helpful.

You don't get to decide what learners value, but you can ask them what they care about, and build that conversation into the learning experience.

Instead of: *Use instead:*

TALK TO YOUR LEARNERS

My last point is that to match your learning design to the internal values and goals of your learners, you need to talk to those learners. Learning experiences where the information is going only one way—the instructor projected at the students—is likely to fail to get to any deep motivators.

You don't get to decide what is important to your learners. You have to learn from them what they care about.

You can do that by talking to people as you design the learning experience, and you can do it as part of the learning experience.

KEY POINTS

- As learning designers, we need to consider not only the amount of motivation but also the durability and quality of that motivation.
- Extrinsic motivation (rewards or punishments) have a role to play in motivation, but they may not be the most durable form of motivation. Also, external motivators risk changing the goal away from the core reasons for the behavior to "get the reward" or "avoid the punishment."
- Motivation is a continuum that goes from amotivated or externally motivated all the way to intrinsically motivated, where someone does something just because they enjoy it, and any situation probably involves multiple types of motivation.
- Guilt, shame, or ego can be useful motivators, but they're still more externally focused. Guilt and shame can also motivate people to avoid engaging altogether.
- Motivation that is tied to peoples' identities and values is likely to be more sustained.
- People resist or disengage if they feel that they have no autonomy.
- Relatedness is a powerful motivator, and talking to your learners, during both the design and execution of the learning experience, can help you understand their values and goals.

RESOURCES

Deci, Edward L., Richard Koestner, and Richard M. Ryan. "Extrinsic Rewards and Intrinsic Motivation in Education: Reconsidered Once Again," *Review of Educational Research* 71, no. 1 (2001): 1–27.

Deci, Edward L. "Promoting Motivation, Health, and Excellence: Ed Deci at TEDxFlourCity." TEDx video. Posted August 14, 2012. https://www.youtube.com/watch?v=VGrcetsoE6I.

Eskreis-Winkler, Lauren, and Ayelet Fishbach. "Not Learning from Failure—The Greatest Failure of All," *Psychological Science* 30, no. 12 (2019): 1733–1744.

Gawande, Atul. *Better: A Surgeon's Notes on Performance* (New York: Metropolitan Books, 2008).

Gneezy, Uri, and Aldo Rustichini. "A Fine Is a Price," *The Journal of Legal Studies* 29, no. 1 (2000): 1–17.

Kornhauser, Lewis, Yijia Lu, and Stephan Tontrup. "Testing a Fine Is a Price in the Lab," *International Review of Law and Economics* 63 (2020): 105931.

Lepper, Mark R., David Greene, and Richard E. Nisbett. "Undermining Children's Intrinsic Interest with Extrinsic Reward: A Test of the 'Overjustification' Hypothesis." *Journal of Personality and Social Psychology* 28, no. 1 (1973): 129.

Moreno, Roxana, and Richard E. Mayer. "Personalized Messages That Promote Science Learning in Virtual Environments," *Journal of Educational Psychology* 96, no. 1 (2004): 165.

"Overview," *Center for Self-Determination Theory* (website), retrieved January 9, 2023, https://selfdeterminationtheory.org/the-theory/.

Reeve, Johnmarshall. "Autonomy-Supportive Teaching: What It Is, How to Do It," chap. 7 in *Building Autonomous Learners: Perspectives from Research and Practice Using Self-Determination Theory* (New York: Springer, 2016).

Ryan, Richard M., and Edward L. Deci. "Self-Determination Theory and the Facilitation of Intrinsic Motivation, Social Development, and Well-Being," *American Psychologist* 55, no. 1 (2000): 68.

Ryan, Richard M., and Edward L. Deci. *Self-Determination Theory: Basic Psychological Needs in Motivation, Development, and Wellness* (New York: The Guilford Press, 2018), 10.

Song, Zirui, and Katherine Baicker. "Effect of a Workplace Wellness Program on Employee Health and Economic Outcomes: A Randomized Clinical Trial," *Jama* 321, no. 15 (2019): 1491–1501. https://jamanetwork.com/journals/jama/fullarticle/2730614 retrieved 1/9/2023.

Spencer, M. and D. Gulczynski. "Creative Handwashing Campaign in an Orthopedic Surgical Institution," *American Journal of Infection Control* 32, no. 3 (2004): E47.

United States Attorney's Office, Western District of Missouri. "Court Employee Pleads Guilty to $185,000 Scheme to Cheat Health Insurance Program." U.S. Department of Justice press release, October 30, 2013. On the DOJ website. https://www.justice.gov/usao-wdmo/pr/court-employee-pleads-guilty-185000-scheme-cheat-health-insurance-program.

United States Department of Labor. "29 CFR 1926.1101 - OSHA's Asbestos Standard for the Construction Industry." OSHA Slide Presentation, 80 slides. https://www.osha.gov/training/library/materials retrieved 1/12/2023.

Vlaev, Ivo, Dominic King, Ara Darzi, and Paul Dolan. "Changing Health Behaviors Using Financial Incentives: A Review from Behavioral Economics," *BMC Public Health* 19, no. 1 (2019): 1–9.

Wikipedia, s.v. "Overjustification effect," last modified May 1, 2023, https://en.wikipedia.org/wiki/Overjustification_effect.

ANALYZING BEHAVIORS

(IN WHICH WE ASK IF THE ELEPHANT KNOWS HOW, WHY, AND WHAT IT NEEDS)

In the previous chapters, I've talked a lot about value and motivation. Now I want to take a look at the process for analyzing a behavior and mapping the results of that to solutions that might be effective.

Many behavioral models exist. Behavioral science draws from a wide range of fields like psychology, behavioral economics, public health, safety, finance, human factors engineering, and persuasive technology (to identify just a few). Each of these domains has principles and models that frequently overlap with similar material from other domains.

So how do you pick? You might have noticed that this book is NOT titled *A Comprehensive Discussion of All the Possible Models*, so I'm focusing on the model I use most often for my own practice. But I acknowledge that many other models exist that likely overlap with this one, and another model may ultimately be more useful for your own practice.

THE BEHAVIOUR CHANGE WHEEL

Several years ago, a colleague who worked in digital behavior-change design introduced me to the COM-B Model, which is part of the Behaviour Change Wheel. This model came out of an effort to reconcile many different behavior-change models from a variety of domains. Susan Michie and her colleagues from University College London's Centre for Behaviour Change reviewed 19 different models and brought common elements into a single model called the Behaviour Change Wheel. This is the model I've been finding most useful in my work.

As mentioned in the earlier chapters, the field of behavioral design comes from many different disciplines, such as psychology, behavioral science, public health, behavioral economics and so on. Many of the models from those fields may cover similar territory and can certainly be useful.

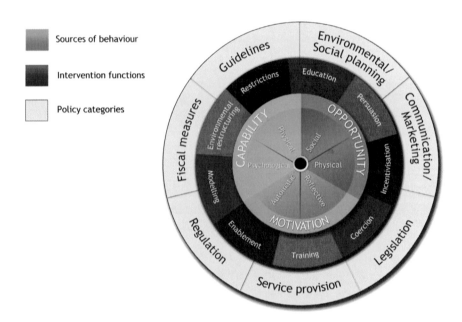

The Behavior Change Wheel is used courtesy of S. Michie, L. Atkins, and R. West (*The Behaviour Change Wheel: A Guide to Designing Interventions.* London: Silverback Publishing, 2014, www.behaviourchangewheel.com). Material related to the Behaviour Change Wheel, COM-B Analysis, Intervention Types, and the Behaviour Change Technique Taxonomy will be used in chapters 6, 8, 9–12, and 14. Some of the examples and specific wording have been adapted to a learning and development context.

UNDERSTANDING THE GOAL

Hopefully, your stakeholders have brought you a problem to solve or an outcome to achieve rather than a solution they want you to implement (I say that with more optimism than confidence).

Ever gotten the kind of request that asks for a solution? You know what it sounds like:

We need customer service training.

The next part of the sentence that you hope to hear starts with "because," so you know what problem stakeholders are trying to solve with customer service training.

Ideally, they would be specific: "We need customer service training because"

- We are getting too many customer complaints.
- Our competitor is stealing clients based on their supposedly super customer service.
- Our customers report having to call multiple times to resolve an issue.

Whatever the reason might be, it can give you a clue to define a desired outcome, which could be something like this:

Desired outcome: Customer satisfaction scores above 90%.

FOCUSING THE EFFORT

It might seem obvious, but if you're going to work on learning experiences to support behavior change, then you need to have actual *behaviors*.

As discussed in Chapter 2, behaviors don't exist in a vacuum. They exist in a complex world, so it's a bit artificial to distill out individual behaviors, but it's also really difficult to design without defining behaviors.

For example, if you ask, "If my goal is to grow a healthy tree, what behaviors are associated with that?"

The answer could be

- Choose a location with good soil and sunlight.
- Plant the seed.
- Water regularly.
- Protect the seedling from pests.

This example is pretty simple, right? But if we zoom out a level, it starts to get a little more complex. Other questions arise:

- What climate zone will the tree be in?
- What other trees or plant life are nearby?
- Should I start from seed outside or with a seedling?
- What are the trends of invasive pests that are spreading to this area?

It's still useful to do that narrow focus on just increasing a desirable behavior or decreasing a less desirable behavior, but it's also important to remember that the narrow focus is limited and needs to be viewed in a broader context.

John Cutler, an expert in product management, describes it this way:

> "One way that I think about it is that to get anything done, we need to reduce the world a little bit.
>
> "That's the difference between oversimplification and focusing. You can have a really complex problem, and you can oversimply it, and that's not great.
>
> "But you can have a complex problem and [think,] 'You know what, I need to hold some things constant. I'm not going to make any progress unless we hold some things constant to do that.'" (Cutler, 2023)

DEFINING "A BEHAVIOR"

For the purposes of this chapter, I define a behavior as

> An (observable) action or set of actions done in response to internal and/or external stimuli.

I put "observable" in parentheses because it is possible to have a cognitive behavior that isn't observable. For example, I could have a behavior like this:

> When reading politically charged print media, learners will evaluate the reliability of the material.

This behavior could happen without any externally observable cues. In this chapter, the focus is on *observable* actions.

So what about these? Are any of these behaviors?

- Participants will have a skeptical view of social media advertising.
- Patients will have more stable blood sugar levels.
- Employees will be more customer-focused.
- Participants will enthusiastically embrace a plant-based diet.

Each of these statements have behaviors *associated* with them, but they aren't really concrete behaviors themselves. Unless somebody is hugging tomato plants, "embrace a plant-based diet" is a metaphor, not a behavior.

Defining behaviors can be really difficult. For example, I've seen quite a lot of diversity, equity, and inclusion materials that focus on attitudes or beliefs. While attitudes and beliefs are important, they aren't specific enough to be the basis of a behavior-change intervention.

In a 2012 study, researchers at the University of Wisconsin-Madison attempted to identify actual behaviors that would reduce the implicit biases of study participants.

For example, when you have a thought that is based on racial stereotypes, stop yourself and use one of these strategies (Devine, 2012):

- **Stereotype replacement:** Stop, recognize a thought is based on stereotypes, and consciously replace it with a nonstereotyped version.
- **Counter-stereotypic imaging:** Imagine in detail someone who counters the stereotype. These individuals can be abstract (for example, smart people in a racial group), famous (for example, world leaders, academics, or artists in that racial group), or nonfamous (for example, a personal friend).
- **Individuation:** Obtain specific information about people in that racial group, so you can see them as individuals rather than representative of a stereotype.
- **Perspective taking:** Picture the world from their perspective.

These behavior-based interventions significantly reduced the participants' racial bias measure on the Implicit Association Test (IAT, https://implicit.harvard.edu), which attempts to measure different kinds of unconscious bias. While the IAT is not a perfect measure of racial bias, reducing the IAT measure of bias is a result that many diversity and inclusion interventions fail to accomplish.

IDENTIFYING BEHAVIORS

The simplest question I use when I'm talking to stakeholders and they say things like, "We want retail staff to be more customer-focused," or "We want people to be self-directed learners," is

> If I took a picture or a video of someone being [customer-focused], what would I be filming?"

Many behaviors support retail staff being more customer-focused:

- Greeting customers when then come into the store
- Checking in with customers to see if they need anything
- Offering to get other items for customers
- Calling to find an item at a different store
- And so on

If we want learners to be more self-directed, what behaviors would support that? A few possibilities include

- Using links in the corporate intranet to access learning content
- Creating a plan for how to develop a skill or ability
- Participating in professional communities to develop their professional skills
- Using tuition reimbursement to take classes that expand their skillsets

How do you identify the behaviors to design for? There are a number of ways to identify behaviors. The following sections look at a few strategies.

CONSULTING EXPERTS

Experts or researchers might have already compiled lists of desirable behaviors for the situation you're working with. For example, if you are looking at ways for people to manage their blood pressure, you can find a wealth of data and research into behaviors that support that outcome, from taking medication to increasing exercise to reducing sodium consumption. There may be new ways added to the list, but you shouldn't need to start from scratch to identify behaviors. You could talk to experts or do a survey of available research literature.

BRAINSTORMING

If the outcome is in a domain that is more emergent, identifying behaviors may require more brainstorming. For example, if the goal is to promote civil engagement in multiplayer online games, the research into that topic is still relatively new, and the constantly evolving technology could introduce new strategies all the time. For something like that, out-and-out brainstorming and prototyping could be a productive strategy.

One technique involves putting an outcome on a whiteboard and brainstorming as many potential behaviors as you can. For example, if you work for a food company and your goal is to create more innovative cupcake toppers, you can probably brainstorm dozens of behaviors to support that. (I may have been watching a lot of baking shows while writing this book.)

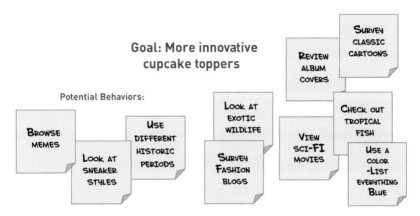

It's possible you may want to work with multiple groups. For example, cupcake topper brainstorming could be something you do with expert staff, but it might also be valuable to engage a group of social media bakers or a group of average customers for a brainstorming session. Consider the different audiences who might have useful input. Also consider the power dynamics when mixing groups. Might home bakers feel intimidated if you mix them with professional experts?

FOLLOWING PERFORMERS

One crucial method to identify behaviors to support an outcome is to engage with people currently doing the behavior. What are they doing? It's helpful to look at different kinds of performers:

- **Star performers:** Who are the people who are currently crushing it, and what are they doing? For example, if you look at behavior to support the goal of improving salesperson-customer relationships, ask who currently has the best customer relationships and follow those salespeople around to note their actions and behaviors.

- **Regular performers:** It's also worth spending time with people in your audience who are not the rockstars so you understand what their situation and behaviors are. Sometimes the star performers have attributes that are not easily replicable. For example, if someone is rated a good teacher because they are funny and charming and captivate their audience, that's great, but you can't just tell a new teacher to "be captivating." You can note that a good teacher also spends 20% more time prompting students to ask questions than the average teacher, and that's a behavior a new teacher *could* replicate.

- **Positive deviants:** On their website, the Positive Deviance Collaboration defines positive deviants as "Individuals, groups, or entities who are the least likely to prevent or overcome a widely shared problem but are successful despite facing the same or worse challenges and barriers. They have access to the same or fewer resources than other colleagues, peers, or entities." Basically, who is being successful right now? This may overlap with star performers, but it's not necessarily the people who are being lauded for accomplishment. I originally encountered the idea of positive deviants in Atul Gawande's book *Better* with the story of Jerry and Monique Sternin, who used the approach in Vietnam to address childhood malnutrition. They looked at which people in the community had the best-nourished children and noted what those parents did differently. Rather than focusing on the problems within the community, they looked at what was going right in the community in order to amplify it.

PRIORITIZING BEHAVIORS

Once you have a list of behaviors, you may have more than you can ever address, so you need to prioritize the behaviors you are going to work on.

One framework you can use is the APEASE criteria (see Table 6.1), which are also part of the Behaviour Change Wheel process.

Table 6.1   APEASE Criteria

Criteria	Definition
Acceptability	How far is it acceptable to key stakeholders? This includes the target group, potential funders, practitioners delivering the interventions, and relevant community and commercial groups.
Practicability	Can it be implemented at scale in the intended context, given the available material and human resources? What would need to be done to ensure that the resources and personnel were in place, and is the intervention sustainable?
Effectiveness	How effective is it (likely to be) in achieving the policy objective(s)? How far will it reach the intended target group, and how large an effect will it have on those who are reached?

Affordability	How far can it be afforded when delivered at the scale intended? Can the necessary budget be found for it? Will it provide a good return on investment?
Spill-over effects (side-effects)	What extraneous adverse (or beneficial) outcomes might it lead to? How important are they, and what is the likelihood that they will occur?
Equity	How far will it, or is it likely to, increase or decrease differences between advantaged and disadvantaged sectors of society?

Source: Achieving Behaviour Change: A Guide for Local Government and Partners

You can use these criteria to rate different behaviors. For example, if you are creating nutrition curriculum with a goal to reducing sodium intake for controlling high blood pressure, you could evaluate these two behaviors:

- Purchase low-sodium substitutes for common items
- Eliminate processed snack foods at home

If I was the target audience, and I just scored these behaviors for my own purposes, the numbers could look like this:

Option	Acceptability (0 to 10)	Practicability (0 to 10)	Effectiveness (0 to 10)	Affordability (0 to 10)	Spill-over effects (−5 to +5)	Equity (−5 to +5)	Total
Purchase low-sodium substitutes for common items	7	7	8	7	4	—	33
Eliminate processed snack foods at home	8	8	3	10	1	—	30

So my ratings are based on a few things. First, I don't really buy many salty snacks right now to eat at home (my junk food indulgences are other things), so even though that would be any easy behavior to commit to, it wouldn't be terribly effective at impacting my sodium consumption. Purchasing low-sodium substitutes (for example, canned goods) would probably help more with my home cooking. To really look at effectively reducing my sodium consumption, I'd probably also need to look at processed meals and habits when eating outside the home.

Because I was rating for myself, I didn't score the equity items, but you'd want to consider that for a different audience. For example, if you were helping a particular population, you might want to consider practicality and equity issues about access to grocery stores that stock low-sodium items, costs of cooking at home, or adapting to a culturally acceptable diet.

You can also use a low–medium–high categorization, if that format is more useful. Here's an example:

Option	Acceptability	Practicability	Effectiveness	Affordability	Spill-over effects	Equity
Purchase low-sodium substitutes for common items	Medium	High	High	High	Medium	N/A
Eliminate processed snack foods at home	High	High	Low	High	Low	N/A

DEALBREAKERS

You want to evaluate a behavior on acceptability and practicality, but some behaviors are dealbreakers. You really can't address the outcome without addressing these behaviors. For example, if your outcome is infection prevention control (preventing the spread of disease in healthcare settings), and you *don't* address hand washing, you won't be dealing with one of the main issues and are likely not going to have enough impact without it. So no matter what score you assign to acceptability and practicality, handwashing is going to be included.

Some other behaviors may be *very* effective but really not practical. For example, if someone is trying to reduce the amount of sodium in their diet to help lower their blood pressure, cooking all their food from scratch would be an effective behavior but not necessarily a practical one. In that case, we would want to figure out if there are other acceptable behaviors that would support the outcome of lower sodium intake.

SPILLOVER BEHAVIORS

Some behaviors support spillover behaviors. So if you DO start cooking more at home because you are trying to reduce your sodium consumption, you may also increase your consumption of fruits and vegetables, serve yourself portions that are closer to your appetite than typical restaurant portions, save money by eating out less, or make it more likely that your whole family eats at the same time. Cooking at home would then be a behavior that supports several adjacent desirable behaviors.

SPECIFYING THE BEHAVIOR

Once you have used prioritization to select the behavior(s), you want to be as specific as possible about the performance and conditions of each behavior. You can do this using a behavioral statement.

Behavioral statements can be written in a "Mad Libs" style format using the following template:

- **Who:** Target audience
- **Will do what:** Target behavior
- **To what extent:** Engagement pattern (amount, frequency, intensity, duration)
- **In what context:** Where, when, with whom, to whom (does the behavior occur)
- **For what outcome to occur:** Outcome goal metric the behavior will affect

So, for example,

> Managers (**who**) will do one-on-one check-ins with their direct reports (**what**), monthly (**extent**), using the new performance management system (**context**), to support improved employee engagement as measured by the biannual engagement survey (**outcome**).

(Source of Behavioral Statement Format: Dustin DiTommaso, used with permission)

Interview with Matt Wallaert, author of *Start at the End* and founder of BeSci.io (Behavioral Science in organizations)

Q: What kind of baseline measures do you use on projects? Where do you start?

I think the first step has to be shifting that mindset from, "What do people know?" to "What do people do?"

You can't have good measurement if you haven't figured out what you actually want people to do in the first place. And it's amazing how often people are throwing around euphemisms. One of my favorites is *engagement*. "Well, I want people to be engaged." What does that mean? When you say you want somebody to love your class, do you mean you want them to recommend it? To come again? To rate it highly? To agree to pay for it? All of those are different potential forms of love.

But what I would do as an intervention to get you to come to another class is very different than what I might do to get you to pay, or to get you to recommend it. So you need to know what outcome you want.

Q: What if it's very difficult to get a behavioral measure?

Even if you don't actually end up asking or measuring "doing," you want to know that what you are measuring correlates to behaviors. So a good example is something like the Clover Five [a series of five employee survey questions asked at regular intervals], which included questions like, "Do I like who I work with?" and "Do I trust who I work for?"

Trusting and liking are not behaviors, but I know they correlate to the behaviors that I want. So, I've done the work to show that trusting your manager correlates to whether or not you stay at the company. The behavior I care about is staying at the company, and I know it correlates with liking your manager.

So step one has to be, "What do we want people actually physically literally to do?" Two, what things that are measured can be measured directly? If so, great. If we can't measure them directly, what other things correlate with those direct measurements that I could use as a proxy? And so I think that's the sort of two-part plan there, what do you want to do? And then how are you going to measure that doing? And if you can't do it directly, what indirect measures do you have?

Q: You talked about onboarding. Many learning and development people have been tasked with creating onboarding training, and the goals are often pretty fuzzy for what they want it to accomplish.

Well, in a lot of companies that I interact with, they haven't done the work to know what they want. And so if I was designing onboarding, you have to figure out what is the thing I care about? Oh, what I care about is 180-day retention. Cool—now we have a measure. What correlates with 180-day retention? Do you even know? There might be a totally reasonable case for you to focus on 401k enrollment, because it turns out that maybe at your company, the biggest predictor of 180-day retention is 401K enrollment. But, if you don't look, if you don't measure, and if you don't know that 180-day retention is the thing that you care about, how would you ever get to that?

COM-B

A foundational part of the Behaviour Change Wheel is the COM-B model, which stands for capability, opportunity, motivation-behavior. This outlines the necessary conditions for any behavior to be enacted.

Once you have behaviors selected, you can analyze them using the COM-B categories (Michie et al., 2011). The next sections look at each one.

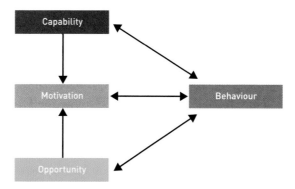

NOTE: Each of the COM-B categories I cover in the following sections are used courtesy of S. Michie, L. Atkins, and R. West (*The Behaviour Change Wheel: A Guide to Designing Interventions*. London: Silverback Publishing, 2014, www.behaviourchangewheel.com).

CAPABILITY

Is the person capable of performing the behavior? Do they know what to do and have the physical capability to do it?

This breaks down into two categories:

Physical capability, which is defined as "physical skill, strength, or stamina."

For example, if the behavior you are trying to support is nurses turning patients more regularly to prevent pressure ulcers (which nobody wants), does a 5'2" nurse have the physical ability to turn a 6'4" bedridden patient? Possibly not.

Psychological capability, which is defined as "knowledge or psychological skills, to engage in the behaviour."

If you know the history of the *Oregon Trail* videogame franchise, how to negotiate a contract, or how to swear in Lithuanian, then you have psychological capabilities. It can be knowledge or cognitive skills. It can also be the stamina to stay focused on a task. For example, the copy editor editing this book may need a certain amount of psychological stamina (ability to concentrate and stay focused and attentive) to deal with my somewhat eccentric use of capitalization.

OPPORTUNITY

Opportunity also breaks down into two categories:

Physical opportunity, which is defined as the opportunity afforded by the environment involving time, resources, locations, cues, and physical "affordance(s)."

For example, a behavior I've frequently heard clients want is for people to look up the answers to technical problems on the support website to try to answer the question before calling the help desk. And then I've looked at how the search function works on the support website, and I'm pretty sure I know why people are calling the helpdesk.

The whole field of user experience design has grown up around the idea that if systems are designed better, people will be able to do things better, faster, and more efficiently.

For example, estimates of handwashing hand hygiene compliance in healthcare settings dramatically improved with the introduction of alcohol-based hand rubs. The improvement was less about persuading healthcare workers to change their behavior and more about the introduction of an alternative that was quicker and easier to use and could be placed in clinic settings more easily than added plumbing.

Social opportunity, which is defined as the opportunity afforded by interpersonal influences, social cues, and cultural norms that influence the way that we think about things.

Social opportunity looks at how well your social environment supports the behavior. For example, lots of people like to participate in Dry January, which is a sobriety challenge that involves not drinking alcohol for the first month of the year. It began as a part of a public health campaign in 2013 by the nonprofit group Alcohol Change UK.

Many people like it as a break after the holidays, but social opportunity can influence whether it's a maintainable behavior for people.

For example, meet Moe. Moe is doing Dry January, and we can look at how social opportunities might influence Moe's behavior.

Image Credit: Disabled and Here.

If it turns out that Moe is doing Dry January with their partner Kai, and everybody in the household is participating, then it could be easier for Moe to maintain the behavior.

Moe might be encouraged by seeing other people posting on social media about their own Dry January participation, and that might make Moe feel like they are part of something. But Moe might also see their sister's husband (who Moe finds super annoying) lecturing people on social media about the evils of drinking and proclaiming that Dry January is just a "super-duper easy thing" for somebody with his willpower, and Moe might find that annoying enough to feel slightly put off by the whole topic.

But if Moe goes to the big holiday party put on by their employer that was pushed to the second week of January, and their boss is handing out glasses of champagne as Moe comes into the venue, and the party organizers got sparkling apple juice but only one bottle because they didn't think that many people would want it, and the other Dry January people have already claimed all the apple juice glasses, and only champagne is left if Moe wants to participate in the big toast, well, that may make Dry January a bit more challenging.

If Kai is with Moe at the work party, that may increase the likelihood that Moe will skip the champagne because Dry January is something they are doing together, but if Kai skipped the party because she thinks Moe's work events are deathly boring, then Kai's influence might be a little less.

So you can see that social opportunity can have many complicated interacting influences on whether someone maintains a behavior.

MOTIVATION

Motivation is broken down into reflective motivation and automatic motivation.

Reflective motivation, which is processes involving identity, values, and beliefs, as well as goals and planning.

Reflective motivation is motivation that you can talk about and reflect on. It's the motivation that is related to goals you might set or values you might have.

If you set a goal to finish a book chapter by a certain date, and you can't quite get it done, you might set a revised deadline to ensure it doesn't drag on. This would all be part of reflective motivation.

Automatic motivation, which is automatic processes involving emotions, drives, and habits.

Automatic motivation might be the draggy feeling around finishing your expense report, the excitement that causes you to be a bit inattentive the last hour before you'll be on vacation for a week, or the reluctance to check a voicemail from a client for reasons you can't quite explain but later realize is because that particular client only calls when they are unhappy about something. While the rider is busy setting goals and evaluating beliefs, the elephant is feeling all the automatic motivations.

USING COM-B TO ANALYZE BEHAVIORS

Let's take a few behaviors and consider which COM-B elements might be involved.

EXAMPLE: WORKER SAFETY

Remember Jerome? He's dealing with updating safety guidelines and training materials for agricultural workers working at heights.

The particular behavior that he's identified is

Workers need to identify and log working-at-heights safety hazards.

We'll interview Jerome to help us understand what capabilities, opportunities, and motivations workers need.

Question	Jerome's Response
What physical capabilities do workers need to perform this behavior?	"Well, it's not really a physical task. We're asking them to flag safety hazards, so it's about them recognizing problems when they see them. The need to know if it meets the definition of a working-at-heights hazard and log that. Logging it is part of how we track safety data."
What psychological capabilities do workers need to perform this behavior?	"They need to know what is and is not a hazard. Anything over a certain height or that has a falling risk is considered a hazard. "Mostly they estimate the height by just eyeballing it (not measuring), and I think they are not great at that. I think they frequently underestimate how high something is. In some of the buildings, it's obvious because the top of the ground floor sheeting is about the height of the safety limit, but not all buildings have that sheeting. "Also, many of the workers don't speak English, and I think that makes it harder for them to log hazards. The form is a bit hard to understand."
How does the physical environment support the behavior?	"Huh, nobody has asked me that before. Hmm, I know that when they are working at the main facility, the safety equipment is right there, but if they are working at one of the farther-out locations, they don't always want to come back to the main facility to get the safety equipment. It takes too long, so they don't log the issue."
How does the social environment support the behavior?	"Social environment? Do you mean how the other workers react? Mostly I think people are supportive. Nobody wants anybody to get hurt. I do see some impatience at the end of a shift though. People want to get done and home, and don't want to stay late because somebody has to drive over and get the safety gear."
What is the reflective motivation of the workers? For example, do they have goals or beliefs about this?	"Well, let's be honest. Most of these workers have done stuff at heights and gotten away with it. If it's an obviously unsafe thing, they'll log it and get the gear, but if it feels like it's just a little over the height limit, I think they see it as rules for the sake of having rules. "Goals? Other than 'don't get hurt' or 'don't get yelled at for breaking the rules'? No, I don't think they have goals about it. "One thing I've noticed, though—a lot of people change when they start supervising. They start to see the reasons behind the rules, and how keeping people safe is part of them being a good boss and a professional supervisor."
What automatic motivation (feeling, habits, biases) do you think influence the workers?	"Like I said, it's more of a problem when it's on the edge. If they are 30 feet in the air, they know they are going to die or be really hurt if they fall. Eight feet up doesn't feel as scary, but if you fall the wrong way, or onto something sharp, you can still be seriously injured. "Also, people get into habits, right? Just ways of doing things. If you take a serious fall or see someone who does, you do NOT mess around with falling risks after that, but a lot of these young kids haven't had that experience."

Obviously, just talking to Jerome probably isn't enough to fully understand the problem. Other sources you should consider investigating include the following:

- **Interviewing workers:** Talk to an assortment of people in your target audience.
- **Observing them doing the behavior:** Watch workers doing the behavior now.
- **Consulting subject matter experts:** See how safety experts can enlighten your understanding of the behavior.
- **Reviewing the research literature:** Read studies from academic researchers looking at questions around safety behaviors.

For simplicity's sake, we will assume that we've done the additional research, and it aligns pretty well with what Jerome told us.

The COM-B analysis can be broken down into observations:

COM-B Diagnosis	Observations
Physical Capability	Physical capability is not an issue here.
Psychological Capability	Workers need to be able to accurately identify situations that qualify as a working-at-heights hazard, including the ability to estimate edge cases visually.
Physical opportunity	Workers need a simple, language-appropriate way to log hazards.
	Visual cues in the environment could help workers estimate and recognize working-at-heights hazards.
	Ready availability of safety equipment may increase willingness to log hazards.
Social opportunity	Personal acquaintance with people who have had accidents can influence behavior.
Reflective motivation	Workers do not have goals or associate professional competence with the behavior but do develop that as supervisors.
Automatic motivation	Workers may have an inaccurate feeling about what is a dangerous working-at-heights hazard, particularly in the absence of personal experience.

I discuss how to match these to solutions in later chapters, but several of the items are blatantly "not a training problem" but are part of the environment or the system, such as difficulty logging problems or access to safety equipment.

Once you have the diagnosis, you can explore which aspects will have implications for your learning design, and you may need to make decisions about which items are in scope or out of scope for your project. A few items that could have implications for learning design are the following:

- The workers need to be able to recognize that hazards could be something to be addressed in training. In particular, the ability to "eyeball" the height is probably something that workers overestimate; it might be really useful to create an opportunity for them to practice and find out just how not-accurate their guesses are.

- Part of the learning experience could be a more visceral or experience-based understanding of the danger of even low-height hazards and could leverage stories about people falling from relatively low heights.
- Workers don't have a strong sense of proficiency or professional identity around this job skill, so a learning activity could help make that connection for them. ▪

KEY POINTS

- Behaviors always exist in a larger context. You might focus on a narrow behavior to understand it closely, but you also need to step back and take a wider view.
- For a behavior-change initiative, make sure that you've defined actual behaviors, not intentions, outcomes, or vague high-level goals.
- COM-B is a model that examines behaviors by looking at capability, opportunity, and motivation.
- To identify a behavior, you could ask, "If I took a picture or a video of someone doing that thing, what would I see?"
- Identifying the right behaviors can come from many sources, including brainstorming with subject matter experts or observation, academic research, or interview data.
- Capability can be physical or psychomotor capability, or it can be psychological capability, which can include mental stamina.
- Opportunity can involve physical opportunity—how the environment and systems support the behavior—and social opportunity—how social connections and social environment influence the behavior.
- Motivation can be reflective—related to goals, beliefs, and values—or it can be automatic, which is related to emotions, impulses, and automatic responses.

RESOURCES

Alcohol Change UK. "The Dry January Story," *Alcohol Change UK* website, accessed January 17, 2023, https://alcoholchange.org.uk/help-and-support/managing-your-drinking/dry-january/about-dry-january/the-dry-january-story.

Cutler, John. "What Differentiates the Highest-Performing Product Teams | John Cutler (Amplitude, The Beautiful Mess)," in *Lenny's Podcast*, produced by Producer Lenny Rachitsky, podcast audio, January 15, 2023, 140:44, https://www.lennyspodcast.com/what-differentiates-the-highest-performing-product-teams-john-cutler-amplitude-the-beautiful-mess/.

Devine, Patricia G., Patrick S. Forscher, Anthony J. Austin, and William TL Cox. "Long-Term Reduction in Implicit Race Bias: A Prejudice Habit-Breaking Intervention," *Journal of Experimental Social Psychology* 48, no. 6 (2012): 1267–1278.

Gawande, Atul. *Better: A Surgeon's Notes on Performance* (New York: Metropolitan Books, 2008).

Kasinger, Chona. "Disabled and Here." https://affecttheverb.com/gallery/disabledandhere/coupleshot/.

Michie, Susan, Lou Atkins, and Robert West. "The Behaviour Change Wheel." *A Guide to Designing Interventions,* 1st ed. (Sutton, UK: Silverback Publishing, 2014). www.behaviourchangewheel.com.

Michie, Susan, Maartje M. Van Stralen, and Robert West. "The Behaviour Change Wheel: A New Method for Characterising and Designing Behaviour Change Interventions." *Implementation Science* 6, no. 1 (2011): 1–12.

Pascale, Richard, Jerry Sternin, and Monique Sternin. *The Power of Positive Deviance* (Brighton, MA: Harvard Business Press, 2010).

Positive Deviance Collaboration, s.v. "positive deviants," accessed January 17, 2023, https://positivedeviance.org/terms.

Public Health England. *Achieving Behaviour Change: A Guide for Local Government and Partners*, PHE publications gateway number: GW-834, November 2019, https://www.gov.uk/government/publications/behaviour-change-guide-for-local-government-and-partners.

Wallaert, Matt. "The Clover 5: Measuring Employee Happiness" from "Clover Off the Charts," Medium.com, September 12, 2018, https://medium.com/clover-off-the-charts/the-clover-5-measuring-employee-happiness-cob4dc23df83.

Widmer, Andreas F., Martin Conzelmann, Milanka Tomic, Reno Frei, and Anne M. Stranden. "Introducing Alcohol-Based Hand Rub for Hand Hygiene: The Critical Need for Training." *Infection Control & Hospital Epidemiology* 28, no. 1 (2007): 50–54.

DETERMINING IF IT'S A TRAINING PROBLEM

(IN WHICH WE CHECK IN WITH THE ELEPHANT TO SEE WHAT ELSE MIGHT BE CAUSING AN ISSUE)

Pretty much everyone who has worked in an organization creating training materials has gotten a request for something that makes them wonder "Is this really a training problem?"

Although I use COM-B as an analysis tool to understand a whole problem, I also have a list of the common issues that go along with those training requests that show up in L&D inboxes. I specifically want to look at these because they so commonly seem to be attached to learning requests, and it can be useful to set expectations about what training

131

can and cannot accomplish at the beginning of a project. This chapter is focused on workplace learning scenarios, but many of the principles should still apply in other contexts.

DIAGNOSIS OF THE PROBLEM: WHAT ARE THE CAUSES, AND CAN LEARNING HELP?

The following are problems that may have a training component, but they're not first and foremost about teaching learners how to do the behavior. Sometimes training can help, but often other issues in the environment or the system also have to be addressed for the behavior to change:

- Lack of feedback
- Unclear goals
- Unlearning an existing behavior
- Unawareness of consequences/bigger picture
- Lack of environment or process support
- Anxiety/fear/discomfort
- Lack of confidence/belief about capabilities
- Mistrust
- Social proof
- Lack of autonomy/ownership
- Learned helplessness
- Misaligned incentives
- Lack of identity or value alignment
- Emotional reaction

Let's work through this list by revisiting the handwashing example from Chapter 5.

Handwashing compliance in healthcare is an ongoing challenge, so each of the following sections takes a look at one of these common issues in the context of handwashing.

If you work in healthcare, you might be asked to design learning for a learning objective like this:

> Learners will be able to wash their hands according to the organizational guidelines.

Disclaimer: Since we are using handwashing as an example here, I want to start by acknowledging that while I have worked on curriculums related to handwashing in the past, I don't claim special expertise on this topic and fully expect that the details may vary in different locations and that understanding of the challenges will change as more is learned in the future.

LACK OF FEEDBACK

One of the most common characteristics I see in cases of "they know what to do but still aren't doing it" is delayed or absent feedback.

For example, if Joe starts a new job and his start time Is 9:00 a.m., he will probably try to show up by 9:00 a.m. every day because he wants to make a good impression. But let's say that sometime in his second week, his bus is delayed, and he gets to work at 9:15 a.m. and *nobody says anything about it*. He might persist with being timely because he wants to be a responsible worker or because he doesn't want to push his luck, but after a few months, it becomes apparent to Joe that when he has transportation delays, nobody is going to comment at all on when he comes in. Joe's rider intellectually knows that his start time is 9:00 a.m., but his real-world experience elephant knows a different story.

EH. ANYTHING UP TO 9:30 IS FINE...

DOES THIS APPLY TO OUR HANDWASHING EXAMPLE?

Let's look at our handwashing example. How does someone get feedback on handwashing?

If your hands are visibly dirty and you wash them, you can see the difference. But in healthcare settings, that isn't really the standard. Often, healthcare workers know they need to wash their hands based not on visible cues but because they've touched surfaces that likely have germs.

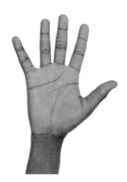

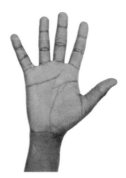

Hand after moving the trash can
to retrieve the tuna fish sandwich
wrapper that fell behind it.

Same hand after washing in
accordance with guidelines
for healthcare workers.

So, with many cases of handwashing, there is no visible difference before and after the hands have been washed, and the only way that you know there's a difference is if you have an understanding of germ theory. This is something the rider knows about, but the elephant doesn't really understand.

I DUNNO, LOOKS
PRETTY GOOD TO
ME.

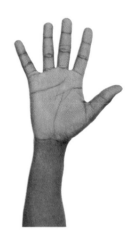

Hand after moving the trash
can to retrieve the tuna
fish sandwich wrapper that
fell behind it.

You are relying on the rider to drag the elephant along every time a person needs to wash their hands in accordance with guidelines and not because their hands look or feel dirty. You can attach penalties when someone fails to comply with hand-washing guidelines, but that's still only going to catch a percentage of incidents.

Additionally, if a healthcare worker fails to wash their hands at 3:15 on a Thursday after-noon, that could cause a patient to get an infection, but it's almost impossible for that worker to connect their behavior with that outcome. There are too many people and moving parts to the healthcare system to ever draw a direct line between handwashing behaviors and the outcomes. The outcomes can only be inferred.

IS THIS A TRAINING PROBLEM?

Mostly, no. Delayed or absent feedback is typically a systems problem. When there's no feedback, it can be possible to engineer something with technology. For example, it typically would take weeks to see some physical evidence of progress after stepping up your level of aerobic exercise, so instead you may rely on fitness trackers or equipment settings to show that you are improving.

In Six Sigma programs, there's a concept called the visual workplace that is about systematically trying to make the status of systems visible and obvious. It could be as simple as a tool board with outlines so a worker can feel confident they are putting a tool in the right place.

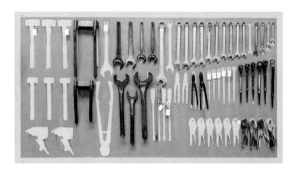

At a nurses station, it could be an electronic board that shows the vitals of all the patients on the ward with alerts that let the nurses know if there's an issue. Both of these examples aren't *just* feedback systems, but looking for ways to make the status or behavior easier to see can also provide useful feedback.

In workplace settings, providing feedback often comes down to whether managers are paying attention or if there's someone who can coach the employee to change the behavior.

WHAT CAN TRAINING DO?

- **Create feedback tools.** Is there any kind of checklist, scorecard, or rubric that participants could use to track their own results?
- **Practice with feedback.** If the learner is going back to an environment where there's no feedback, is there a way that they can get enough practice in the training environment that the behavior starts to become automatic?

- **Support managers.** Often for a worker to be successful, they need to have the support of their manager. That often means the manager also needs to change some of their behaviors. When that's the case, you should consider the managers to be a secondary audience you are designing for. For example, if a manager needs to provide feedback on a behavior change, the learning designer should ask what tools or support can be created that makes it more likely the manager will be able to provide that feedback effectively. It's worth remembering that the people reinforcing the behaviors have their own 37 Other Things competing for their attention, so anything you can do to make feedback and reinforcement easier for them is worth considering as part of the design process.

UNCLEAR GOALS

Sometimes the issue is that the goal is fuzzy or vague. Is there a defined standard of performance? If not, you need to find a way to clarify the goals.

For example, I've seen many training classes that had objectives about things like "proactive leadership" or "bias awareness." For both of these, how would you know if you were doing them well? Are you at a 25% level for proactive leadership? At 50%? At 90%? If you become more aware of your own biases, are you identifying a few, some, or most of them?

There's probably no way to answer these questions, so you need to operationalize them to be able to measure them. What behaviors are associated with these goals? What outcomes are associated with these goals?

DOES THIS APPLY TO OUR HANDWASHING EXAMPLE?

In terms of our handwashing example, I think we would actually *not* consider it to be an example of unclear goals. The standard of performance is quite well defined by several medical organizations.

IS THIS A TRAINING PROBLEM?

Sort of? Theoretically, unclear goals are not a training problem but an operational or management problem. The reality, though, is that in many organizations, specific performance *hasn't* been defined, and although stakeholders know there's an issue with current performance, they often can't tell you exactly what they want instead.

In many ways, learning and development is a logical partner to ask these questions and to help define performance standards as part of the design process. The methods discussed in Chapter 6 about identifying clear behaviors are relevant here.

WHAT CAN TRAINING DO?

The question of how to become a better partner to management or operations to define performance is the topic of a whole other book, but there are a few strategies to consider:

- **Define performance.** Creating a definition of performance is part of the analysis process, and it can be helpful to ensure that stakeholders know that defining performance will be part of the learning design process.
- **Illustrate tacit goals with enough case examples.** One way to communicate a goal or expectation is to look at enough examples to start to tacitly understand what is and is not representative. For example, I was working with a client that had "integrity" as a company value, and it was actually used to guide decision-making in the organization. But my client explained that the meaning of "integrity" not only referred to being ethical but also to making decisions that had "structural integrity"—that is, solutions that were sustainable or solved the root cause of a problem. While I understood this explanation, I didn't really understand how the company used that value until I had seen multiple examples of it in action in the course of work.
- **Use goal-setting learning activities.** If specific performance is hard to define, it may be useful to have the learners work through how to operationalize the goals themselves. You can have activities in which they define and plan how to use the goals and define their own standards of performance.
- **Use rubrics and tiered performance goals.** Many goals aren't all or nothing. Rubrics or tiered performance goals that explain what a starter, intermediate, and expert level looks like can give learners the ability to gauge where they are on the continuum and understand what improving could look like.

UNLEARNING AN EXISTING BEHAVIOR

One of the common problems when it comes to behavior change is that the new behavior fights with existing behaviors, and some of those existing behaviors might be so familiar, they are mostly automatic, which means it's hard to stop doing them.

If you've ever had the experience of trying to drive in a country where traffic lanes are reversed (you drive on the side opposite of what you're used to), you understand this pretty well. (I can't do it—every time we make a left turn, I think we're going to die.) Driving is a behavior that is so automatic, it can be very difficult to force yourself to do it differently.

I will note that people don't actually "unlearn" things. There's no big eraser that comes along and rubs out the neuronal connections for a particular behavior. Overwriting the existing behavior might be a better analogy.

DOES THIS APPLY TO OUR HANDWASHING EXAMPLE?

Assuming the handwashing guidelines or environment haven't changed, this probably isn't a big issue for our handwashing example, but this issue shows up in all sorts of other domains—for example, how you process paperwork, enter a customer record in a system, handle a tool, or talk to a client.

IS THIS A TRAINING PROBLEM?

Oh yeah, this is *definitely* a training problem. Designing sufficient practice opportunities is absolutely a responsibility of the learning designer. One of the biggest issues I see in many training environments is that we provide enough practice to understand how something works but not enough practice to actually develop some fluency with the behavior.

WHAT CAN TRAINING DO?

A few strategies include the following:

- **Observe performance and note automatic behaviors.** Watch or video people performing and identify where there is a high degree of automaticity. If you are someone who doesn't do the job you're observing, the places where autopilot is in control will be all the places where you can't quite follow what the person is doing because they do it with an ease or speed that's too fast for you. Knowing where there's automaticity in the existing process can help you pinpoint where learners need to practice the new behavior. Of course, sometimes the answer is *all of it.*
- **Use implementation intentions.** This is having learners identify the trigger for the new behavior and having them form an intention for what they'll do differently ("if x, then I'll do y"). For example, I have an implementation intention around being a pedestrian in the UK. As I mentioned, I'm not good at the whole "driving on the other side of the road" thing, and that also extends to being a pedestrian. (My expectations about where the cars are coming from are usually wrong.) So, my implementation intention is "When I feel the urge to jaywalk, I make myself wait for the walk signal."
- **Practice forming the new habit.** You want people to practice enough that they start to have some fluency with the new behavior. It's unlikely that you'll get people to full automaticity in a training class, but getting people to the point that they recognize they're getting better can help them have momentum and motivation after the class.
- **Create learning activities to compare the old and new behavior.** For example, you can have an activity where participants are given or shown the

steps in the new process, and they have to identify how that's different than the existing process. They can identify for themselves where problems might occur and help develop some troubleshooting plans for implementing the new process.

UNAWARENESS OF CONSEQUENCES/BIGGER PICTURE

I try to be a good recycler. I understand that the efficacy of the world recycling system is tremendously complex, but the only part of it that I control is what I purchase and how I recycle.

Despite reading the materials sent from the city, I've always had some hesitancy about certain recycling choices. I clean out the containers, but does it need to be squeaky clean, or just reasonably rinsed out? What about all those bottle caps? And so on.

So I did a deep dive into the world of recycling center videos available online and learned that I shouldn't be flattening milk cartons because it makes sorting harder (according to my local recycling authority) and that black plastic is trash because the way the optical scanners work.

By the time you read this, the guidance might be different, but I changed several of my behaviors because I had a better sense of the downstream consequences of my actions. I'd read the rules but struggled with some of the behaviors until I had a better sense of the consequences.

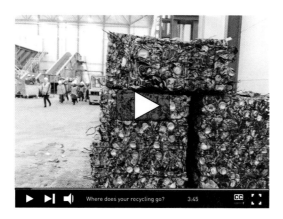

In complex organizations, unawareness of consequences happens a lot. The customers filling out an application might skip or guess at an answer if they are unsure of what is being asked. The people who are doing data entry for the customer application might have some shortcuts they use when the customer didn't fill out the information in the right format. The person evaluating the application might apply guidelines that the customer had no idea would be relevant. All of these people might behave differently if they understood the consequences or the bigger picture.

DOES THIS APPLY TO OUR HANDWASHING EXAMPLE?

If we look at our handwashing example, there is potential for unawareness of consequences to be an issue. Clinical staff like doctors and nurses are likely to understand the scientific consequences of unwashed hands, but other healthcare or facility staff may or may not know what can happen.

IS THIS A TRAINING PROBLEM?

Yep, this is a training issue. Part of the analysis process should be asking about consequences or the bigger picture for the behaviors. Because consequences are often obvious to subject matter experts, it can be easy for them to forget to explain them. One of my favorite questions to ask while doing analysis is "What bad thing can happen if they don't do this right?"

WHAT CAN TRAINING DO?

- **Show consequences.** The obvious answer is to explain or show the consequences. It can be useful to create scenarios where learners can try behaviors and then see what happens.
- **Make consequences salient, or emotionally resonant.** There's a concept in charitable giving called "the identifiable victim effect" (Lee, 2016) where people are more likely to donate if the appeal focuses on the plight of a single individual, rather than multiple people or a reported number of people impacted. We connect with personal stories, so learning about consequences that feel real or personal may have a greater effect on behavior. Even without an emotional hook, just seeing consequences you can relate to and comprehend can help. One of the better recycling videos I watched followed a single yogurt container through the whole recycling process, which made things more salient for me than watching mountains of plastic recycling be moved through the process.

LACK OF ENVIRONMENT OR PROCESS SUPPORT

Sometimes the issue is that the environment or process does not support the behavior. (I've alluded to this issue several times in the book so far.)

For example, I was filling out a survey that asked me to rate my experience at a retail store in comparison to similar retail stores in the area. However, I hadn't been in any other stores in the area (I was visiting family for the holidays), and the form wouldn't let me skip the question. My choices were to abandon the survey altogether or pick a rating at random. I assume the goal of the survey was for customers to provide accurate information, but the survey designers made it impossible for me to do so.

Poorly designed environments or processes happen ALL THE TIME, and it's the domain of people like user experience or service designers to make things better.

DOES THIS APPLY TO OUR HANDWASHING EXAMPLE?

Often yes, it does. Improvements in hand-cleaning compliance saw a significant uptick in the United States when alcohol-based hand rubs became widely available. Researchers have spent a huge amount of effort on how to design healthcare settings to better support hand hygiene. Handwashing compliance efforts in other parts of the world are hampered by lack of access to clean water and handwashing supplies.

IS THIS A TRAINING PROBLEM?

Mostly it's not a training problem, but that unfortunately doesn't let us off the hook. A significant portion of the training I worked on in the first several years of my career would not have been necessary if the systems or environment had been better designed.

For example, I remember one software training project where the instructions to add another item were "Hover your mouse below the other items and a gray box should appear. Click the gray box to add an additional item." Why would the interface be designed with a phantom button you could see only when you hover in the correct spot rather than an actual visible button? No amount of pleading could get them to replace the ghostly box with the button labeled Add Item.

+ Add Item

WHAT CAN TRAINING DO?

- **Emphasize troubleshooting strategies.** Sometimes you just need to acknowledge that we live in an imperfect world and emphasize strategies that can help people troubleshoot when things don't go as intended.
- **Add job aids to the environment.** For example, put prompts or clear, easy-to-read instructions at the point of use.
- **Give learners tools to audit their own environments or processes.** Can you give learners a checklist of items to change in their environment to promote the desired behaviors? Or can you have learners work in class on a plan to modify, adjust, or troubleshoot processes back in their own environment?

ANXIETY/FEAR/DISCOMFORT

It might be my midwestern U.S. background, but negotiation is *hard*. I've consumed a lot of training materials, articles, and other media about negotiation over the years, and when it comes time to actually negotiate, I'm usually still filled with overwhelming discomfort.

I've gotten better over the years and worked out strategies that I can execute on, but the discomfort hasn't completely gone way.

Any time that a new behavior is accompanied by anxiety, fear, or discomfort, the design of the learning experience needs to take that into account.

DOES THIS APPLY TO OUR HANDWASHING EXAMPLE?

In our handwashing example, anxiety, fear, or emotional discomfort probably don't prevent people from following handwashing guidelines, but physical discomfort is a very real challenge for healthcare workers who wash their hands repeatedly throughout the day. Hands can be become dry, cracked, and painful. Even with the best will in the world, that discomfort can turn into a little bit of reluctance.

In some of the other behaviors associated with hand hygiene, anxiety, fear, or discomfort can be an issue. For example, in one country where I worked on a hand-washing curriculum, there was a social convention around shaking hands with a patient and the concern that handwashing immediately afterward would appear rude. Another related behavior was the need to say something to a coworker if they did not wash their hands, but that situation was incredibly difficult to navigate when the coworker had more authority or was at a higher status in the organization.

IS THIS A TRAINING PROBLEM?

Yeah, probably. It's not just up to training to solve this problem, but it definitely should be a concern for learning design. Often, familiarity is crucial for something to feel more comfortable. Strategies like observation (seeing the behavior modeled) and practice may be vital to learners feeling more comfortable.

WHAT CAN TRAINING DO?

- **Provide practice.** If you're anxious about performing a particular behavior, it's best if you aren't trying it out for the very first time in a high stakes situation. I don't think I've ever encountered a workshop participant who would say they just *love* a role-play activity, but it's often the best way to practice.
- **Use scaffolding.** Scaffolding is a long-standing practice in education. Basically, it provides support for a learner as they attempt the new behavior. Training could start the learner with an easy version of a task, or it could provide support, like a checklist to follow or prompts to keep them on track. Scaffolding is often gradually removed until a student is ready to perform on their own.
- **See the behavior being modeled.** Can you arrange for learners to see other people model the behavior? For example, when I was traveling in China for the first time, negotiating a price with a street merchant was a completely expected behavior, and I struggled with it until I was able to watch some other travelers demonstrate how they did it. I never got particularly good at it, but seeing someone else was critical for me to even *try*. Being able to watch someone else demonstrate the behavior can be enormously important for allaying anxiety or discomfort.

- **Address misconceptions.** Sometimes learners have misconceptions about the behavior—that it's difficult or complicated or unpleasant or not really helpful. Training and practice can help learners understand what is really involved or help learners reframe the behavior to make it feel more achievable.

LACK OF CONFIDENCE/BELIEF ABOUT CAPABILITIES

Someone's lack of confidence or a belief that they don't have the necessary capabilities can hamper their motivation, and this often overlaps with fear, anxiety, and discomfort. As discussed in the motivation chapter, if you believe you are being asked to do something that you believe you don't have the capability to do, then you are likely to be amotivated.

For example, I believe I am not musical. I like listening to music, and I played the violin (badly) for a while in grade school, but I do not currently play an instrument or sing. I acknowledge that I could be much better at music if I put in time and effort, but I'm not inclined to try.

The good news is that it 100% does not matter if I don't engage in creating music. I can still enjoy listening to it, and I have other hobbies that I enjoy more (probably because I'm somewhat less bad at those other hobbies).

So my belief about my musical capabilities limits my motivation to perform the behavior, which in this circumstance is fine. But if you have fixed beliefs about your capabilities to do things like be organized, or to work with other people, or do difficult tasks, your beliefs can be limiting.

Researcher Carol Dweck talks about having a fixed versus a growth mindset. An example of a fixed mindset is "I'll never be good at music," and a growth mindset is more like "I can improve my musical abilities."

DOES THIS APPLY TO OUR HANDWASHING EXAMPLE?

Belief about capabilities is probably not a significant factor in our handwashing example. While it's possible that some people are better at handwashing than others, the level of proficiency for anyone following the directions is likely sufficient.

IS THIS A TRAINING PROBLEM?

This issue is at least partially a training problem. You can't control what beliefs people bring to the process, but it is the responsibility of the learning designer to ensure that what is being asked of the learners isn't out of reach of their capabilities, and providing opportunities for learners to feel smart and capable is part of a good learning experience.

WHAT CAN TRAINING DO?

- **Provide practice, modeling, and scaffolding.** Similar to anxiety/fear/discomfort, these strategies can help improve someone's beliefs about their capabilities.

- **Start with tasks near the learner's capability level.** One of the classic mistakes I see made by people new to creating learning is that they want to put tricky questions up front. This is never a good idea, and it's particularly bad when confidence or belief is an issue. Front-loading too many really easy things is also a problem (training can get boring), but if you find it hard to hit the exact right point, defaulting to easier challenges is a better choice.

- **Assess level of confidence.** One of the strategies that Will Thalheimer discusses in his book *Performance-Focused Learner Surveys* is to gather data on learners' level of confidence. Are they completely new to the behavior, are they aware of the behavior but not confident, are they confident with support, do they consider themselves to be fully competent, or are they experts? This can help you understand where learners believe they are coming into a learning experience. It also helps you gauge the change in their confidence between when they start the training and when they finish.

- **Coach employees to troubleshoot.** Gabriele Oettingen, in her book *Rethinking Positive Thinking*, describes how picturing success may be less useful than picturing and planning for potential obstacles.

MISTRUST

We've all experienced it. The program, initiative, or class that's presented in glowing terms, but you know the goal is about money or convenience or some other base reason. You're told it's good for you, but you know that it's really good for them, and they are trying to sell you a bill of goods.

Sometimes the promise of a benefit is completely sincere, but we distrust it because of experiences we've had in the past. For example, you join a gym and they suggest purchasing personal training sessions. They might mean it in a very sincere and helpful way, but if you've had bad experiences in the past with people trying to upsell you at a previous gym, you might mistrust the effort.

DOES THIS APPLY TO OUR HANDWASHING EXAMPLE?

Probably not too much. Other health behaviors (for example, mask-wearing or vaccinations) are very much influenced by how much the audience trusts the source of the message.

IS THIS A TRAINING PROBLEM?

Not really. There's usually some larger context influencing someone's beliefs. You can try to understand your audience and craft your messages carefully, but your audience is still bringing concerns from their previous experiences to the situation. Sometimes you can address mistrust head on and have an honest conversation with learners about why they might be skeptical to answer questions about doubts they have or help them reframe the behavior in a more positive light. And if the organization is doing training *instead of* making more difficult or costly changes to fix a problem, it can even increase a feeling of mistrust.

WHAT CAN TRAINING DO?

- **Involve participants in problem-solving.** People become attached to solutions *they* come up with. Rather than handing them predetermined actions, get their input into what and how to address the goal of the change. If they have had input on the plan, they are much more likely to trust the solution.
- **Identify how the behavior aligns and supports their identity or values.** Even the most annoying compliance guideline was put into place for a reason. Try to see where those reasons match up with values or goals that the learners already have.
- **Tell the truth.** Okay, I shouldn't need to say this explicitly (and I am positive, gentle reader, that you already know this), but DON'T LIE TO PEOPLE,

particularly if there is already an issue with mistrust. Sometimes organizations implement changes that are beneficial to the organization but kind of a hassle to the individual worker. Don't pretend otherwise. Help them understand why it's important, and work to minimize the hassle, but don't pretend "It will be great!"

- **Test messages with pilot groups**. Before you roll messages out to a group where mistrust may be an issue, test the message with a pilot group, and let them tell you how it really lands with them.

SOCIAL PROOF

I helped out on a project many years ago that was training for flight attendants. There was a list of safety checks that flight attendants needed to perform during the preflight period, and there was job aid available to help them make sure they didn't miss anything. New flight attendants weren't using the job aid consistently.

The training materials focused heavily on the very-very-bad-no-good-awful things that could happen if safety checks weren't done correctly, but when I talked to the designer on the project, he told me that one of the problems was that experienced flight attendants didn't use the checklist. They didn't really need to. They had done the same safety checklist hundreds of times and could probably recreate the checklist with their eyes shut. The problem was that new flight attendants saw the experienced staff not using the checklists and tried to emulate that. Because why wouldn't they want to do what the experienced people did?

The problem is obvious, right? The new people wanted to model their behavior on what the experienced people did, but they didn't have the ingrained knowledge that the experienced flight attendants had. Nobody was deliberately trying to be unsafe or circumvent the process, but the behavior being modeled was setting the wrong example.

DOES THIS APPLY TO OUR HANDWASHING EXAMPLE?

Very possibly, but it depends on the particular environment. If people see senior workers cutting corners about handwashing, that will almost certainly spread the problem.

IS THIS A TRAINING PROBLEM?

Not really, but it should be taken into account when designing and reinforcing learning. Using positive modeling is extremely underutilized in workplace training environments, and it can be a very effective way to support the behavior.

WHAT CAN TRAINING DO?

- **Make success stories visible.** Using actual success stories can help engage participants during the learning experience, but they are also a really nice way to reinforce and refresh the key learning points.
- **Enlist experienced people to model the correct behavior.** As discussed in the motivation chapter, experienced people often react poorly to being told things they already know (annual compliance training is an example of this). However, if you involve them in the conversation on how to spread the behavior with the less-experienced participants, that gives them a different reason to buy in to the behavior and shows respect for their existing knowledge and experience.

LACK OF AUTONOMY/OWNERSHIP

I was doing a workshop at a Large Tech Company a few years ago, and one of the workshop participants told me he taught daylong workshops on a technical topic. When he first started teaching the topic, he would begin with a slide entitled "Why the [topic] is important" with a list of reasons.

Then he told me that he'd recently switched the slide to a blank slide with the title "Why is [topic] important?" He said, "The whole day goes differently." Students were much more engaged if they'd had the opportunity to weigh in on why they thought the topic was important rather than being told.

Previous chapters cover quite a bit about autonomy, but lack of autonomy comes up a lot in high-compliance environments, where there are rules for the sake of having rules. In some of these situations, people can become passively disinterested at best and actively resistant at worst.

DOES THIS APPLY TO OUR HANDWASHING EXAMPLE?

Very possibly, but it really depends on the organization or environment. In command-and-control organizations, treating handwashing as a mandatory action with harsh punishment can work against the behavior if people feel like they need to hide infractions or if they only do the behavior when they think they are being observed. If the environment supports worker autonomy and those employees are invested in the mission or purpose of the organization, then a lack of autonomy or ownership probably won't be a factor in their handwashing behaviors.

IS THIS A TRAINING PROBLEM?

Mostly not. This is really an organization or systems problem. That doesn't mean you can't foster autonomy in your learning experience, but if autonomy is poorly supported in the larger organization, it's still going to be an uphill climb for all the people involved.

WHAT CAN TRAINING DO?

- **Talk to employees.** Make sure you are talking to the people in your audience about their experience. They need to believe that you are listening to them and responding to what they tell you rather than just shouting at them from a distance.
- **Have them talk and listen to what they say.** Have them tell you what their challenges are and how they think they can solve the problems. Have them put reasons into their own words, and make their own plans for how to proceed. Sincerely being interested in their views is important. People can tell if you really want to know or if you are just asking because you got to that slide in the presentation.
- **Give them some decision-making authority whenever possible.** Sometimes it's not possible or practical to let employees decide things, but default to letting them have control whenever possible. Even small things like deciding what they are going to learn first can help foster a feeling of autonomy and control.

LEARNED HELPLESSNESS

Sometimes when I'm consulting or teaching a workshop in an organization, everybody has a reason why the strategies I'm suggesting will not work in that organization: *IT won't let us do that*, *we tried that but management wouldn't support it*, or *that never works here.*

This sounds like lack of confidence, but it's actually a bit different. This is a phenomenon called *learned helplessness*. It's a result of having tried something in the past but having had that past effort shut down or punished by something in the system or organization. This makes people reluctant to try again.

The concept of learned helplessness comes from some unappealing research from Martin Seligman in the late 1960s (Seligman, 1972). Seligman and his colleagues put dogs into cages where they would receive electric shocks from the floor. Some of the dogs had the ability to stop the shocks with a lever, but some dogs could not do anything to stop the shocks. They would then put the dogs into a box where half the floor would shock the dogs. The dogs could jump over a barrier that was only a few inches high to get away from the shocks. The dogs that had control over the initial shocks would jump over the barrier almost immediately. The dogs that had been forced to endure the shocks without control would not even try to escape. They engaged in what Seligman describes as "escape-avoidance behavior."

DOES THIS APPLY TO OUR HANDWASHING EXAMPLE?

This one doesn't apply to the handwashing example as far as I can tell, though it could depend on the environment in which people work.

IS THIS A TRAINING PROBLEM?

This is a hard one, because here's the thing: *people aren't wrong when they demonstrate learned helplessness*. Their attitude is preventing them from acting, but the attitude comes from direct experience. In some cases, the learned helplessness bleeds out to other people in the organization who haven't had the direct experience, but it still stems from someone's actual experience.

In Seligman's trials, the researchers tried treats and encouragement to get the escape-avoidant dogs to jump over the barriers, but ultimately, the only thing that would change the dogs' behavior was actually picking them up and moving them through the physical motion of jumping over the barrier. Twice.

So this probably *isn't* a training problem, and there's probably not much you can do when you're working with trainees. Practicing a simulated version of the new behavior during training isn't going to convince people that response back in the workplace will be different.

When a training request comes in, it's worth pointing out that this isn't a training problem. To undo learned helplessness, people need to have an actual (not simulated) positive experience. Possibly more than once.

WHAT CAN TRAINING DO?

- **Ensure that management is supporting the new change.** It shouldn't need to be pointed out, but the support of management and stakeholders is *crucial* to the success of countering learned helplessness.
- **Roll out changes slowly, rather than all at once**. If you can start with things that are small and low stakes, people may be more willing to try the new behavior, and you can build a small accumulation of positive experiences. Be sure to verify each change before adding a new one.
- **Over-reinforce positive examples.** Make sure there is enthusiastic coaching and encouragement for the first few times the employee tries the new behavior and that this support is visible to the whole audience.
- **Engineer the experience of positive examples.** There are anecdotes about managers setting up chances for employees to call them out on safety issues to prove that no one is an exception. Are there ways you can arrange for positive examples to happen and provide concrete proof that circumstances have changed?

MISALIGNED INCENTIVES

I had this conversation with clients at a multinational insurance company several years ago. We were working on an elearning program for the people who entered client data for insurance policies into the computer system:

CLIENT: Can we put something in the training about the importance of accuracy? They don't always pay attention to the accuracy of the information they are entering.

ME: Sure, we can do that. Tell me, how are they evaluated on job performance?

CLIENT: Oh, the number of applications they do per hour.

ME: Okay, and do they get any feedback on their accuracy?

CLIENT: Huh, no...I don't think they do.

You see the problem, right? When your incentive and feedback systems don't align with the behavior, it's unlikely you'll see much of that behavior with some other powerful motivators being involved.

DOES THIS APPLY TO OUR HANDWASHING EXAMPLE?

Again, it depends on the organization, but it probably comes up in terms of how people are incented to use their time. My primary care physician has learned to talk *really quickly* at our annual checkups because she's only allowed so much time per patient, but she also wants to have a meaningful conversation to understand what has been happening in my life and what the broader context is for my health. She has competing priorities/incentives: stay on time because she doesn't want to shortchange other patients later in the day but also take time with each patient.

While misaligned financial incentives are unlikely to have an impact on hand-washing, the priorities of getting everything done while still spending time on handwashing probably do compete with each other.

IS THIS A TRAINING PROBLEM?

No, but having the conversation about why a training solution will not fix an incentive problem is something that is part of the role of a performance consultant.

WHAT CAN TRAINING DO?

You can analyze the problem and give feedback to management about the limitations of what a training course can achieve.

LACK OF IDENTITY OR VALUE ALIGNMENT

A few years ago, after a presentation at a conference, someone came up to me and asked, "How do we change people's values about the environment?"

I told him "You don't. You show them how behaviors related to the environment support values they already have."

Researchers have found that, with certain audiences, framing environmental messages using the language and values of that particular ingroup can increase their willingness to engage in pro-environment behaviors (Wolsko et al., 2016, 2017). We will talk more about this in later chapters, but it's always worth understanding what your audience's values are.

Identity also impacts how people view certain behaviors. For example, consider these different views of workplace safety:

"I know the safety regulations exist to keep everyone safe, and that's really important. But sometimes the rules are a little ridiculous. You feel like they were written by people who never did the actual job. Rules for the sake of having rules, I guess."

"It's my job to keep myself safe, and to keep my coworkers safe."

"What these kids coming up don't understand is that safety is part of being good at the job. They should be proud of it. Getting better at safety is part of being a better carpenter or a better plumber or a better electrician."

None of these people are wrong, but they each see a different relationship between their identity and safety behaviors. The first view frames safety regulations as an externally imposed rule set coming from someplace quite separate from the job identity, and the last one frames safety as an intrinsic part of professional identities.

DOES THIS APPLY TO OUR HANDWASHING EXAMPLE?

Values and identity are absolutely part of the handwashing example. Not every last person who works in healthcare does so because they feel a sense of mission or values around caring for people, but many, many healthcare providers do.

When I was working on a handwashing curriculum several years ago, I was talking to one of the nurse practitioners about washing hands for 20 seconds. She told me it doesn't sound like a long time, but it can be hard to make yourself wash that long, particularly on a busy day.

She said, "Sometimes I have to think to myself *I'm a good nurse. I can wash my hands for 20 seconds.*"

That was one of the most clear invocations of identity to support a behavior that I'd ever heard.

IS THIS A TRAINING PROBLEM?

Yes and no. You don't get to decide what someone's values are, and changing someone's values takes time and is unlikely to succeed. But you can frame behaviors in terms of the audience's values if you understand what they care about. Be careful of anything that sounds glib or pat, and test your messages with people in the audience before releasing widely. We've all seen the advertising messages that get this wrong.

WHAT CAN TRAINING DO?

- **Identify how the behavior aligns and supports identity or values.** Whenever possible, have the audience do this identification themselves.
- **Amplify the message from people in the actual audience.** A classroom instructor who has never done the job is the wrong person to deliver the message. Try to have it come from people in the audience. This could be a discussion in the classroom, or testimonials from others in the same field.

EMOTIONAL REACTION

When I was working on an infection prevention curriculum, one of the doctors said, "Even with all that I know about the importance of preventing infection, I sometimes find myself tempted to take shortcuts at the end of long day. I know better, and it *still* happens. Why is that?"

This woman was one of her country's national experts on preventing infection in healthcare, and even *she* sometimes felt the temptation to skip a few steps or do the easier thing.

Any behavior that is a challenge to do will likely be harder when we are tired/hungry/sleepy/stressed/distracted/bored/angry/frustrated/unhappy.

DOES THIS APPLY TO OUR HANDWASHING EXAMPLE?

Yep. As mentioned previously, it clearly does.

IS THIS A TRAINING PROBLEM?

Absolutely. In the ideal world, you'd also make changes to an environment or system to reduce negative emotions, but training should prepare learners for the real environment and situations where they will be executing the behaviors.

WHAT CAN TRAINING DO?

- **Help learners recognize and respond to emotional reactions.** Have learners practice identifying physiological signs of emotional arousal and create the routine of recognizing and regulating the emotion (for example, learning a breathing routine to calm themselves in a stressful situation).
- **Stress inoculation.** If learners are expected to operate in high stress environments, try to allow them to practice in increasingly stressful simulations, so they can become accustomed to operating in those circumstances. For

example, stress inoculation is used when training people for military combat situations. They practice in simulated exercises—either in real or virtual environments—so they can learn to manage their physiological reactions.

HANDWASHING TOTAL UP

So, for handwashing, it seems that we should definitely consider the following causes:

- Lack of feedback
- Environment or process support
- Discomfort
- Emotional reaction
- Lack of identity or value alignment

Depending on the organization, we may also need to consider the following:

- Unlearning an existing behavior
- Unawareness of consequences/bigger picture
- Social proof
- Lack of autonomy/ownership
- Misaligned incentives

It's likely that we don't need to worry too much about the following things:

- Anxiety/fear
- Lack of confidence/belief about capabilities
- Learned helplessness
- Mistrust

Again, none of these are absolute truths about handwashing. All of these depend on the particular context and audience.

EXAMPLE: NETWORKING FOR COLLEGE GRADUATES

Let's take another look at another behavior. Imagine you are creating learning experiences for recent college graduates on how to get started on their professional career.

The particular behavior we want to analyze is networking at in-person events. You are tasked with working with a group of 20 recent graduates from the liberal arts program. Let's see which of these issues might apply.

Issue	Impact
Lack of feedback	This may be an issue. Networking is the kind of thing where it doesn't pay off immediately, so it might be important to help the learners assess how well an interaction went and what constitutes success.
Unclear goals	Yes, this is likely to be an issue. People who have been operating in a professional community for a while will have a mental image of what networking looks like, but new graduates may need it spelled out clearly.
Unlearning an existing behavior	This one is likely to be an individual issue. Some college students may have some behaviors that need to be unlearned or revised.
Unawareness of consequences/bigger picture	This is probably an issue. College students who haven't already been through this kind of curriculum are unlikely to understand just how important building a professional network is and what it can look like.
Lack of environment or process support	This one also depends. Some professional organizations deliberately create activities or opportunities for people to network, and some have mentors or other structures in place to support new members.
Anxiety/fear/discomfort	Yes. Some college students might be comfortable in social situations, but it's very likely that many of the students may feel uncomfortable putting themselves forward in professional situations.
Lack of confidence/belief about capabilities	This is likely an issue. Despite the ubiquitous advice to "fake it 'til you make it," most recent graduates are not going to feel a high level of confidence in networking environments.
Mistrust	Again, assuming students have opted in to the class, mistrust probably won't be a significant issue.
Social proof	This depends on what opportunities individual students have had to see how networking works in professional environments. For example, if a student had an internship in a large company, they may have some awareness, but other students may not have seen anything relevant.
Lack of autonomy/ownership	Assuming this is a class students have opted in to, autonomy or ownership probably isn't an issue.
Learned helplessness	This could be an issue, but it probably depends on the individual student.
Misaligned incentives	This probably isn't too much of an issue, though students may need help understanding that quality is more important than quantity, and that the goal is to form real connections, not to get the biggest number of LinkedIn connections possible.

| Lack of identity or value alignment | Again, it depends, but it's very possible that students will have a hard time connecting this behavior to their values or identity. |
| Emotional reaction | Possibly. Stress and anxiety about social interaction could play a role here. |

We'll take a look at how we consider all these factors in the design of learning in the next few chapters. Next, we will look at how the results of a COM-B analysis map to intervention domains and how to begin selecting behavior-change strategies.

KEY POINT

Training is often the first go-to option for behavior-change challenges, and part of the role of a performance consultant or learning designer is to analyze the relevant variables and to help stakeholders understand what training can and cannot do to address a particular challenge.

RESOURCES

Dooley, Roger. "How the Cootie Effect Can Reduce Virus Transmission," https://www.neurosciencemarketing.com/blog/articles/reduce-virus.htm.

Lee, Seyoung, and Thomas Hugh Feeley. "The Identifiable Victim Effect: A Meta-Analytic Review." *Social Influence* 11, no. 3 (2016): 199-215.

Oettingen, Gabriele. *Rethinking Positive Thinking: Inside the New Science of Motivation* (New York: Penguin Random House, 2014).

Seligman, Martin E.P. "Learned Helplessness." *Annual Review of Medicine* 23, no. 1 (1972): 407-412.

Thalheimer, Will. *Performance Focused Learner Surveys: Using Distinctive Questioning to Get Actionable Data and Guide Learning Effectiveness* [Second Edition] (N.p.: Work-Learning Press, 2022).

Västfjäll, Daniel, Paul Slovic, Marcus Mayorga, and Ellen Peters. "Compassion Fade: Affect and Charity are Greatest for a Single Child in Need." *PloS one* 9, no. 6 (2014): e100115.

Wolsko, Christopher. "Expanding the Range of Environmental Values: Political Orientation, Moral Foundations, and the Common Ingroup." *Journal of Environmental Psychology* 51 (2017): 284-294.

Wolsko, Christopher, Hector Ariceaga, and Jesse Seiden. "Red, White, and Blue Enough to Be Green: Effects of Moral Framing on Climate Change Attitudes and Conservation Behaviors." *Journal of Experimental Social Psychology* 65 (2016): 7-19.

8

MAPPING TO SOLUTIONS

(IN WHICH WE MATCH THE ANALYSIS TO SOLUTIONS FOR BOTH THE RIDER AND THE ELEPHANT)

The Behaviour Change Wheel has nine general types of intervention (definitions source: UFG Guide). Some of them have obvious alignment with learning and development. In this chapter, we take a look at which ones are more or less likely to be part of the learning experience design.

MEET MIGUEL AND LISA

Miguel and Lisa are nurse educators for a large hospital chain. Because of staffing shortages, they have a large influx of new nurses and nursing assistants.

Although their hospital chain has had a good record regarding pressure ulcer prevention, there has been an uptick in the incidence of pressure ulcers in the last few months, and Miguel and Lisa have been asked to create solutions to help train the new staff about pressure ulcer prevention. Pressure ulcers are injuries to skin and underlying tissue resulting from prolonged pressure on the skin, also known as bedsores.

Using the COM-B framework, Lisa and Miguel discuss the different aspects of helping new staff with the behaviors to support pressure ulcer prevention:

Question	Response
What physical capabilities do workers need to perform this behavior?	**Miguel:** There are several things, but the first main physical capability is that they need to be able to turn and position patients correctly. Sometimes, if a patient is physically large or unable to move themselves, nurses may need extra support to turn and position the patient effectively. They also need to be able to physically examine patients for signs of pressure ulcers.
What psychological capabilities do workers need to perform this behavior?	**Lisa:** They need to know the protocol for preventing pressure ulcers and how to assess patient risk. Since we've been hiring from a wider field of people lately, we've been finding a lot of variability in the type and amount of training that new staff have had in the past. Of course, we want them to know what the standard of care is in our hospital system. The other skill that our most experienced nurses have that the new nurses don't is the ability to talk to patients about pressure ulcer prevention. The patients aren't just bodies to be moved around. They can participate in their own care and help us know what they need. But that works best if the nurse communicates with them about what's happening and coaches them on what to do or watch out for and what to continue to do after they leave the hospital. Not all patients are cooperative, so it's really important to help those patients understand why regular turning is necessary. Talking to patients is a skill I'd really like to develop with the new nurses.
How does the physical environment support the behavior?	**Lisa:** We invested in high-density foam mattresses, but there are some alternatives that may actually be more effective, so we are testing some other options. We've also added patient status whiteboards by each patient bed where nurses and nursing assistants put the last turn time, in addition to recording it in the patient chart. That started out well, but I've noticed some staff have been skipping the whiteboard and just putting the time in the chart. **Miguel:** But let's be honest. The real problem is we are overstretched. Staffing is very difficult, and there are so many demands on each nurse's time. And we are better off than some other facilities, but it's so difficult right now.

How does the social environment support the behavior?	**Miguel:** With so many new staff, not everyone knows everyone else, and I think that makes it hard to know who to ask if there's a question. It used to be that we had fairly low staff turnover, so there would always be a few experienced people on each shift who could keep an eye on a new person, but that's just not possible right now.
What is the reflective motivation of the workers? For example, do they have goals or beliefs about this?	**Lisa:** We've done some attitude measures, and their attitude toward pressure ulcer prevention doesn't really seem to be an issue. They know that it's important.
What automatic motivation (feeling, habits, biases) do you think influence the workers?	**Miguel:** It does depend a bit on whether they have a lot of direct experience with pressure ulcers. If you've seen how bad they can get, you REALLY know prevention is important.
	Years ago, I was told that a deep pressure ulcer can cost upward of $70K to treat, and I'm sure it can be a lot more now, and that doesn't even get into the health impact on the patient.
	Intellectually, they know, but we still need them to *feel* that urgency, no matter how busy and overloaded things get.

INTERVENTION TYPES

After doing a COM-B analysis, the next step in the process is to identify the types of intervention that are likely to be effective. Here, we look at each of the nine types of intervention, even though some of them are not likely to be part of a training intervention.

> **NOTE:** The intervention types are used courtesy of S. Michie, L. Atkins, and R. West (*The Behaviour Change Wheel: A Guide to Designing Interventions.* London: Silverback Publishing, 2014, www.behaviourchangewheel.com).

INTERVENTION TYPES MORE LIKELY TO BE PART OF TRAINING

EDUCATION

Increasing knowledge and understanding by informing, explaining, showing, and providing feedback.

This is the knowing part of the learning equation.

LISA: We will definitely have an education component as part of the pressure ulcer campaign. Everybody needs to be on the same page about what needs to happen, and what our standard of care is.

TRAINING

Increasing the skills needed for a behavior by repeated practice and feedback.

This is the doing/applying part of the learning equation.

MIGUEL: We need to have a clearer way for new staff to practice turning patients with coaching and feedback. In the past, the experienced staff would just keep an eye out, but I think we need to formalize that a bit more.

LISA: Also, talking to patients about pressure ulcer prevention is a skill! We need to figure out how new people can see good examples and how they can practice and get coached on that.

PERSUASION

Using words and images to change the way people feel about a behavior to make it more or less attractive.

This is pretty much anything we would do to motivate or persuade the learner.

MIGUEL: I think the persuasion will really be around the importance of prevention and how easily it can get away from you. It's about vigilance. If you've been treating a patient every day for a week and haven't had any issues, it's only human nature to get a little less vigilant, but that can cause something to be missed.

MODELING

Showing examples of the behavior for people to imitate.

LISA: Modeling is going to be crucial for the part about how to talk to patients. Several of our experienced nurses are amazing: They are so good at coaching patients and at getting the uncooperative patients to cooperate. Seeing how they do it is going to be the best example for our new staff.

ENVIRONMENTAL RESTRUCTURING

Constraining or promoting behavior by shaping the physical or social environment.

This one is a little less obviously part of a learning experience but could still be involved.

MIGUEL: I don't know if we will do much with this in the training part, but the hospital is definitely looking at ways to improve the environment and tools.

LISA: You know what does come up here? The bolsters and foam wedges they use often don't make it back to the storage space until much later. I'd like to do an activity in the training class about how to solve that problem. I'm sure if we involved the nursing staff in that discussion, they would have ideas.

THE INTERVENTION TYPES THAT ARE LESS LIKELY

Some of the other types of intervention are somewhat less likely to be used because they are typically outside of the control of learning and development, though obviously that depends on who is responsible for what in any particular organization.

INCENTIVIZATION

Changing the attractiveness of a behavior by creating the expectation of a desired outcome or avoidance of an undesired one.

LISA: I can't imagine that we would want to tie an incentive to pressure ulcer prevention. That doesn't sound appropriate at all.

MIGUEL: Probably not, though we could celebrate a month of no pressure ulcers or something. I wonder if we could do an incentive around updating the whiteboards, though? Bring in bagels if all the whiteboards are updated when we spot check?

LISA: Hmm, maybe. Let's think on that.

COERCION

Changing the attractiveness of a behavior by creating the expectation of an undesired outcome or denial of a desired one.

LISA: So, like a punishment? There are certainly consequences if people aren't doing their jobs, but that's really not our responsibility. I do think we need to work with managers on how they are reinforcing the behavior, though.

RESTRICTION

Constraining performance of a behavior by setting rules.

MIGUEL: A colleague in a different health center was telling me that they restricted the ability of nursing assistants to update the patient record when they turned people. They had to get a nurse to verify, so the nurses could make sure that all the patients had been turned on schedule. I understand what they were trying to do, but apparently it turned into a bureaucratic mess.

ENABLEMENT

Providing support to improve ability to change in a variety of ways not covered by other intervention types, such as supplying nicotine patches to support people trying to quit smoking.

LISA: I think the only thing that might fall into this category is the video support option. If staff is concerned about a spot on a patient, and a senior staff member isn't available, they can do a quick video consult using their tablets.

MAPPING COM-B TO INTERVENTION TYPES

Generally, the interventions map this way:

Intervention Type	Capability	Opportunity	Motivation
Education	X		X
Training	X	X	X
Persuasion			X
Modeling		X	X
Incentivization			X
Coercion			X
Restriction		X	
Environmental Restructuring		X	X
Enablement	X	X	X

(Source: *Michie S, Atkins L, West R. (2014)* The Behaviour Change Wheel: A Guide to Designing Interventions. *London: Silverback Publishing. www.behaviourchangewheel.com.*)

BEHAVIOUR CHANGE TECHNIQUES (BCTS)

After you have identified the relevant intervention types for your behavior, you can look at specific techniques to leverage in the training design.

Along with the Behaviour Change Wheel, there is a taxonomy of Behaviour Change Techniques (BCT) that can be applied to your learning design. There are 93 different techniques in the taxonomy, and not all the BCTs will be relevant for learning design. The next four chapters look at specific techniques that can be applied in a learning context.

NOTE: The BCTs are used courtesy of S. Michie, L. Atkins, and R. West (*The Behaviour Change Wheel: A Guide to Designing Interventions*. London: Silverback Publishing, 2014, www.behaviourchangewheel.com).

The categories for BCTs are as follows:

- **Goals and planning:** This involves encouraging learners to set goals or make plans regarding the behavior and includes strategies like problem-solving barriers to the behavior and behavioral contracts.
- **Feedback and monitoring:** This involves using different kinds of feedback strategies to help reinforce the behavior and could include strategies like self-monitoring or using digital tracking applications.
- **Social support:** This involves arranging for social support of the behaviors and could include both emotional and practical support.
- **Shaping knowledge:** This is the main category about education strategies and also includes learning about causes and attribution.
- **Natural consequences:** The strategies here involve information about consequences, which could be physical, emotional, social, or environmental. It also emphasizes the salience of the consequences (how vivid or tangible the consequences seem).
- **Comparison of behaviors:** This category includes strategies like demonstration of the behavior and comparing your behavior to others in your social group or other people who are similar to you.
- **Associations:** This category uses strategies such as using prompts or cues to remind or "nudge" the behavior. This category also has strategies such as associating something positive with a desirable behavior or something negative with an undesirable behavior or exposing people to a stimulus to make it less frightening, like letting a child visit a hospital in advance so it will be less scary when they go in for a surgical procedure.
- **Repetition and substitution:** These strategies are critical for learning and practice design and include rehearsal of the behavior, habit formation, and graded tasks where you start people with easy versions of the behavior and work up to more difficult versions.
- **Comparison of outcomes:** This involves strategies like examining the pros and cons for a behavior, imagining future outcomes, or hearing about outcomes from a credible source.

- **Reward and threat:** This category involves incentives (a promise of a benefit if they do the behavior) or rewards (a benefit that rewards a behavior after it's been done), as well as different types of punishment.
- **Regulation:** This category involves managing emotional reactions or physical sensations. It could include pharmacological support (such as medication to reduce cravings to smoke), self-regulation techniques, or techniques to conserve mental resources so learners aren't battling too much cognitive load.
- **Environment:** As we've already discussed, this category involves options for modifying or restructuring the environment to make the behavior easier to do or increase the likelihood of the behavior.
- **Identity:** Strategies in this category include prompting the person to think about how they are a role model, framing or reframing how they identify, and considering how their current values or identity support the behavior.
- **Scheduled consequences:** This category includes different types of rewards or punishments, including removing punishments or denying rewards to reinforce the behavior.
- **Self-belief:** Sometimes people's own beliefs about their capabilities stand in the way of success. This category uses strategies like persuading people they can be successful, mental rehearsal of successful performance, and helping people identify past successes that indicate they can do the future behavior.
- **Covert learning:** This strategy uses techniques like imagining rewards or punishments or vicariously picturing consequences from other people's experiences.

In the next few chapters, we will take a closer look at the most useful BCTs.

RESOURCES

Catania, Kimberly, Cheryl Huang, Polly James, Michelle Madison, Molly Moran, and Misty Ohr. "PUPPI: The Pressure Ulcer Prevention Protocol Interventions," *The American Journal of Nursing* 107, no. 4 (2007): 44–52.

Michie, S., L. Atkins, and R. West. *The Behaviour Change Wheel: A Guide to Designing Interventions* (London: Silverback Publishing, 2014).

Michie, Susan, Michelle Richardson, Marie Johnston, Charles Abraham, Jill Francis, Wendy Hardeman, Martin P. Eccles, James Cane, and Caroline E. Wood. "The Behavior Change Technique Taxonomy (v1) of 93 Hierarchically Clustered Techniques: Building an International Consensus for the Reporting of Behavior Change Interventions," *Annals of Behavioral Medicine* 46, no. 1 (2013): 81–95.

Moore, Zena Eh and Declan Patton. "Risk Assessment Tools for the Prevention of Pressure Ulcers," *Cochrane Database of Systematic Reviews* 1, no. 1 (2019): CD006471.

USING PERSUASION AND MOTIVATION TECHNIQUES

(IN WHICH WE PERSUADE THE ELEPHANT THAT IT REALLY HAS ALL IT NEEDS TO MAKE THE CHANGE.)

MEET EVAN

This is Evan. He works for a professional association for authors and freelance writers. He's been tasked with creating material to help association members plan for retirement.

Here's the particular challenge that he's dealing with:

"Authors often have pretty variable income. Our members are authors with traditionally published books, but the overwhelming majority of them don't make their whole incomes from book writing. Some of them have full-time day jobs and write in their free time, but many of them of them are combining several different income sources, which include book royalties, freelance writing gigs, teaching, or editing work. Some of them are also content creators in other media, like blogs, podcasts, or videos channels.

"It means that most of them don't have access to a retirement savings program where they just allocate part of their paychecks every two weeks. Figuring all this out for yourself can be really overwhelming.

"Our mission as an organization is to help support writers personally and professionally, so that means we're creating learning materials to help them understand the options for retirement savings and hopefully help them take action to ensure their financial outlook."

AUDIENCE RESEARCH

To make sure he understood the challenge, Evan talked to association members about their current retirement planning.

Here are some of the key things he heard:

From Ritesh, a long-time magazine writer who recently published his first non-fiction book:

"Oh, wow. Retirement. Yeah, I really need to get on that. For the longest time, I was barely making enough to cover city rent and keep up with my student loans. But my partner and I got married last year and are now expectant parents! Which is great, but also terrifying. The good news is that with the book, I've jumped up a lot in terms of freelance rates, and I got a good advance for the book. But it's time to act like a grown-up, so retirement planning is part of that, right? What do other people in my situation do? I don't really know where to start. Pointers would be helpful because I guess I should get to it before the baby comes and there's no time for anything. Also, how much is enough? How can you even tell?"

From Teresita, a video blogger with a popular dog training channel:

"For the longest time, I was waiting tables and living at my folks while I built my channel. It's only been lately that I've had a more reliable income from video advertising and my patron subscriptions. I never thought I'd have a book deal too, though I didn't get a big advance. I'm saving to be able to afford my own place, but it needs to be somewhere I can have my dogs, so that might take a while. Depending on what's going on, some months are good, and some are not as good. I'm not sure if I can manage retirement savings if I don't have a reliable income. It's kind of exhausting just to think about."

From Bernadine, who was a veteran middle school teacher in Philadelphia until recently and is now a new full-time author with her three-book paranormal romance series that is breaking out on the bestseller lists.

"For the longest time, I was clear about exactly what I needed to do—I made my monthly retirement donation. This is the most money I've ever had at one time, and I'll admit my main impulse is to just stash it in savings until I know what being a full-time writer looks like. As soon as you start searching on options, there are so, so, sooo many. It's overwhelming! Until I'm sure I know what I really need to do, I'll probably just put it in a money market or something."

ANALYSIS RESULTS

Let's look at a summary of the COM-B analysis for one of the key behaviors, choosing a plan for retirement saving.

COM-B Domains	Observations
Physical capability	N/A
Psychological capability	Members often have a hard time knowing what options are best and how much they can or should invest in retirement savings.
Physical opportunity	Often, systems and information about retirement investing is too complicated or overwhelming.
Social opportunity	Members don't have insight into what others in similar situations are choosing for retirement savings. A few members talked about how the people in their personal networks try to be supportive and helpful about financial decisions, but those family and friends didn't really understand the complexity and variability of writers' incomes.
Reflective motivation	Most of the members that Evan talked to understand that saving for retirement is a good idea but have difficulty making decisions, which seems to make them reluctant to choose options or prioritize saving.
	Younger members, in particular, don't believe that the little amounts they could save would make much difference and think there will be time later when they are making more money.
Automatic motivation	Members mentioned feeling overwhelmed, which may prompt feelings of reluctance and a desire to just avoid the issue.

Evan then worked with some of the stakeholders to identify intervention functions and look at the overall strategy:

"We know that we want to have an education function, but persuasion is going to be just as important. The members we talked to were all very concerned about their retirement planning stacked up against a "typical" member. All our members' situations are so different that I'm not sure we actually have any "typical" members, but we can definitely use comparisons for motivation. We also know that planning so far ahead just feels fuzzy and intangible for a lot of people, particularly our younger members. We need to figure out how to make it not be intimidating and how to help people have confidence that they can actually do it."

Since Evan has some strategies in mind, he's going to look through relevant Behaviour Change Techniques (BCTs) to see if they would help him design learning or support materials to help the association members.

BEHAVIOUR CHANGE TECHNIQUES

We are going to take a look at which Behaviour Change Techniques (BCTs) would be helpful for Evan's challenge. Each BCT will have the definition, an example, and a comment from Evan about how he might use it. I focus on four categories of techniques in this chapter, but none of these solutions exist in a vacuum, so I'll also pull some techniques that are also discussed in other chapters.

In real-world projects, you would consider all the relevant BCTs based on your COM-B analysis, but in this chapter, the focus is these main categories:

- Consequences
- Comparisons (behaviors and outcomes)
- Self-belief

Other categories include

- Covert learning
- Environmental restructuring
- Antecedents

> **NOTE:** All BCTs used or adapted from S. Michie, L. Atkins, and R. West (*The Behaviour Change Wheel: A Guide to Designing Interventions.* London: Silverback Publishing, 2014, www.behaviourchangewheel.com).

Evan already has a partial plan for this technique:

Instruction on how to perform a behavior (BCT 4.1)	Advise or agree on how to perform the behavior (includes "skills training").	Example: Explain how to create a retirement account.

"We definitely need an instructional component. Fortunately, we were able to buy into a really good, clear financial literacy online curriculum, so I have the basic content, but it isn't specific to the needs of our audience. The crucial part for me is to make it relevant for our members."

Let's look at some of the BCTs that Evan could apply. You'll see cards for different techniques, and see how Evan might use them.

CONSEQUENCES

Information about consequences (BCT 5.1)	Provide information (e.g., written, verbal, visual) about consequences of performing (or not performing) the behavior.	Example: Show the potential consequences of untreated high blood pressure.

"The curriculum tools that we bought have retirement calculators, which is good, but I think it might be good to have several profiles of sample plans that some members already have, so people can put it into context."

Salience of consequences (BCT 5.2)	Use methods specifically designed to emphasize the consequences of performing the behavior with the aim of making them more memorable (goes beyond informing about consequences).	Example: Produce cigarette packets showing pictures of health consequences, such as diseased lungs, to highlight the dangers of continuing to smoke

"*Planning for retirement is all numbers and percentages, and it's hard to make it feel real.* There's this great activity that one of the financial advisors did in a webinar. She gave members 20 different aspects of retirement, and they could sort them into must-have, nice-to-have, and not important.

"Items included 'having as much time to write as they wanted' and 'being able to focus on their interests' and 'being able to travel.' She encouraged people to visually picture their retirement and add any other items that hadn't been on the list.

"She then talked about the kind of retirement planning they would need to do to have a few, some, or all of the items they had put on their must-have or nice-to-have lists. It was great that she could connect it to things they had prioritized."

Salience of Consequences

Do you believe what you know intellectually or what your senses tell you?

A few years ago, I took a tour of the Stanford Virtual Human Interaction Lab (VHIL), and as part of the tour, I got to try a VR demo. In the demo, you walk across a virtual plank above a giant pit:

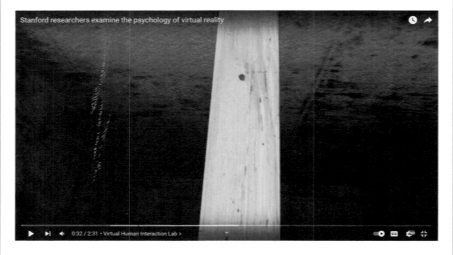

Image credit: Stanford Virtual Human Interaction Lab

Even though I *KNEW* beyond all doubt that it was a carpeted floor in an ordinary campus building and not really a skinny plank above a huge pit, I could. Not. Do. It.

The only way I could do it was to look up, and then I could walk forward. But as long as I was looking down toward the floor, there was no way that my rider could override my elephant.

Because so much behavior change involves delayed or absent consequences, we are asking our learners to override their elephant all the time, with pretty mixed results. As we discussed in the tangibility section of Chapter 4, the rewards for many of these behaviors are often abstract, delayed, or uncertain.

In the classic behavior economics book, *Nudge*, Thaler and Sunstein describe it this way:

> "If you have personally experienced a serious earthquake, you're more likely to believe that an earthquake is likely than if you read about it in a weekly magazine. Thus vivid and easily imagined causes of death (for example, tornadoes) often receive inflated estimates of probability, and less-vivid causes (for example, asthma attacks) receive low estimates, even if they occur with a far greater frequency (here a factor of twenty). So, too, recent events have a greater impact on our behavior, and on our fears, than earlier ones."

In the BCT Taxonomy, the technique to address this is "Salience of Consequences."

HANDWASHING EXAMPLES

We've already talked about handwashing quite a bit, since it's a pretty classic example of abstract consequences. If they aren't visibly dirty before washing, your hands usually look the same before and after; germ theory is very intellectual, and it's not something you can perceive with your senses. So let's look at some of the ways curriculum designers have made the consequences of inadequate handwashing more salient.

Black Light

A common strategy in well-resourced classrooms is to use black light. Participants rub a gel that glows under black light on their hands. They then wash their hands as they would normally and check them under black light to see that much of the gel remains in the same way bacteria would.

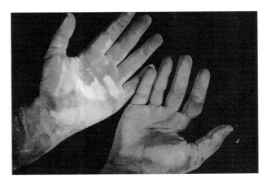

Participants can then vividly see the limitations of so-so handwashing.

PAINT ON THE PATIENT

In a video titled "Wash Your Hands - It Just Makes Sense," a doctor examines a patient in a normal way, but the patient is covered in green paint. The video then asks what would happen if the doctor didn't wash his hands after seeing the patient. We see the consequences vividly as the doctor moves around the clinic spreading the green paint to many different surfaces.

Offer to Shake Hands

I was working on a handwashing curriculum for healthcare providers that didn't have the resources to do black light or show videos, and one of the subject matter experts explained what they would do instead: The instructor would ask for a volunteer to come to the front of the room. The instructor would cough dramatically into their hand and then offer that hand to the volunteer to shake. The volunteer would almost always be comically horrified by the prospect.

All of these are ways to make something that is abstract (germ theory) and make it more vivid and tangible and *salient* for learners.

HOW CAN WE USE THIS?

If motivation is one of the clear struggles that your audience is having with the behavior, it's worth asking if making the rewards or consequences more salient may make a difference for learners. For example, in the saving-for-retirement example, can we make life at retirement age more salient for people?

In a study also done at the Stanford VHIL (Hershfield 2011), researchers looked at whether spending time in virtual reality as your retirement-age self would change your choices about saving for retirement. They created VR avatars of each test subject and then artificially "aged" the image to be retirement age.

 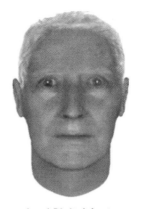

Nonaged Digital Avatar   Aged Digital Avatar

Image credit: Stanford Virtual Human Interaction Lab

Some of the subjects would then explore a virtual environment as their retirement-age selves. They would move around the environment and see "themselves" in a virtual mirror. Other subjects would explore the same environment as their current-age selves.

Afterward, they were given a hypothetical money allocation, were told to imagine that they had just unexpectedly received $1,000, and were asked to allocate it among four options:

- Use it to buy something nice for someone special
- Invest it in a retirement fund
- Plan a fun and extravagant occasion
- Put it into a checking account

Participants who had spent time as their retirement-age selves allocated more of the hypothetical funds to retirement savings than participants who spent their time as their current-age selves.

While creating a full VR environment may not always be a practical strategy, stories, images, and experiences are all ways to increase the salience of the experience for learners.

BCT	Anticipated regret (BCT 5.2)	Induce or raise awareness of expectations of future regret about performance of the unwanted behavior.	Example: Ask the person to assess the degree of regret they will feel if they do not quit smoking.

"After they spent all that time picturing the nice things they could have and do in retirement, the financial advisor pointed out that if people weren't actively saving for retirement, they would need to start crossing items off the list. She asked how they would feel if they got to retirement age and they just didn't have the resources for those items. I could tell it was really hitting some of the people—they'd spent all this time imagining what it could look like, and having to cross items off made them think."

COMPARISON

BCT	Demonstration of the behavior (BCT 6.1)	Provide an observable sample of the performance of the behavior directly in person or indirectly (for example, via film or pictures) for the person to aspire to or imitate (includes modeling).	Example: Demonstrate to nurses how to raise the issue of excessive drinking with patients via a role-play exercise.

"We've been developing examples of different types of members and their retirement profiles. They are anonymous, of course, but based on recognizable scenarios for our members. We've been testing them out, and it's really interesting to see members' relief to have something clear that they can understand. So much of the stuff from the financial curriculum is written really clearly, and isn't that hard to understand, but it's too abstract. I think people are just grateful to have specific examples."

BCT	Social comparison (BCT 6.2)	Draw attention to others' performance to allow comparison with the person's own performance.	Example: See how your energy usage compares to similar households.

"We've got some survey data of what different types of members are doing, and people can see how they compare to their peer group. That seems to be effective with our more established members.

"But it turns out the saving rates are still pretty low with our junior members, so when we showed them the numbers, they were like, 'Whew, it's okay I'm not saving yet,' which I don't think is what we want to communicate.

"We are probably going to have to be careful which segments we use that message with. For the younger audience, I think we want to find messages from younger members who have gotten started with retirement savings and feature that instead."

BCT	Information about others' approval (BCT 6.3)	Provide information about what other people think about the behavior. The information clarifies whether others will like, approve, or disapprove of what the person is doing or will do.	Example: Tell the staff at the hospital ward that staff at all other wards approve of washing their hands according to the guidelines.

"Hmm, I'm not sure what we could do with this. I guess we could do some testimonials from influential members, but I'm concerned that people would feel like, 'Of course those really successful authors can save for retirement. Did you see their last publishing deal? What does that have to do with me?' I guess I'll need to think on that one a little more."

BCT	Credible source (BCT 9.1)	Present verbal or visual communication from a credible source in favor of or against the behavior.	Example: Young athletes hear about the importance of drug-free performance from top athletes in their sport.

"As I mentioned, we had some financial advisors on a panel who didn't really understand the situations for our members. I've managed to find some other advisors who specialize in working with creatives and freelancers. I think they'll have much more credibility with our audience."

BCT	Pros and cons (BCT 9.2)	Advise the person to identify and compare reasons for wanting (pros) and not wanting (cons) to change the behavior.	Example: Advise the person to list and compare the advantages and disadvantages of using a password manager.

BCT	Comparative imagining of future outcomes (BCT 9.3)	Prompt or advise the imagining and comparing of future outcomes of changed versus unchanged behavior.	Example: Prompt the patient to imagine and compare likely or possible outcomes from having or not having an annual mammogram screening.

"So it's interesting. Most of the pro/con materials in the curriculum we received focus on the pros and cons of saving for retirement at all, but that's not really the issue we are hearing about from our members. They already buy in to the pros of saving for retirement. The issue is really more about the pros and cons of saving for retirement right now. I was thinking we could have some scenarios where members could see the impact of delaying. What if you start this year with a little, versus next year, versus five years from now?"

SELF-BELIEF

BCT	Verbal persuasion about capability (BCT 15.1)	Tell the person that they can successfully perform the wanted behavior, arguing against self-doubts and asserting that they can and will succeed.	Example: Tell the person that they can successfully increase their physical activity, despite their recent heart attack.

"I was genuinely surprised at how many people expressed doubt in their ability to manage all this. Our members are generally pretty smart folks and are used to researching and figuring things out. In one of the webinars, we asked them how they would handle it if they were researching retirement options for an article or book and had them brainstorm what they would do. I think just bringing them into their researcher mindset made it a little less intimidating for them."

BCT	Mental rehearsal of successful performance (BCT 15.2)	Advise to practice imagining performing the behavior successfully in relevant contexts.	Example: Ask them to imagine what it would look like to order a nonalcoholic drink at their next social event.

"There's a calculator in the curriculum materials where they can pick options for some different scenarios. I think just doing it for some fictional situations made them feel more confident about their ability to make their own choices. Then we had them think about what they could do to get started."

BCT	Focus on past success (BCT 15.3)	Advise to think about or list previous successes in performing the behavior (or parts of it).	Example: When asking them to do a complicated task, have them think about complicated things they have accomplished in the past.

"Our members are people who have finished writing books. Most people who start books never finish them, but all our members have successfully done this really hard thing that involved logistics, planning, and diligence. I want to see if reminding them that they have that capacity will help them believe they can tackle this other thing that is comparatively much easier."

COVERT LEARNING

BCT Imaginary reward (BCT 16.2)	Advise to imagine performing the wanted behavior in a real-life situation followed by imagining a pleasant consequence.	Example: Have the patient picture the increased flexibility they'll have if they complete their physical therapy series.

"Writers never picture a time when they stop writing. It's not like some grim job where people are counting the days until they can stop working. But they do get excited about the idea of having freedom to write, or to be able to focus on topics they are passionate about. When people picture some of those really great things for their retirement, you can see their attitude shift to feel more positive about the whole thing."

OTHER BCTS

BCT Goal setting (BCT 1.1)	Set or agree on a goal defined in terms of the behavior to be achieved.	Example: Agree on a daily walking goal (for example, 3 miles) with the person and reach agreement about the goal.

"We've created this pop-up page for members who are browsing the resources. It says, 'Looks like you are interested in retirement options. What's your next step?' and it gives them options that range from 'research options' to 'open an account' to 'increase my automatic deduction' and several options in between. Then they can opt in for email or text reminders of their goal to help keep them on track."

BCT Environment (BCT 12.1)	Change, or advise to change, the physical environment to facilitate performance of the wanted behavior or create barriers to the unwanted behavior (other than prompts/cues, rewards, and punishments).	Example: Advise patients trying to reduce their dietary sodium to have only a small container of salt in the house.

"Look, the education is great, but no matter how much education we do, people probably still won't get started unless it's easy.

"We don't really get involved in the actual financial service they use—that's up to them—but we have negotiated some reduced-cost memberships to some of the financial service platforms, and there's this great app for our younger members where they adjust their savings amount to whatever their financial situation is that month. It shows them a streak if they put something away each month—even if it's only five dollars.

"We started out trying to collect as many resources as we possibly could for our members, but found that too many options contributed to the feeling of overwhelm, so we've curated the list down to the best options."

BCT	Avoidance/reducing exposure to cues for the behavior (BCT 12.3)	Advise on how to avoid exposure to specific social and contextual/physical cues for the behavior, including changing daily or weekly routines.	Example: Suggest to a person who wants to quit smoking that their social life focus on activities other than pubs and bars, which have been associated with smoking.

"One strategy that some people really liked was identifying a few things they wouldn't buy so they could put that money toward retirement instead. The big one was coffee shops. A lot of writers work while they're in coffee shops and therefore spend a lot on coffee. We talked about other places they could write, like public libraries, and cheap beverages they could buy, like plain coffee, rather than expensive coffee drinks.

"That strategy was really more about avoiding the behavior of spending money, but I think it really helped them feel some simple changes, like avoiding places where they spend unnecessary money, made it feel more possible to find money for retirement savings."

RESOURCES

Hershfield, Hal E., Daniel G. Goldstein, William F. Sharpe, Jesse Fox, Leo Yeykelis, Laura L. Carstensen, and Jeremy N. Bailenson. "Increasing saving behavior through age-progressed renderings of the future self." *Journal of Marketing Research* 48, no. SPL (2011): S23-S37.

Marwaha, Seema. "Wash Your Hands - It Just Makes Sense." YouTube video. September 30, 2011. https://www.youtube.com/watch?v=M8AKTACyiBo.

Stanford's Virtual Human Interaction Lab. "Stanford Researchers Examine the Psychology of Virtual Reality." YouTube video. August 20, 2014. https://www.youtube.com/watch?v=IIGFGF1hQmw retrieved 5/8/2023.

Thaler, Richard H., and Cass R. Sunstein. *Nudge: Improving Decisions About Health, Wealth, and Happiness.* (New York: Penguin, 2009), 25.

USING PLANNING, PRACTICE & FEEDBACK

(IN WHICH WE RECOGNIZE THE ELEPHANT IS A CREATURE OF HABIT AND WE TEACH AN OLD ELEPHANT A FEW NEW TRICKS)

MEET ANGELIKA

Angelika is a learning experience designer for a company that manufactures cleaning supplies for commercial use. She specifically works with the sales division, creating training materials to help salespeople learn and improve their sales skills.

Here's the particular challenge that she's dealing with:

"We've been moving away from selling individual products to focusing on suites of products. We offer different suites of products to address a customer's particular needs.

"It's a slower sales cycle and really requires a consultative sales approach. We've got a lot of people in the sales group who have been there for years and years. They are very good at what they do, but this is a different kind of selling.

"Honestly, I thought we'd get a lot of resistance and skepticism from our salesforce, but that actually hasn't been the case. Times have changed, and I think they understand that to be successful, they have to sell in at a different level. They aren't demoing for a kitchen manager how well the grease-cutting agent works anymore. Instead, they're talking to a purchasing agent for a chain of restaurants about cost per use.

"But while I think they are mostly on board with the idea, many of the salespeople are struggling to change their practice. Old habits are hard to break, and all that. There's a lot of backsliding."

AUDIENCE RESEARCH

To make sure she understood the challenge, Angelika talked to stakeholders and salespeople already piloting the new process.

A few themes emerged from her interviews. Here are some examples of the key things she heard.

From Reuben, a senior salesperson:

"I genuinely thought I could pick the best suite for my clients. I've worked with them for so many years, I really thought I had a clear picture of their needs, but I found that the clients were thrown off by me just switching to a product suite. I hadn't really brought them along with me, so I started having more of the qualifying conversations and found that it helped my customers understand the logic behind the shift. I also found out that I didn't know quite as much about their situations as I had assumed. I'll be interested to see what experiences other senior folks are having."

From Estrella, a sales manager, after observing some of her sales team:

"The salesperson would start with the qualifying questions, but then a customer would say something that the salesperson had a product solution for, and they just couldn't help themselves; they'd go down the path of selling that specific product. It was like watching a switch get flipped. They'd sound a little awkward working through the new process, and then you could see them relax into their old familiar patter for a particular product. They are very good at making it sound natural, but I could tell they were slipping into old habits. I also think we really need to figure out a way for the team to see what good looks like for this, and how to catch themselves when they go off track."

From Charles, a more recent addition to the sales team:

"It's tough to switch from measuring success by just product sales. Don't get me wrong—I completely understand the logic behind the shift, and it's the kind of sales I want to be doing. I think it's a little easier for me than some of the team who've been selling these products for years, but you don't necessarily walk away from even a successful consultative call with a string of new orders, so I have a hard time gauging whether I'm moving the needle enough. I've heard they might revise sales goals to match this new direction, but nothing has happened with that yet."

ANALYSIS RESULTS

Let's look at a summary of the COM-B analysis for one of the key behaviors: qualifying a client to identify the product suite options.

COM-B Domains	Observations
Physical capability	N/A
Psychological capability	Salespeople know the process but not with any fluency yet. They also need the capability to "catch" themselves when they go off track.
Physical opportunity	The sales tracking systems do not reflect the new behaviors and goals, and salespeople are having a hard time judging "success."
Social opportunity	Salespeople may not currently have the opportunity to see "what good looks like" (modeling). Additionally, there's probably an opportunity for social support of the change within the sales team.
Reflective motivation	While most salespeople may buy into the overall process, not all of the salespeople are convinced that they need to do the specific behavior of qualifying customers (asking questions to assess their needs) because they believe they already know what long-standing clients need. Several salespeople also report not feeling comfortable or confident with the new methods.
Automatic motivation	Existing habits of salespeople are getting in the way of the new behaviors, particularly the ability to recognize and catch themselves when they default to old habits. Some of the salespeople also mentioned feeling offended that their current efforts weren't being respected, and anxiety about being forced to change what's working while being held to existing sales quotas.

BEHAVIOUR CHANGE TECHNIQUES

Angelika worked with some of the stakeholders to identify intervention functions and look at the overall strategy.

"Of course education and training are going to be part of this. They need to learn the new model and practice it. I think it's going to be just as important, though, to have goals and planning and then feedback and monitoring of progress. We also want to look at how we need to adapt the environment to support them. And we want to make sure that there's modelling and social support. Our salespeople care a lot about what their peers are doing, and if there isn't good support for this change coming from the teams, it's going to fail."

Since Angelika has some strategies in mind, she's going to look through relevant Behaviour Change Techniques (BCTs) to see if they would help her design learning or support materials to help the salespeople.

As mentioned in the previous chapters, you could consider all the relevant BCTs, but for the purposes of this chapter, I focus on the following four categories of techniques, along with a few other relevant techniques:

- Goals and planning
- Feedback and monitoring
- Repetition and substitution
- Shaping knowledge

I also look at some techniques from these categories:

- Associations
- Social support
- Environment

We'll also assume that Angelika already has good material in place for this technique:

BCT	Instruction on how to perform the behavior (BCT 4.1)	Advise or agree on how to perform the behavior (includes skills training).	Example: Any form of instructing learners how to do something.

"Oh yeah, we already have good instruction on the methods in place. I think we are fine there."

Since Angelika already has a strong instructional module in place, let's look at some of the other behavior change techniques that she could apply. You'll see cards for different techniques, and see how Angelika might use them.

GOALS AND PLANNING

BCT	Goal setting: behavior (BCT 1.1)	Set or agree on a goal defined in terms of the behavior to be achieved.	Example: To save money, plan to cook dinner at home at least three times per week.

"I've been looking at how to do goal setting in the class. I think it makes sense to have them set their own goals for how they want to implement the new process, and to have a way to track and maintain that. I wanted to do something in the sales tracking system, but I don't think we'll be able to add functionality to that this quarter, so we are creating planning workbooks for the salespeople to make their plan and track the results so they can review them with their managers."

BCT	Graded tasks (BCT 8.2)	Set easy-to-perform tasks, making them increasingly difficult, but achievable, until behavior is performed.	Example: To start running, follow a couch-to-5K plan that starts with running for one minute at a time, and gradually moves up to running 5K after six weeks.

"I've been thinking about this. The original plan was to just switch everything over, but that's pretty overwhelming. I've been talking to the management team, and we've agreed that salespeople will pick two or three clients—the ones most ready for this approach—and test the water with them. Then after a few weeks, they'll work with their managers to add more clients into the program, saving the really challenging client accounts for when they are more comfortable with the process."

Using Graded Tasks in Learning Environments

Psychologist Mihaly Csikszentmihalyi described the phenomenon of flow state, which is that feeling of intense engagement where time just seems to fly by. One of the characteristics of flow is a balance between challenge and ability, as shown in the illustration.

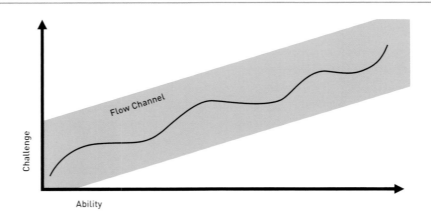

In a learning environment, if something is too difficult, it's frustrating. If something isn't challenging enough, it's boring. So finding ways to gradually increase the challenge as learners' proficiency increases is your best bet for creating engaging practice.

You can ramp up challenge by making things faster or more complex or by requiring more accuracy.

You can also make the learners' performance more challenging. For example, you can move learners through these steps:

- Recognition
- Critique
- Performance

For example, if you are teaching managers how to interview job candidates without violating any hiring laws, you could go through these steps like this:

- **Recognition:** Have learners go through a list of questions and sort out which are legal and which are not
- **Critique:** Have learners watch an interview and identify where there were legal issues, and what they should have asked instead
- **Performance:** Have learners draft interview questions for one to three job descriptions and then role-play interviews with feedback

There are other ways to gradually increase difficulty, but this can be a way to build competence and confidence in learners.

PROBLEM SOLVING & ACTION PLANNING

BCT	Problem solving (BCT 1.2)	Analyze, or prompt the person to analyze, factors influencing the behavior and generate or select strategies that include overcoming barriers and/or increasing facilitators (includes relapse prevention and coping planning).	Example: To keep better track of financial spending, anticipate barriers or challenges (for example, difficulty tracking vacation spending) and create a strategy in advance to address the problem if it happens.

"We've added a problem-solving component to the workbook. The pilot group gave us some ideas for the challenges that the larger team will face, and the team is coming up with some of their own anticipated barriers. We've added some brainstorming activities where the whole class can create troubleshooting plans for the anticipated barriers or difficulties."

BCT	Action planning (BCT 1.4)	Prompt detailed planning of performance of the behavior (must include at least one of context, frequency, duration, and intensity). Context may be environmental (physical or social) or internal (physical, emotional, or cognitive) (includes implementation intentions).	Example: To exercise more regularly, plan the performance of a particular physical activity (such as running) at a particular time (such as before work) on certain days of the week.

"One thing they definitely need a plan for is when the conversation starts to go down the old product route. We've been coming up with lists of the things that should tell them that the conversation has gone off track, and they've been coming up with their own plan for how to get it back on track."

Implementation Intentions

Habits are a hot topic in behavior change right now, and require practice to really become part of someone's daily life. In learning environments, the best option is to set learners up with a plan they can implement back in the workplace or relevant environment.

Researcher Peter Gollwitzer has a strategy called implementation intentions that I've found to be helpful in learning experiences.

In its simplest form, it's a plan:

If X happens, I'll do Y.

These work best if learners create them for themselves.

For example, if the behavior is to protect mornings for deeper work by avoiding distractions, some implementation intentions could be

When I arrive at work, I'll silence my devices.

If a coworker wants to talk, I'll schedule an afternoon time with them.

If I get a morning meeting invite, I'll propose an alternative time.

You can give learners a template and have them create their implementation intentions as part of planning for their return to the workplace or application environment.

CONTRACTS AND COMMITMENT

BCT	Behavioral contract (BCT 1.8)	Create a written specification of the behavior to be performed, agreed on by the person, and witnessed by another.	Example: To start to give up vaping, sign a contract with your best friend that you will not vape for at least one week.

BCT			
BCT	Commitment (BCT 1.9)	Ask the person to affirm or reaffirm statements indicating commitment to change the behavior.	Ask the person to use an "I will" statement to affirm or reaffirm a strong commitment (that is, using the words *strongly, committed,* or *high priority*) to start, continue, or restart the attempt to take medication as prescribed.

"Hmm, the idea of contracts or commitments is interesting, but I actually think it's overkill here. The salespeople are mostly on board with the idea, so I don't think they'd like being asked literally sign on. I can understand why this might be a strategy for more personal goals, but I don't think it makes sense for our team."

PRACTICE

If I ask the question "Why do we want learners to practice?" it might sound like a the-answer-is-blatantly-obvious-why-even-ask situation?

But actually, practice can have a few benefits, and it's worth identifying which one you are aiming for.

SUPPORT REMEMBERING

The first reason you want to have practice is it helps people remember things, particularly processes. If you are doing a process that involves some kind of psychomotor element, like priming an IV infusion device or making a sandwich to order in a restaurant, then practicing can make it easier to remember the necessary steps. You could also support that memory by using a job aid or some other kind of guidance in the environment, but practice can also help the learner be faster or more accurate.

CREATING EASE

Another reason you might want someone to practice is to help the learner develop more ease and confidence with the task. If something feels too hard, learners are going to be reluctant to try.

For example, several years ago, I worked on the teacher training materials for a substance abuse prevention program for seventh and eighth grade students called Project ALERT.

The program designers explained that a lot of drug-prevention curriculums had historically focused on the dangers of drug use but hadn't made much of a dent in actual behavior. One of the strategies they had found to be more effective was to repeatedly have the kids practice how to handle the awkward social moment where they get offered something.

Even if that kid has no intention of accepting the substance, it's still a challenging social situation to handle smoothly. Project ALERT had many different ways over a 13-week curriculum for kids to practice how they would respond in that situation. That practice probably won't change the mind of a kid determined to try an illegal substance, but it would greatly increase the comfort level of the kids who did not want to try anything.

Image Source: Project ALERT/RAND Corporation, used with permission

The goal wasn't necessarily to have the kids remember exactly what they were going to say but rather to have ease and familiarity so they aren't caught off guard when they encounter the situation.

DEVELOPING AUTOMATICITY

Sometimes, you are trying to use practice to reduce the perceived or actual effort of performing the behavior.

Remember this elephant?

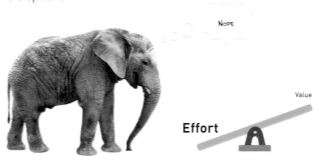

There are a few different models for how a skill or behavior moves from familiar to automatic. I prefer these stages from Gloria Gery:

- Familiarization
- Comprehension

- Conscious effort
- Conscious action
- Proficiency
- Unconscious competence

If we apply this model to learning to drive, it will likely follow this progression:

- **Familiarization:** Getting familiar with the controls on the car (steering wheel, transmission, brake, and so on) and what sequence of events needs to happen to do basic driving.
- **Comprehension:** The would-be driver knows what to do for basic driving.
- **Conscious effort:** Our driver-to-be can drive a bit but has to pay conscious attention to everything they do to stay in control and may or may not be successful. When I was learning to drive, my dad started by taking me to an empty parking lot on a Sunday afternoon so I couldn't run into anything during what I now realize was my "conscious effort" stage.
- **Conscious action:** This is the point at which the driver can successfully execute but still has to pay attention to everything they're doing, which is cognitively very effortful. At this point in my driving training, my dad would let me drive around the block. Carefully. And slowly.
- **Proficiency:** This is the point where the driver can execute without having to consciously control everything they're doing, and they're ready for the driver's exam. For more complex skills, there's quite a bit of practice between conscious action and proficiency.
- **Unconscious competence:** This is the point where someone can execute at a high level of proficiency and may not need to pay much conscious attention at all. They've reached a high level of automaticity for the task (it's become automatic). You know what this feels like if you've ever driven home from work and pulled into your home driveway only to realize that you HAVE NO MEMORY OF THE DRIVE HOME. After many years of driving on a well-practiced route with no unexpected events, you can execute with very little conscious control. If you had encountered a detour or an accident on your way home, you would have heightened your conscious control to manage the unexpected complication.

By making the action automatic, it becomes much easier and changes the effort-to-value equation.

This is also one of the reasons change can be so difficult for people. If they are used to a task feeling easy, and having a high level of confidence in their ability, it can be very dysregulating to be thrown back into feeling like a beginner.

SET A GOAL FOR PRACTICE

You might structure practice differently depending on your goal:

- **Support memory:** If you are trying to support memory, it could be practice with gradually reduced guidance until learners can operate without support, or to a certain level of speed or accuracy.
- **Create ease:** If you are trying to get learners to feel more confident or comfortable, you might start with a very easy version and add complexity or variety as they practice.
- **Develop automaticity:** If you are trying to develop automaticity, then it's likely you'll have the learner do multiple repetitions over time, and automaticity isn't likely to really occur until a learner leaves the classroom, unless it's something where it's required for safety reasons (for example, airline pilots practicing in a simulator).

BCT			
	Behavioral practice/ rehearsal (BCT 8.1)	Prompt practice or rehearsal of the performance of the behavior one or more times in a context or at a time when the performance may not be necessary to increase habit and skill.	Example: People newly diagnosed with diabetes can get comfortable testing their blood sugar by practicing going through the process at their doctor's office with help and support.

"We did a warm-up activity where everyone used some of the analysis questions to understand something from their regular life. One guy did a hilarious one where he used the questions with his teenage son to negotiate his son cleaning his room. He reported back to us that it worked really well!"

BCT			
	Habit formation (BCT 8.3)	Prompt rehearsal and repetition of the behavior in the same context repeatedly so that the context elicits the behavior.	Prompt patients to take their statin tablet before brushing their teeth every evening.

"We did a practice activity in class where we watched recordings of sales calls, and everybody would shout when the salesperson got sidetracked on a product tangent. It got a little rowdy, but it was fun, and I really think everyone got tuned to listen for those going-off-track moments.

"Once they got good at recognizing the cue of the going-off-track, they all wrote down a question or two they could use to bring things back on track."

Habit Formation

There are a number of different definitions of *habit*. In her excellent book *Good Habit, Bad Habit*, researcher Wendy Wood gives this definition:

> "a mental association between a context cue and a response that develops as we repeat an action in that context for a reward"

She goes on to explain:

> "A habit turns the world around you—your context—into a trigger to act. That easy, fluid, automatic feeling of acting on habit isn't accidental or secondary to the way habits work. Effortlessness is a defining property. The situation you're in triggers the response from memory, and you act. It can essentially bypass your executive mind."

So, for example, a flossing habit could be triggered by morning teeth brushing if you have the habit of flossing after brushing. Or a habit could be checking your phone if you are bored during a lull in conversation—the feeling of boredom could be an internal trigger, or the environmental trigger of being stuck in a line could lead to the habitual behavior.

HABITS VERSUS ROUTINES

There seems to be some distinction between a routine—which can be more complex or deliberate than a habit—and a habit. It seems to hinge on how automatic or specific the action(s) are.

I've been setting up my desk every morning to work on this book. It involves unpacking and connecting my computer, plugging everything in, and getting coffee, which is a routine. Despite my intention to start writing immediately, I still find myself checking my email within a few minutes of sitting down. That's probably due to habit.

Most habits are fairly specific behaviors. "Ensuring work site safety" is not a habit, but "scanning the work site for hazards at the beginning of a shift" could be a habit.

SUPPORTING HABIT FORMATION

Some ways to support habit formation in learning experiences include helping learners, as shown in the flowchart:

- **Identify the actual habit behavior:** "Being a better manager" is not a habit, but "giving feedback promptly after witnessing an issue" could be.

- **Identify the trigger(s) in the environment:** What triggers could a manager use to cue the "providing prompt feedback" habit? The manager could look out for emails containing updates from the team or give feedback after each team member reports in during an update meeting. Triggers should be something that learners themselves identify based on their own knowledge of the context and environment.
- **Increase motivation:** What could learners do to increase motivation? This is a personal thing, so learners should help determine what could support motivation for the habit.
- **Decrease barriers:** If the manager is concerned there won't be enough time in the update meeting for feedback, they can extend the meeting time to support it.
- **Hack the environment:** For example, managers would put reminders in their calendar to make sure they provide feedback at least once a week or set up one-on-one check-ins with their team to make sure feedback happens.
- **Chain it to an existing habit:** If you have a reliable event that's already happening, you can try to chain a new habit to it. For example, taking the dog out first thing in the morning is a reliable event for me, so I've tried to do some stretches while I wait for the dog.
- **Make feedback/tracking visible:** If possible, use something that creates a form of feedback or tracking. For example, the manager could note feedback in a journal with a page for each team member, so they can see if they are being consistent.

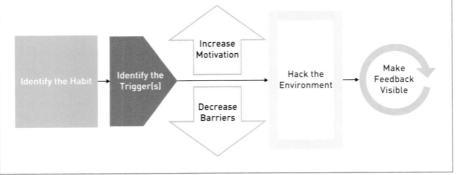

FEEDBACK AND MONITORING

BCT	Review behavior goal(s) (BCT 1.5)	Review behavior goal(s) jointly with the person and consider modifying goal(s) or behavior change strategy in light of achievement. This may lead to re-setting the same goal, making a small change in that goal, or setting a new goal instead of (or in addition to) the first; there may also be no change.	Example: If you are trying to meditate more regularly and you have been meeting your goal of 5 minutes each morning, you might revise the goal to be 7 or 10 minutes each morning.

"We are going to build this into check-ins with their managers. We've actually created a brief rubric for what needs to happen to signal that the salesperson is ready to move to the next part of the process and use the new strategies with a wider section of their clients."

BCT	Discrepancy between current behavior and goal (BCT 1.6)	Draw attention to discrepancies between a person's current behavior (in terms of the form, frequency, duration, or intensity of that behavior) and the person's previously set outcome goals, behavioral goals, or action plans (goes beyond self-monitoring of behavior).	Example: If you are working with a health coach and set the goal of walking 30 minutes daily, but during your check-in with the coach, you acknowledge that most walks are 15 to 20 minutes, you can discuss what needs to change.

"Generally the salespeople are on board, but you know there are going to be people who lag when it comes to implementation. I've been discussing the follow-up plan with managers, and I think it's important that salespeople understand that managers are going to pay attention and will check in with them if they don't implement the plan. Managers will do weekly one-on-ones with sales staff and have salespeople describe how they are using the new methods with at least three customers.

"We've rolled out some initiatives in the past that nobody ever followed up on, so it's important that salespeople agree to the strategy and believe that the strategy will have follow up. They need to believe that managers will notice if salespeople aren't implementing the change."

BCT	Monitoring of behavior by others without feedback (BCT 2.1)	Observe or record behavior with the person's knowledge as part of a behavior change strategy.	Example: You and a friend agree to share your progress on your productivity goals at the end of each day so you know someone is seeing how you do.

"We're trying out a buddy system. Basically, the salespeople will be matched with another salesperson, and they will report back to each other how they are progressing. They aren't checking each other's work or anything. It's really just about feeling like someone is paying attention and is in it with you."

BCT	Feedback on behavior (BCT 2.2)	Monitor and provide informative or evaluative feedback on performance of the behavior (such as form, frequency, duration, intensity).	Example: Using a smartwatch to track sleeping habits over time.

"We are going to do role plays as part of the training. We do them with three people: one to be the salesperson, one to play the client, and one to observe how well they implement the process and give feedback. When I've used that in the past, the person giving the feedback also learns a lot through watching how the feedback is delivered. Then the people rotate, so everyone does each role. I'm also working with Estrella on support materials for the managers, so they can give effective feedback when they shadow their staff on client calls."

BCT	Self-monitoring of behavior (BCT 2.3)	Establish a method for the person to monitor and record their behavior(s) as part of a behavior change strategy.	Example: Use a streak-tracking app to record your daily flossing behavior.

"The workbook will provide a way for the salespeople to track their own progress. I'd love to have something in the sales system to track some actual performance data, but that will probably not be possible until Q3 at the earliest."

	Self-monitoring of outcome(s) of behavior (BCT 2.4)	Establish a method for the person to monitor and record the outcome(s) of their behavior as part of a behavior change strategy.	Example: Checking blood pressure outcomes after taking blood pressure medication as prescribed for a specific time period.
BCT			

"Outcomes? You mean does it impact their sales numbers? I certainly hope it will, but honestly, there are so many other things that also impact sales numbers, so I'm not sure how to connect the dots on that. You better believe that salespeople will be watching their outcomes, though. Everybody is prepared for there to be a dip in sales numbers in the short term—maybe a quarter—but ultimately this needs to improve overall numbers. We are encouraging salespeople to look for other measures to track, like client engagement or more cross-selling opportunities."

	Behavioral experiments (BCT 4.4)	Advise on how to identify and test hypotheses about the behavior, its causes and consequences, by collecting and interpreting data.	Example: A pediatrician counsels a set of parents of preschool-age children on behavioral strategies, uses a periodic survey to measure results compared to other parents, and adjusts their counseling strategy based on results.
BCT			

"Ooo, I like the idea of behavioral experiments. We emphasize that our salespeople manage their territories as their own business, so I like the idea that they would study and adapt to find what works for them. I think that could be a really good follow-up module. Once they have implemented the process, how can they experiment with different strategies to take it to the next level? I'm writing that down to do as a follow-up workshop. Change is a process, not an event, right?"

SOME ASSOCIATED BCTS

	Behavior substitution (BCT 8.2)	Prompt substitution of the unwanted behavior with a wanted or neutral behavior.	Example: When trying to drink less caffeine, find an herbal iced tea that you like to drink instead of caffeinated soda.
BCT			

	Habit reversal (BCT 8.4)	Prompt rehearsal and repetition of an alternative behavior to replace an unwanted habitual behavior.	Example: When trying to be more alert in the afternoons at work, take the stairs instead of the elevator.
BCT			

"I've been having the salespeople think about what they should do instead of getting sidetracked by product requests. Just ignoring it doesn't feel right to most of the team. They've come up with a few different strategies. Mainly, they either note it for later and then do a follow up with the client or somehow track it. A couple of salespeople have found they like pulling the product sheet when it comes up; then they have a stack of things to go over at the end of the call."

BCT			
	Social support (practical) (BCT 3.2)	Advise on, arrange, or provide practical help (for example, from friends, relatives, colleagues, "buddies," or staff) for performance of the behavior.	Example: To stretch more regularly, have a weekly Zoom yoga session with friends who are accountability partners.

"We've been using buddies and small groups to work on the change and have created message threads in the sales track-ing system for them to discuss what they are doing. Not every group has really engaged in the message threads, but some groups have been really active. They definitely have a "we're all in it together feeling" about it, which is good to see. I'd like to figure out how the team can do more knowledge sharing even after this initiative. We tried something for social networking a few years ago, and it didn't really go anywhere, but this one seems to be working better because there's something specific they are working on."

BCT			
	Prompts/ cues (BCT 7.1)	Introduce or define environmental or social stimulus with the purpose of prompting or cueing the behavior. The prompt or cue would normally occur at the time or place of performance.	Example: To remember to set the alarm when leaving the building, put a note by the door.

"We created a note-taking job aid that prompts the different parts of the conversation for them to use while they talk to clients. Hopefully if it feels awkward at all, they can just move on to the next category on the job aid and get back on track."

Incentives, Rewards, and Punishments

Okay, so there's another metaphorical elephant in this room. It's this question: How should a learning designer deal with incentives, rewards, and punishments?

I'll admit this is a tough one for me. I became a learning designer because I really like helping people, and I really love learning, so using strategies that feel like bribes or punishments to force people to learn or perform the behavior just feels like something I shouldn't be involved with.

At the same time, these are part of the systems our learners operate in, so we do need to discuss it. Here are a few issues to consider:

- **Incentives versus rewards:** An incentive is a deal you are making with the participant: "Do X, and you'll get Y." As we discussed in the motivation chapter, this sets up a scenario where people are going to figure out how to optimize for the incentive. Sometimes this may not matter. For example, if you only need them to do the behavior once (for example, create a login in the new knowledge-sharing system), it might not matter if they are only doing it for the incentive. If you need them to make this a regular behavior (for example, posting regularly in the new knowledge-sharing system), then you run into the problem of people optimizing for the reward (such as posting slight or nonsensical items in the system), or you may need to up the incentive over time to get people to continue the behavior.
  Rewards, on the other hand, are something you do to reinforce the behavior after it's happened. For example, it could be a gift card and a sincere thank-you from your manager after the first time you post in the new knowledge-sharing system. There was no deal in advance—just a nice acknowledgement afterwards. Rewards are less likely to create problematic motivations, but they also don't inspire the behavior; they only acknowledge and reinforce it afterwards.

- **Behaviors versus outcomes:** If you are going to look into incentives or rewards, you need to decide if you are going to reward the behavior or the outcome. For example, in our sales example, people could do the behavior without immediately producing the outcome of improved sales. Typical sales environments reward outcomes (such as increased sales revenue), but it can make sense to reward the behavior (such as consultative selling) if you need people to persist in that behavior. People control their behaviors but may not control outcomes (for example, sales could be flat because of outside factors like economic conditions or competitor initiatives).

- **Punishments:** Of course, punishments can be part of making a behavior change happen. The threat of legal penalties can be part of having ethical, fair workplaces. Typically, though, if punishments creep into learning experiences, I find it's a symptom of other problems. For example, punishing people who haven't completed training often is a sign of learners who don't see the value of what they are being asked to learn, learners who aren't being given enough time, or learners who are being forced to go through compliance training they don't need or can't use. Punishment may be necessary, particularly when there are issues like legal compliance requirements or significant safety concerns, but it shouldn't be the first option.

BCT	Restructuring the physical environment (BCT 12.1)	Change, or advise to change, the physical environment to facilitate performance of the wanted behavior or create barriers to the unwanted behavior (other than prompts/cues, rewards, and punishments).	Example: To take vitamins more regularly, put the vitamin bottle next to the coffee maker.

"I stay out of the sales compensation conversation, mostly. My only responsibility there is to make sure that new salespeople understand how it works. I have been included in a few of the meetings about the revisions to the sales goals. One thing I'm relieved to see is that they are going to loosen sales requirements while people get used to the new behaviors.

"I don't have opinions about how salespeople should get paid, but we do need to make sure we are incenting the new behaviors, so I'm glad they are talking about how to ensure they are rewarding the right behaviors."

RESOURCES

Csikszentmihalyi, Mihaly, *Flow: The Psychology of Optimal Experience* (New York: Harper & Row, 1990).

Gery, Gloria J. *Electronic Performance Support Systems: How and Why to Remake the Workplace Through the Strategic Application of Technology* (Boston, MA: Weingarten Publications, Inc., 1991).

Haier, Richard J., Benjamin Siegel, Chuck Tang, Lennart Abel, and Monte S. Buchsbaum. "Intelligence and changes in regional cerebral glucose metabolic rate following learning." *Intelligence* 16, no. 3–4 (1992): 415–426.

Michie, Susan, Michelle Richardson, Marie Johnston, Charles Abraham, Jill Francis, Wendy Hardeman, Martin P. Eccles, James Cane, and Caroline E. Wood. "The behavior change technique taxonomy (v1) of 93 hierarchically clustered techniques: building an international consensus for the reporting of behavior change interventions." *Annals of Behavioral Medicine* 46, no. 1 (2013): 81–95.

Project ALERT. https://www.projectalert.com/.

Wood, Wendy. *Good Habits, Bad Habits: The Science of Making Positive Changes That Stick* (New York: Farrar, Straus & Young, 2019), 43.

USING ENVIRONMENTAL AND SOCIAL SUPPORT

(IN WHICH WE LEARN THAT THE ELEPHANT CARES A LOT ABOUT WHERE THEY ARE AND WHAT THE OTHER ELEPHANTS ARE DOING)

MEET ANH

Anh is the training manager for a financial services call center. The company has been expanding through hiring and acquisitions, and they are about to start having remote employees. Up to this point, all employees have been on site, but now people are going to be able to work from home part of the week. The plan is also to start hiring remote workers in other geographical areas.

Here's the particular challenge that Ahn's dealing with:

"Everything has been all over the place with all the new hiring, and my team is bracing themselves for the switch to virtual classes. I know we should be able to do anything virtually if we design it well, but that's easier said than done.

"You want to know what behavior I'm most concerned with? I'll tell you. It's getting people to USE THE DANG RESOURCES. Right now, if someone has a problem they don't know the answer to, they raise their hand, and a supervisor swings by to help. Most people troubleshoot by leaning over the cubicle of their smartest neighbor. There's no leaning over the cubicle if you're working from home.

"Here's the thing: Everything employees need to know is on the intranet. My team has been making sure that the resource library is very complete. It's all out there, but we haven't had control over the main search pages. Corporate required us to use the company template, which is not set up for the kind of quick reference the call center needs. We've begged and begged, and we finally have the approval to redo the resource page to make it work better for everyone. But I'm afraid that the call center reps are too accustomed to ignoring the resource page and just asking Tim. Everybody always wants to ask Tim. But soon, Tim will be working from home and won't be around to answer questions."

AUDIENCE RESEARCH

Anh obviously knows this audience and environment pretty well, but she talked to stakeholders and call center reps about the changes they would like to see to the resource page.

A few themes emerged from her interviews. Here are some examples of the key things she heard:

From Tim, one of the most senior call center reps, and everybody's go-to person for all the questions:

"I'm looking forward to working from home. My daughter is in an after-school program where they learn about robotics, and if I'm home when she's done, that frees up my wife's schedule a lot. I don't know how this new intranet thing will work out. I hope it's good. They've asked me to help with the design of the new pages, so that's nice. It's definitely going to take a lot of getting used to for everyone."

From Shaima, a rep who has been with the company for a few years:

"I'm looking forward to the work-from-home option, but who are they kidding with the whole thing about the resource page? That's magically going to be usable? Oh sure, I'll believe it when I see it. They are going to have to figure out how we can easily reach a supervisor for questions. Can we all put Tim on speed dial?"

From Rachel, one of the department supervisors:

"I told Anh that they are going to have to put everybody through training for the new resource materials. I don't want everyone asking me all the time, and if they are working remotely, they'll have to know how to do it. They need training."

ANALYSIS RESULTS

Let's look at a summary of the COM-B analysis for one of the key behaviors: using the intranet to find the answers to customer service questions.

COM-B Domains	Observations
Physical Capability	N/A
Psychological Capability	Reps know that the information is on the intranet but may have a hard time finding materials or may not even try because they believe the resource isn't navigable.
Physical Opportunity	The format needs to support easy searching and to provide answers quickly.
Social Opportunity	The social modeling in the current environment has shown employees that asking others (or asking Tim specifically) is the best way to get needed information. In the new remote work environment, it will be difficult to observe others.
Reflective Motivation	Some employees are skeptical about the system and don't believe that the intranet resources are actually useful.
Automatic Motivation	Most of the current reps have habits in place for getting answers. In the new remote work environment, they will need to adjust because they'll lose access to asking coworkers in person and need other ways, like the online support tool, to get information when they need it.

Let's see how certain Behaviour Change Techniques (BCTs) can help Anh design learning resources to support the call center reps.

BEHAVIOUR CHANGE TECHNIQUES

I focus on four categories of techniques in this chapter, but none of these solutions exist in a vacuum, so I'll also pull some techniques that are also discussed in other chapters.

The main categories are

- Environment
- Associations
- Social support

Other categories include

- Shaping knowledge
- Repetition and substitution
- Comparison of outcomes
- Scheduled consequences

Anh already has a basic introduction to the new interface as a planned part of the curriculum:

BCT		
Instruction on how to perform the behavior (BCT 4.1)	Advise or agree on how to perform the behavior (includes "Skills training").	Example: Any form of instructing learners how to do something.

"Yes, we will have a quick intro lesson that shows how the new format works. I don't think it will be too complicated. Learning how it works should be pretty easy. Getting them to remember to use it is the hard part."

ENVIRONMENT

Let's talk about environment. Sometimes, it's easier to fix the environment or the system than it is to fix the person.

I did some work for a client that did product distribution and had large warehouses full of conveyor belts, forklifts, and palette movers. The people who worked in the warehouse understood the traffic patterns and where they could safely walk, but people from the office side who came into the warehouse would not necessarily know where it was safe to walk or stand.

They could have created a training course on warehouse safety for the office staff, but some staff rarely went into the warehouse, and would likely not retain the information over time. Instead, they used red carpet.

Basically, they put red carpet on the pathways in the warehouse where it was safe to walk, and then office staff only had to know "Stay on the red carpet."

The whole discipline of user experience design and service design focus on helping people accomplish behaviors by adjusting products or systems or environments, so I won't dig into those methods here, but for the creation of digital resources, I highly recommend Steve Krug's *Don't Make Me Think, Revisited* (New Riders, 2013) as a starting place.

One of my other favorite examples of "fix the environment, not the person" is the Freedom Trail in Boston. Many tourists want to see the historic sites in Boston, and the tourist board wants to help them do that.

To help people with the "see the sights in Boston" goal, the tourist board could provide maps or smartphone apps or street signs.

Or they could make a big red line.

To see historic Boston, you can start at one end of the Freedom Trail, which is basically a big red line of bricks or paint that you follow. Walk along it and it'll take you to all the most important sights in historic Boston. This is similar to the lines on the floors of some hospitals, airports, or transportation stations, where you can follow a line on the ground to your destination.

So, it's always worth asking yourself if the best solution is training or whether it would be better to fix a difficult or complicated system instead. Basically, can you give users a big red line?

BCT	Restructuring the physical environment (BCT 12.1)	Change (or recommend changing) the physical environment to facilitate performance of the wanted behavior or create barriers to the unwanted behavior.	Example: Advise patients trying to reduce their dietary sodium to have only a small container of salt in the house.

"This is the crucial part. We are promising a lot with the redesign of this site, so we really need to make sure that it works for people. We have been having Tim and some of the other senior people track their most common requests for the last several weeks, and we're using those questions as a starting point. We're also working with one of the designers from the UX (user experience) team to help work on the design and create prototypes we can test with some of the reps."

BCT	Restructuring the social environment (BCT 12.2)	Change (or advise changing) the social environment to facilitate performance of the wanted behavior or create barriers to the unwanted behavior.	Example: To save money, try to minimize time with friends for shopping or eating out and focus on friend activities like hiking or craft projects.

"So, we are talking to the senior folks. The truth is this change really relies on their buy-in. We've involved them in the conversation, and the plan we've come up with is that when they get questions, they'll help redirect people to the site. Instead of saying, 'Here's the answer,' they will say something like, 'Let's see where that is on the intranet,' and help the reps find it."

BCT	Adding objects to the environment (BCT 12.5)	Add objects to the environment to facilitate performance of the behavior.	Example: Provide an attractive toothbrush to improve tooth-brushing technique.

"We are getting swag! I don't know if it will help, but we figured it can't hurt. This is a pretty important change, so we're trying a lot of approaches. We've got a character on the website we are calling AnswerBot, and we are going to have little squishy AnswerBot toys people can keep on their desks as a reminder to ask AnswerBot. AnswerBot's shirt has a QR code that links right into the site."

ASSOCIATIONS

BCT	Prompts/cues (BCT 7.1)	Introduce or define environmental or social stimulus with the purpose of prompting or cueing the behavior. The prompt or cue would normally occur at the time or place of performance.	Example: Put a sticker on the bathroom mirror to remind people to brush their teeth.

"We're putting a lot more prompts into the customer record system that link right into the intranet. They make it easier to jump over to the reference materials, but we hope they'll also remind people to use that option.

"And AnswerBot also is going to help remind them to use the system. Don't tell Tim, but AnswerBot looks just a little bit like him."

SOCIAL SUPPORT

BCT	Social support (unspecified) (BCT 3.1)	Advise on, arrange, or provide social support (for example, from friends, relatives, colleagues, "buddies," or staff) or noncontingent praise or reward for performance of the behavior. It includes encouragement and counselling, but only when it is directed at the behavior.	Example: Arrange for a housemate to encourage continuation with the behavior change program.

"We are pulling Tim and some of the other senior people into the planning of the site. That's mostly because we want their input, but we also hope they can talk about it to the other reps in a positive way, so not all the messages come from training or management."

| BCT | Social support (practical) (BCT 3.2) | Advise on, arrange, or provide practical help (for example, from friends, relatives, colleagues, "buddies," or staff) for performance of the behavior. | Example: Ask family members to help the patient with their physical therapy exercises. |

"We've got several people who will support the rollout, including supporting reps with their first few attempts at using the site."

OTHER BCTS

| BCT | Action planning (BCT 3.2) | Prompt detailed planning of performance of the behavior (must include at least one of context, frequency, duration, and intensity). Context may be environmental (physical or social) or internal (physical, emotional, or cognitive). This can include "implementation intentions." | Example: To exercise more regularly, plan the performance of a particular physical activity (for example, running) at a particular time (such as before work) on certain days of the week. |

"We are going to have the reps think about and make plans for what to do when they have the impulse to look for somebody to ask rather than using the site. If they stand up, scan the room, or raise their hands, that's a cue for them think again, and check the website."

| BCT | Behavioral experiments (BCT 4.4) | Advise on how to identify and test hypotheses about the behavior, its causes, and its consequences by collecting and interpreting data. | Example: A pediatrician counsels a set of parents of preschool-age children on behavioral strategies, uses a periodic survey to measure results compared to other parents, and adjusts their counseling strategy based on results. |

"This is an interesting idea. I think people believe that it will take a lot longer to use the online system than just asking somebody, but we could ask them to hypothesize what the result would be and then test it out for themselves.

"If we could have people viewing it as an experiment as they track how it's going—for example, how often they are successful finding what they need or where the system needs improvement—then I think people might have more buy-in.

"Of course, if the results don't support using the new system, that's a problem. Doing this is probably too complicated for us right now, but it's a really interesting idea."

BCT	Behavioral practice/ rehearsal (BCT 8.1)	Prompt practice or rehearsal of the behavior one or more times in a context or at a time when the performance may not be necessary to increase habit and skill.	Example: To help newly diagnosed diabetic patients get comfortable testing their blood sugar, they can practice going through the process at their doctor's office with help and support.

"Okay, let's face it. People have habits. We are going to need to have them practice the new behavior enough that they get comfortable in the new system. We were thinking about info scavenger hunts. They could play in teams and compete to find the most answers or to find answers the fastest. Anything fun to get them to practice using the system."

BCT	Credible source (BCT 9.1)	Present verbal or visual communication from a credible source in favor of or against the behavior.	Example: Young athletes hear about the importance of drug-free performance from top athletes in their sport.

"Have I already mentioned that Tim is kind of our secret weapon? No one has more credibility with this group, so if he supports the change, that goes a long way."

BCT	Restructuring the social environment (CT 12.2)	Change (or advise changing) the social environment to facilitate performance of the wanted behavior or create barriers to the unwanted behavior.	Example: Identifying social opportunities with friends who like outdoor activities as a way to be more active.

"Right now, several of the senior folks—particularly Tim—get questions because they are walking around helping people. We plan to keep them available as we transfer to the new site but have them be just a bit less available. The hope is that by reducing their availability, we encourage greater reliance on the online resource."

BCT	Remove reward (BCT 14.3)	Arrange for discontinuation of contingent reward following performance of the unwanted behavior (includes "Extinction").	Example: Parents agree that they will not reward tantrums from their child with attention. They'll note the upset, but not encourage it.

"The plan is for our helpful people to gradually be just a bit less helpful and more likely to prompt people to look things up rather than to just give the answer, increasing that over time. They will still help but won't be the source of immediate satisfaction. If people are able to consistently get the answer faster and easier from the system, then I think—hope!—they'll use it."

12

VALUES AND IDENTITY

MEET NATE

Nate is the safety training supervisor with an electrical installation company. His company has been working on a new approach to safety within the organization.

"We've gotten a mandate from the new CEO about creating a safety culture in the organization. When I first heard that, I was a little skeptical. 'Safety culture' sounds a little fuzzy, right? But as we've continued to work through the plan, I've really changed my mind. What our CEO is talking about is everyone participating in safety as a team, not as a set of rules to be enforced.

"I really think we had reached the end of what we could do with a 'command-and-control' approach to safety. Workers would follow the rules because they were the rules, not because they saw the value. And who knows what they were doing when no bosses were around?

"So we want to shift our focus. We want workers to think of safety as one of their skills sets that they can improve, just as they improve their skills at electrical work. We'd like them to identify ways they can get better at safety. But this isn't just a mindset shift for the workers, it's also a shift for the managers.

"Managers tend to think of their main purpose as getting the work done. They're there to drive the task to completion—basically, 'Git it done.' But

211

this new shift means that they need to be more focused on developing their staff. I don't think that's how they see themselves. It's going to be a big change to focus less on 'git it done' and more on 'help this person get better.'"

AUDIENCE ANALYSIS

As part of working with the rest of the team on this change, Nate has gotten a lot of input. Here are examples of some of the key things he's heard from the group.

From Manuela, a senior electrician:

"I've been through all the mandatory safety training, and most of it was stuff I already knew. If this is what we are doing, then I'll participate, but I don't really understand what they mean when they say, 'create a safety skill development plan.' That just means 'take more courses,' right?"

From Jeffrey, a supervisor:

"I'm willing to give this a try, but I'll admit I don't really know what this all is gonna look like. These guys are all about getting the job done, and it's my job to help them do that. I'm worried they'll take one look at all this stuff and roll their eyes. But if it makes things safer, then I'm on board. I hate the idea that somebody could get hurt or killed on my watch, so if this works, then great."

From Cliff, an experienced electrical worker who is new to the company:

"I don't know, man. I'm skeptical. In almost 20 years of doing this, I've seen this stuff before, and it's all words to me. I do my job, I try not to get killed, I try not to get anyone else killed. Isn't that enough?"

ANALYSIS RESULTS

So, actually, we have two audiences we're dealing with: the workers and the super-visors. Let's look at a summary of the COM-B analysis for one of the key behaviors for the workers—participating in creating their own safety development plans.

COM-B Domains	Observations
Physical capability	N/A
Psychological capability	Workers likely don't know what a development plan can look like or how to make the decision about what to add to the plan to pursue.
Physical opportunity	Many of the workers are likely deskless. They work on job sites, so there needs to be an easy way to participate in the activities related to safety development planning.
Social opportunity	The current outlook among the staff seems to be skeptical and lacks social reinforcement of the behavior.
Reflective motivation	Workers see their role regarding safety to be compliance-based and practical. They take the mandatory training, follow the rules, and that meets the expectation. They don't see developing their own safety skills as part of their role.
Automatic motivation	Safety can be very habit driven, so development of safety competencies may require workers to recognize and adjust habits.

Nate then worked with some of the stakeholders to identify intervention functions and look at the overall strategy.

Since Nate has some strategies in mind, he's going to look through relevant Behaviour Change Techniques (BCTs) to see if they would help him design learning or support materials to help the association members.

Let's see how certain BCTs can help Nate design learning materials to support both groups.

BEHAVIOUR CHANGE TECHNIQUES

I focus on two categories of techniques in this chapter, but none of these solutions exist in a vacuum, so I also pull some techniques that are also discussed in other chapters.

Following are the main categories:

- Identity
- Regulation

I also look at some techniques from these categories:

- Environment
- Social support
- Feedback and monitoring

Here's what Nate had to say about the instructional materials:

BCT	Instruction on how to perform a behavior (BCT 4.1)	Advise or agree on how to perform the behavior (includes skills training).	Example: Any form of instructing learners how to do something.

"We are working on a workshop on how to develop safety skills and how to create a development plan. We can't assume they've ever done anything like that before. Most of their training as electricians has been technical school curriculum, certificates, licenses, and hands-on work on the job, but the plan for most of that is pretty much spelled out for them; they just have to sign up. Choosing what they want to work on and creating a development plan is going to be a whole new skill. I honestly think that the workshop is just a first step. It's really going to come down to how management and the organization work with them on it.

"We are also planning a workshop with the managers. Even though they've all supervised many junior employees over the years, I think the idea that they will be coaching development planning is not something they are used to."

IDENTITY

I've referenced the importance of identity and values alignment a few times in this book so far. While it's not impossible to change someone's values or sense of identity, doing so is a much more difficult path than figuring out how a behavior aligns with the identity or values they already have.

For example, if we look at the behavior "exercise regularly," the identity that people have can have a big impact on how they view that behavior. Take this example group, who all work in the client relations department at a large nonprofit organization that recently implemented a team-based health and wellness program. They get points for exercise and steps as a team, and their team is in friendly competition with other teams in the organization.

Let's see how they each feel about that based on their experiences and identities related to exercise:

Sondra: I love the idea of a team challenge. I was a swimmer in college, and there's something really special to me about being part of a team. I know this is just a casual thing—it's nothing like being a college athlete was for me—but I'm really looking forward to it.

Yad: Oh man, I was NOT an athletic kid. I was one of those tall gangly uncoordinated kids. Middle school gym class was purgatory. My buddy and I were the "smart kids," and we used those smarts to figure out how to sneak behind the scoreboard so we could skip some of the torture.

Now that I'm a dad, I'm trying to do better, though. I don't want my kids to grow up with the same hang-ups.

Shanita: I was a really active child when I was growing up. I loved being out in the neighborhood playing pickup games with the other kids. I was also a track and field athlete, and I'm still a runner now. I'm training for a half marathon with a group of girlfriends—running is better for me with friends AND with brunch afterward.

Min: My history with exercise? We got lots of exercise as kids, except we called it work. My parents owned an upholstery business, and it was just expected that as a part of the family, you would help out. Do you know how much a bolt of upholstery fabric weighs? Because I do.

Now, I mostly get exercise while I'm gardening. As a gardener, you get plenty of exercise by putting out a dozen bags of mulch. It's worth it, though. I've won awards for my azaleas.

June: I was never an athlete, but I tried a bunch of things over the years to "get in shape." I tried swimming, running, biking, but was never somebody who could stick with it. I never felt like I was doing it right or well enough. When I would do active things with friends, it was more fun, but I was always the one pulling up the rear. I never liked feeling like I was the one slowing them down or holding them back.

The one thing that I have stuck with is yoga. I really like that the instructors emphasize that you adjust your practice to the place you are now. If your hips aren't that flexible, you just sit on a bolster, and there's no shame in that. I really appreciate that yoga meets me where I am.

When you look at the words everyone has used to describe their identity in relation to exercise, you see quite a spectrum:

- "I was a *swimmer* in college"
- "being *part of a team*"
- "being a *college athlete*"
- "I was *NOT an athletic kid*"
- "My buddy and I were the '*smart kids*'"
- "Now that *I'm a dad,* I'm trying to do better though"
- "I was a *really active child*"
- "I was also a *track & field athlete*, and I'm *still* a runner now"
- "as a *part of the family,* you would *help out*"
- "As a *gardener,* you *get plenty of exercise*"
- "I was *never an athlete...* never somebody who could stick with it"
- "I was always *the one pulling up the rear* ... I was the one slowing them down or holding them back"
- "you adjust your practice to *the place you are now*"
- "Yoga meets me *where I am*"

Clearly some of the team members identify much more closely with physical activity than others, and each person has a different relationship with exercise, which will likely influence their participation in the program. Nike's founder, Bill Bowerman, is quoted as saying, "If you have a body, you are an athlete," which is a great inclusive framing for people who don't typically identify with being an athlete (though whether Nike's ongoing products and messaging support that idea is open for debate).

Interview with Dr. Michelle Segar: How Our Stories Shape Our Identities and Behaviors

I talked to Dr. Michelle Segar, an expert in the science and practice of creating sustainable changes in exercise and self-care at the University of Michigan, train-the-trainer, and the author of *No Sweat* and *The Joy Choice*, which show readers how to make sustainable changes in behavior.

Q: How do you understand people's perspectives about exercise?

I organize them around mind, body, and environment. When I was in graduate school for kinesiology, I looked at the problem that cancer survivors exercised for us, but didn't exercise for themselves. And then I wanted to learn about how to change that mindset.

So I went and got a Masters in Public Health, and it was during that program that I looked at the question "What is the universe of problems that prevent people from sustaining exercise?"

At the psychological level, we know, "it's all in people's heads," but the reality is, is that what's in people's heads about exercise, and the experiences they've had, and the way they've approached it, has all come from society's prescriptions, society's magazines, and so the biggest thing that you need to change is that people have downloaded all that culture into their minds, not willfully, but you just can't escape it.

That has created a whole curriculum in people's heads about what exercise is, what it should look like, how they should do it, how it should feel, and why they should do it. And to a great extent, almost the whole downloaded curriculum sets most people up to fail. What we need to do is download a brand-new curriculum that helps people rethink almost every assumption they have about exercise.

Q: What about the fitness industry, which is also an audience for what you do?

In a way, the fitness industry has represented the people who've been successful with what I call "the old story of exercise behavior change." That old story is what's been successful for a lot of those people in the fitness industry, which is made up of people who are not just passionate about exercise, they've been successful with it. So the gap is I (a fitness professional) love exercise, it makes me feel good about myself, and I just have to power through it. I am disciplined.

There's a big difference between that perspective and someone who's tried and tried and tried and for whom exercise feels punishing, and who has self-perceived failures. It's this huge gap. And the industry is recognizing that they have alienated, to a great extent, the very population they have been wanting to attract as members or clients. I've been helping fitness industry people understand it, and I do have to say that when I talked to personal trainers 20 and 30 years ago, the response was very different then to how they respond now to what I'm saying.

They recognize that the old stories about exercise aren't helping many people. And they are willing to ask themselves, "If I want to be more effective, and if I want to help more people be effective and take better care of themselves, then what do I need to do differently?"

People's beliefs and associations will impact how they engage with the behavior. It's not just whether or not they feel positive about the behavior—it's more about internal motivation, identification, and belief about capabilities. Conversations with the people you are designing for should be part of any behavior-change project, but looking at the words people use to describe themselves and their relationship to the behavior can be very enlightening, and you may need to adjust the message to meet people at the place where they are now.

Identity Examples

I DON'T VERSUS I CAN'T

Researchers (Patrick & Hagtvedt, 2012) found that using a framing of "I don't..." was more predictive of participants action toward a goal than "I can't." For example, participants with a goal of exercising more were more successful if they framed it as "I don't skip my workout" rather than "I can't skip my workout."

The researchers theorized that "that using the "don't" refusal frame is more empowering and is more likely to lead to resistance to temptation than the "can't" refusal frame and that "I don't" is more affirming of willpower and control.

SMOKER/NON-SMOKER IDENTITY

Identities aren't just people's individual perception. They're also about connection to groups of people who share that identity.

In a 2015 paper, researchers described how "stronger smoker group-identity (the extent to which the person identifies with the group of smokers) predicts lower intentions to quit, and that stronger smoker self-identity (thinking of the self as a person who smokes) predicts fewer quit attempts" (Høie, Moan, & Rise, 2010 cited in Meijer, 2015). Researchers found that participants who identified with a non-smoker identity (for example, "I am able to see myself as a non-smoker") were more likely to engage with quitting activities.

DON'T MESS WITH TEXAS

In the mid-1980s, the Texas Department of Transportation (TxDOT)—in an effort to curb littering and reverse escalating trash pickup costs—created an anti-littering campaign targeting the audience they believed most likely to litter: young men in their teens and twenties.

Feeling that more traditional anti-littering messages (for example, Keep America Beautiful) weren't likely to resonate with the target audience, the agency working with the TxDOT created the slogan "Don't Mess with Texas." The campaign became prominent with a TV ad during the Super Bowl featuring musician and guitarist Stevie Ray Vaughn. Subsequent ads featured other Texas notables like musicians Willie Nelson and George Strait, athletes like players from the Dallas Cowboys, and actors like Chuck Norris.

The program is credited with significantly reducing highway litter in the late 1980s and 1990s (although Texas introduced other programs at the same time, such as one of the first "Adopt a Highway" programs). The Don't Mess With

Texas campaign ad has been revised and revamped over the years as they address different audiences.

Rather than trying to change the audience's values about the behavior of littering, the campaign showed them how the behavior of not littering aligned with values they already had around their pride in Texas and being Texan and protecting what was theirs.

BCT	Identification of self as role model (BCT 13.1)	Inform that one's own behavior may be an example to others.	Example: Inform the person that if they eat healthily, they may be setting a good example for their children.

"Some of the really experienced people are also—how should I put this—kind of stuck in their ways. They came up in a different work environment and don't really see why—if it was good enough for them—it's not good enough for these new kids.

"I really think we are going to have to talk to them separately about how they are the role models for most of the younger staff. We need to make it clear that we respect their experience, and that they are crucial to making this initiative work. That's not blowing smoke, either. If they don't buy in, it won't work."

BCT	Framing/ reframing (BCT 13.1)	Suggest the deliberate adoption of a perspective or new perspective on behavior (for example, its purpose) in order to change cognitions or emotions about performing the behavior (includes cognitive structuring).	Example: Suggest that someone consider exercise something they "get" to do rather than something they "have" to do.

"Electricians are very familiar with the apprentice/journeyman/master idea. They also know that there are additional safety certifications, but they see those things as belonging to a path to a safety manager job.

"Safety isn't something they really think about being tiered in the same way that other electrical skills and abilities are. They think of it as 'you meet the standard or you don't.' So I'm going to do an activity were they map the ways that people get better at safety over their careers. They can think about how someone's knowledge and actions change as they get more experienced. If we can reframe it as a skill, rather than a set of compliance activities, that will really help."

BCT	Incompatible beliefs (BCT 13.1)	Draw attention to discrepancies between current or past behavior and self-image to create discomfort (includes cognitive dissonance).	Example: Draw attention to a doctor's liberal use of blood transfusion and their self-identification as a proponent of evidence-based medical practice.

"I want to have an honest conversation about why intentions and actions don't match up. If I ask one of these workers 'What's more important? Saving a few minutes on a job or seeing your kids graduate from high school?' of course they would say seeing their kids grow up and graduate. So if that's the important thing, why don't they always act in a way that supports that?

"We all know the answer: You don't think that this is going to be the time something bad happens, or you aren't thinking an action is all that risky, or you've done it a bunch of times before and gotten away with it. I think it could be a really good conversation to highlight the difference between what they say is important and what their actions say for them. If they are going to buy into this whole process, they need to buy into that idea."

BCT	Valued self-identify (BCT 13.1)	Advise the person to write or complete rating scales about a cherished value or personal strength as a means of affirming the person's identity as part of a behavior-change strategy (includes self-affirmation).	Example: Advise the person to write about their personal strengths before they receive a message advocating the behavior change.

"We are going to have everyone identify their strengths— what makes them good at their jobs or good at other things like hobbies. Basically, what are they proud of? And what skills did they learn and develop? They've learned and developed skills in the past. They can do this too."

BCT	Identity associated with changed behavior (BCT 13.1)	Advise the person to construct a new self-identity as someone who used to engage with the unwanted behavior.	Example: Ask the person to articulate their new identity as an ex-smoker.

"Like a lot of this, I think this is going to need to be a discussion. We need to talk about what this approach looks like and what the identity is for someone who embraces a 'safety culture.' I really think that sense of identity will have to come from them if this is going to work. But I'll need to figure out what set of questions can help guide them and seems straightforward because these are not folks who typically spend a lot of work time pondering their 'sense of identity.'"

REGULATION

BCT	Reduce negative emotions (BCT 11.2)	Advise on ways of reducing negative emotions to facilitate performance of the behavior (includes stress management).	Example: Advise on the use of stress management skills—for example, to reduce anxiety about joining Alcoholics Anonymous.

"Safety problems happen when people are tired or frustrated or overloaded. We've also seen a trend where mistakes happen when people are working alone doing nonstandard tasks. And time pressure is always a risk factor. If you add in general grumpiness over compliance requirements that can sometimes feel a little bit arbitrary, you experience a lot of reluctance that makes you feel like it's okay to skip safety steps, especially when skipping a few steps feels like 'no big deal.' And I think our culture leads people to 'tough it out' rather than admit that they're tired or stressed.

"As long as our audience feels like safety is something that is being done to them, rather than feeling like it's something they are choosing to do, there's going to be some resentment, and we are hoping to reframe that.

"Managing to stay safe when you are fatigued or stressed is a development skill people can practice and get better at, though if you talk to a lot of our folks about 'stress regulation,' they will probably give you a pretty skeptical look. I was reading an article about some of the ways they train soldiers in the military to manage their stress reactions. I'd like to look at whether there's anything we can use from that because I think something that comes from military training will resonate more with our 'tough' audience."

BCT	Conserving mental resources (BCT 11.3)	Advise on ways of minimizing demands on mental resources to facilitate behavior change.	Example: Advise to carry food calorie content information to reduce the burden on memory in making food choices.

"I think it's important we don't overwhelm people with options on how to do their development planning. If we make it sound too complicated, I think they'll just check out and disengage. We are going to start with a fairly simple set of options for people to choose from for their development plans. Ideally, we'd like to end up with them bringing their own ideas to the table, but I don't think that's feasible with this first round. We'll have a fairly basic set of goals and actions they can choose from, and then bring them in six to eight weeks later for a follow-up workshop, and then again a few months after that. I think we'll get there, but we need to keep the process from being too demanding until people have more experience with it."

Other BCTs

BCT			
	Social support (practical) (BCT 3.2)	Advise on, arrange, or provide practical help (for example, from friends, relatives, colleagues, "buddies," or staff) for performance of the behavior.	Example: To stretch more regularly, have a weekly zoom yoga session with friends who are accountability partners.

"The social support and modeling are pretty crucial. That's why we are pulling in the most experienced and most influential folks and involving them in the overall design. If they don't buy in, nobody will.

"In some teams, it's not the most experienced who are the most influential. We did a quick text survey with the teams and asked them who they would probably ask if they had a safety question or issue. A lot of the answers were what we expected, but there were some surprises too, so I'm happy we have those people involved."

BCT			
	Restructuring the environment (BCT 12.1)	Change or advise to change the physical environment to facilitate performance of the wanted behavior or create barriers to the unwanted behavior (other than prompts/cues, rewards, and punishments).	Example: To take vitamins more regularly, put the vitamin bottle next to the coffee maker.

"We know that we'll have to have an easy way to track these plans. Everyone can work on them during the workshops, but most of these workers don't have desks or easy ways to manage paperwork.

"They have service tablets, and we are creating an app on the tablets that will track their plans and goals. We are also designing posters for team stand-ups, where supervisors can track the goals that the teams are working on together. They'll be able to write on the posters with whiteboard markers, and update them as they go. None of this works if they forget about it the moment they walk out of the workshops."

BCT	Goal setting - behavior (BCT 1.1)	Set or agree on a goal defined in terms of the behavior to be achieved.	Example: To save money, plan to cook dinner at home at least three times per week.

"We want people to take ownership for their own development wherever they can, so we are building some opportunities for them to create their own goals and planning. We'd want to help them pick development goals that are attainable and interesting enough to be compelling."

RESOURCES

Meijer, Eline, Winifred A. Gebhardt, Arie Dijkstra, Marc C. Willemsen, and Colette Van Laar. "Quitting smoking: The importance of non-smoker identity in predicting smoking behaviour and responses to a smoking ban." *Psychology & Health* 30, no. 12 (2015): 1387–1409.

Nodjimbadem, Katie. "The Trashy Beginnings of 'Don't Mess With Texas,'" *Smithsonian Magazine*, March 10, 2017, retrieved 3/28/2023, https://www.smithsonianmag.com/history/trashy-beginnings-dont-mess-texas-180962490/.

Patrick, Vanessa M., and Henrik Hagtvedt. "'I don't' versus 'I can't': When empowered refusal motivates goal-directed behavior." *Journal of Consumer Research* 39, no. 2 (2012): 371–381.

Segar, Michelle. *No Sweat: How the Simple Science of Motivation Can Bring You a Lifetime of Fitness* (New York, Amacom, 2015).

Segar, Michelle. *The Joy Choice: How to Finally Achieve Lasting Changes in Eating and Exercise* (New York: Hachette Go, 2022).

Smithson, Nathaniel, "Nike's Mission Statement & Vision Statement (An Analysis)," Updated on June 3, 2022, retrieved 3/28/2023, https://panmore.com/nike-inc-vision-statement-mission-statement.

Wikipedia. 2023. "Don't Mess with Texas." Wikimedia Foundation. Last modified January 27, 2023. https://en.wikipedia.org/wiki/Don%27t_Mess_with_Texas.

13

DESIGNING RESPONSIBLY

(IN WHICH WE CONSIDER THE WELL-BEING OF BOTH THE RIDER AND THE ELEPHANT)

I once gave a talk on techniques to support behavior change. After the talk, someone came up and explained they were looking to encourage the behavior of employees working more than 40 hours per week.

My response:

Umm...

Not one of my more profound moments. But I didn't really know what to say, considering *I didn't think this was a good idea.*

My impression was that the employees were knowledge workers, so it wasn't a situation where paid overtime was likely. People who are exhausted and overworked often have diminished productivity, so in addition to being a bad policy for employees, it was also likely a bad policy for the organization.

I've had more than a few weeks where I've worked more than forty hours (there have been a few while writing this book), but they have always been in service of a goal or objective, not a policy. But mostly I don't work excessive hours because I don't think it accomplishes the right things. (To be fair to the person who asked the question, I may have misunderstood something about what they were trying to do, given that we talked for only a few minutes.)

But it does raise an important issue. Not every behavior is worth changing.

ETHICAL ISSUES WITH BEHAVIOR-CHANGE DESIGN

Behavior-change efforts frequently have a persuasive component or operate at the unconscious level of habits or biases, which we often have less explicit insight into. In my opinion, this heightens the need for us to consider the ethical implications of our design choices.

If we look at steps in a design process, it might look like this:

There are many different design processes in the world, and most of them are different arrangements of the same activities. I expect the material in this book to add to the process that works for you now rather than replacing it altogether. This particular set of steps helps us frame the conversation around ethics, but if you do things a bit differently, then adjust as needed.

At each step, there are some questions I try to consider when I'm working on a behavior change project.

PROBLEM DEFINITION

IS THIS WORTH DOING?

Is the objective a worthwhile one that matches up with the values or mission of the organization or of the people involved? As I mentioned in the previous story, I didn't think the goal of getting people to work more than 40 hours was a goal worth doing, at least based on what I understood about the circumstances. Of course, context matters. In a healthcare emergency, for example, figuring out how to support healthcare workers who are desperately needed more than 40 hours per week may be something that *is* worth doing.

Some goals may have unintended consequences. For many technology platforms, the goal was (and is) creating "engagement," which seems like a reasonable goal. However, on many of the social media platforms, engagement is driven through promoting the most alarmist messages possible. It turns out that fear and anger are engaging, so a goal of engagement (at any cost) may not match up to other values.

If your organization has a mission statement or a set of organizational values, it can be worth asking if this behavior change is aligned with those values. It's also worth watching carefully during implementation to ensure that unintended consequences aren't cropping up.

ARE THE INTERESTS ALIGNED?

In addition to asking whether the goal is aligned with the values of the organization, it's also worth asking if the goals of the organization are aligned with the goals of the people affected by the change. For example, if the goal at a management level is to increase the number of customers served per hour, but the goal at the employee level is to feel good about ensuring they are helping customers, then those goals might not be aligned. Or the goal of the legal department might be avoiding catastrophic legal liability that could bankrupt the company, but the goal of the audience might be getting through the day with minimal paperwork. This question doesn't assume one goal is better than the others, but if interests are misaligned, that is something that needs to be discussed.

We talk about the issue of misaligned incentives in Chapter 7, but sometimes you will be in the position of asking an audience to do something that has no clear benefit for them but has a benefit for the broader organization. It's better to be honest about that rather than pretending it will magically be better for everyone.

ANALYSIS

DO I KNOW MY AUDIENCE WELL ENOUGH?

One of the ways things can go wrong is if you do not understand enough about your target audience. You can build something with the best possible intentions, but if you haven't spent enough time with your audience to understand what they care about and what their reality is like, then you can build things that are counterproductive for everyone.

Several years ago, I worked on a teacher training product. It was designed for the learners to do a short module as part of their lesson prep each week. It turned out, though, that the only way teachers could get paid to do the training was to do it on their in-service day, so they viewed all the modules back to back on a single day, which was not an ideal experience. If we had known that would happen, we would have built it differently.

I had talked to teachers and tried to ask the right questions, but we didn't find out about this issue until the pilot. We were able to make some adjustments, and the training has been revised since then, but it was still initially a failure to understand their context well enough.

AM I PROTECTING THE RESEARCH PARTICIPANTS?

When you do research, such as interviews with members of the target audience or job shadowing, you want them to trust you enough for them to tell you the real story. You want to know how the work actually gets done—not how the work is SUPPOSED to get done. But if you are asking people to be upfront with you about these things, you also need to ensure that they aren't punished for what they're telling you. You can do this by anonymizing results, sharing only summary data, or making sure that the design group and stakeholders agree that the purpose of research isn't to blame and shame.

SOLUTION STRATEGY

IS THIS A SUPPORTABLE STRATEGY?

When you pick a strategy (or strategies), is it based on good science or accepted practice? I'm not opposed to creative solutions, but those solutions should have some basis in evidence-informed practice. If a designer is working on educational materials to help healthcare consumers take their medication regularly, then it is the responsibility of that designer to review the abundant research literature on that topic and not to spend time, money, and patient effort on solutions that are already known to be unsuccessful.

You may be working in an area with little or no existing research. If that's the case, you should have a plan for testing as you work through the design process, so you can eliminate as many dead ends as possible.

IS THIS GOING TO BE TRAUMATIC FOR LEARNERS OR MAKE THEIR LIVES MORE DIFFICULT?

I've worked on a few electrical safety curriculums over the years, so I've been in the room for a few different discussions about "How scary is too scary?" when it comes to showing the consequences of electrical shock. I don't remember much consensus, but it seemed to be somewhere between the cartoonish illustration where you could see the character's skeleton as they got shocked (not scary enough) to actual photos of injured or dead workers (too scary, and inappro- priate for a whole host of reasons). In addition to being inhumane, emotionally overwhelming your audience is a bad learning experience. A small amount of stress in learning can help focus learners' attention, but large amounts of stress can block their ability to take in necessary information and learning.

As highly immersive environments like virtual reality become more prevalent, we are going to need to have ongoing conversations about what are and are not okay experiences to put learners through.

DESIGN

ARE YOU TESTING, EVALUATING, AND ITERATING?

Behavior is complicated stuff, and the likelihood that your very first design pass is going to be exactly right is really, really unlikely. The most common sort of review of learning materials is to have a subject matter expert give you feedback, which is great for ensuring content is technically correct, but it's not enough to tell you whether the materials are producing the right outcomes for behavior change. The best way to judge that is to test solutions with people in the target audience and to iterate on those results. Exactly what type and how much testing is required depends on the project, but a good starting place is the kind of usability testing done by UX researchers, where you watch learners go through the materials to see how they react. Testing probably should go on from there, depending on the type of behavior, but that's a place to start.

ARE YOU AVOIDING DARK PATTERNS?

Dark patterns is a term for deceptive and misleading design strategies. If you've ever found yourself signed up for something you didn't intend on a website or had your personal information used in a way you were unhappy about, you've been subject to dark patterns. *Nudges* has been a popular term in behavioral economics since the book *Nudge* by Richard Thaler and Cass Sunstein was published in 2008, and many nudges are useful, benign, or ineffective, but some forms of nudging can fall in the category of deceptive patterns.

For example, if a human resource department uses defaults (a common nudge) to enroll people for a life insurance benefit automatically unless that person noticed and deliberately opted out, that could come from a well-intentioned place. The benefit could be a really inexpensive bargain for the employee, but if that employee already has coverage through their spouse, it might not be a good program for them. In that example, it would be important to make sure they know they can opt out, and make it easy to do so.

IMPLEMENTATION

SHOULD WE DISCLOSE WHAT IS HAPPENING?

Probably. I was doing workshops for A Very Big Tech Company in several of their locations around the world, and they had free snacks and meals available for all the staff. The company, in an effort to support healthy food choices, had used several different nudges (for example, sugared beverages on the bottom shelf of the refrigerator or vegetables and salads at the beginning of the cafeteria line) to encourage employees to make healthy choices. However you view that strategy (and I've heard reactions that varied from "Wow, that's cool" to "Um, that's not the employer's business and is not okay"), everyone I ever encountered at the company was very aware of the strategy. There may be some instances where it's not possible to disclose (though I can't think of any right now), but you are almost always on sturdier ethical ground if you aren't hiding information or "tricking" your learners.

ARE WE WATCHING FOR ISSUES?

As mentioned earlier, unintended consequences can happen when dealing with the complexities of human behavior. Part of any implementation effort should be some way to monitor outcomes and ensure that we didn't accidentally cause negative outcomes.

ARE YOU WATCHING FOR BIAS IN YOUR PILOT AUDIENCE?

There's a significant conversation happening right now in the social sciences about the limits of test audiences for a lot of research and how that may bias results. If you are an academic psychology researcher at a university, the most abundant audience for research is all the college students right outside your office door, but there are several characteristics of college students that may not be present in more general audiences. Similarly, research that relies on survey response means you're hearing only from people who answer surveys.

Pilot testing in workplaces or organizations may not have these issues, but a common issue I see is that it can be difficult to get pilot materials in front of actual members of the target audience, often due to the cost of "taking people off the floor" or away from their "real jobs."

Aside from the ethical issues of releasing an untested solution to an entire audience, it is very unlikely that a solution for a complex behavior change will work perfectly without some testing and iteration. If stakeholders are unwilling or unable to make people in the target audience available for that testing, then it's important to make the stakeholders aware of the impact that may have on project outcomes.

EVALUATION

HOW DOES DATA COLLECTION IMPACT LEARNER PRIVACY?

The ethical issues associated with data collection and data privacy are beyond the scope of this book, but a behavior-change project should involve collecting data about participants' behavior. At a minimum, you need to have a plan for how you collect, secure, and use that data. Don't encourage people to lie by making outcomes unreasonably punitive. Also, don't take advantage of people being candid; otherwise, they'll learn to tell you whatever won't get them in trouble.

WHAT IF A BAD OUTCOME HAPPENS?

It can be useful to have clear guidelines for the results you're looking for and the ability to pull the plug if needed. I've seen many training efforts over the years where people stake their reputations to get the necessary organizational support to make a training initiative happen. This. Is. Not. Good.

There is too much uncertainty in human behavior. Even with the best evidence base in the world, certain solutions just *may not work* in your particular context. As my friend Karl Fast, an expert in information design, says, "If someone says 'Well, you're the expert,' that is not a compliment. That is setting you up for blame."

These kinds of initiatives should be set up as an opportunity to learn and improve, and that requires the possibility that what you may learn is what *doesn't* work.

KEY QUESTIONS TO ASK

- Is this a worthwhile objective that matches up with the values and missions of the organization?
- Are the goals and objectives aligned with the goals and priorities of the audience?
- Do I understand what my audience values, and do I understand what kind of environment and situation they are dealing with?
- Am I ensuring that the people participating in the research are protected?
- Is the strategy for the solution based on good science or accepted practice?
- Is this experience going to be traumatic for learners?
- Is it going to make the learners' lives more difficult?
- Are we testing our solution before rolling it out?
- Are we using any hidden or deceptive practices?
- Have we considered whether we should disclose to our audience?
- Are you piloting with an appropriate group?
- Does data collection protect learner privacy?
- Is there a plan if things don't go well?

Additional resources on the ethical application of behavior-change interventions are available at https://usablelearning.com/elephant.

RESOURCES

Jun, Gyuchan Thomas, Fernando Carvalho, and Neil Sinclair. "Ethical Issues in Designing Interventions for Behavioural Change" (conference contribution, Loughborough University, Loughborough, UK, March 19, 2018), https://hdl.handle.net/2134/32265.

Organization for Economic Co-operation and Development (OECD). "Tools and Ethics for Applied Behavioural Insights: The BASIC Toolkit" (Paris: OECD Publishing, 2019), https://www.oecd.org/gov/regulatory-policy/tools-and-ethics-for-applied-behavioural-insights-the-basic-toolkit-9ea76a8f-en.htm.

14

PUTTING IT ALL TOGETHER: A CASE EXAMPLE

(IN WHICH THE TEAM PONDERS ALT TEXT AND TACOS)

In this chapter, we take the tools from the previous chapters and work through an example of how this could all play out.

A Few Quick Notes About This Chapter

I want to show a start-to-finish process as best I can, so this case example is going to use pretty much all the tools, models, and check-lists we've already talked about. In the real world, you will probably prioritize some steps, and you may not do everything. What you do will depend on the context of the behavior and importance of the initiative. Your mileage may vary.

Also, the topic of this chapter is about behaviors around improving access to digital materials. This story is a snapshot of where a fictional company is at in a moment in time. The characters are not necessarily accessibility experts, and by the time you are reading this, the best practices and language around accessibility may have changed. I consulted with people more knowledgeable than I am about this topic, but any mistakes are my own. The intention is for this case study to be an example of how the process works, not to be a model of how to implement accessibility, and feel free to let me know if there are any updates that should be made.

MEET RITA

Rita works for Tilija Design, a small media consultancy with 60 employees. They create materials for clients, focused mostly on content marketing. Rita is the human resources person who is most often responsible for staff training initiatives.

The company has just received some sizable contracts with the federal government to do a media and communications plan for a federal agency. Rita is in a meeting about how to prepare for projects, and she's just presented on staffing needs for the contracts.

UNDERSTANDING THE CHALLENGE

DONALD, CEO: Is there anything else we need to address?

RITA, HUMAN RESOURCES: Did you see the requirement about digital content accessibility? We need to make sure we meet the government requirements for accessibility. Really, we should be doing it regardless. I've added knowledge of digital accessibility guidelines to the job descriptions, but does everyone here know how to do that?

MARCUS, LEGAL: That's a good point. There have been some new lawsuits moving through the courts about ensuring that digital content is accessible to people with things like visual, auditory, or physical access needs and so forth. We absolutely need to ensure we get that right if we want to do more government contracts in the future.

DONALD, CEO:	I thought we addressed that. Didn't everybody do a training last year? Are there still issues?
ANISHA, DESIGN DIRECTOR: 	My team knows that all consumer-facing content needs to go through an accessibility review, and we've used a few audit services to ensure we aren't missing anything.
RITA, HUMAN RESOURCES:	It's not just the official consumer-facing content that we need to think about. It really needs to be part of everything we do.
MARCUS, LEGAL:	She's right. Some of the legal cases have talked about social media content, presentations—even some internal paperwork.
ANISHA, DESIGN DIRECTOR:	Whoa, everything? Okay, I see why that would be the right thing to do, but that's a lot more than our people are accustomed to doing. I don't think any-one will disagree, but we need to figure out how we are going to make it happen.
DONALD, CEO:	So the goal is to have a more comprehensive prac-tice around accessibility, and ensure everyone is up to speed and able to execute. Honestly, this is some-thing we should be doing as a modern organization anyway. Rita, why don't you work with Anisha to figure out what the training plan would be and let me know what resources you need. Marcus can help you with legal requirements. We have a few months before the contracts begin to make this change.

CHOOSING THE BEHAVIOR(S)

Anisha and Rita pull in Jeong, the operations person, to brainstorm behaviors for the accessibility initiative.

JEONG:  I go on vacation for a week and you two start a whole new company-wide initiative?

ANISHA: Well, we considered a tacos-for-everyone initiative, but we thought that ensuring our materials are accessible to everyone was more important than tacos.

JEONG: I'm not sure anything is more important than tacos, but I'm on board with this. What is it we are trying to accomplish today?

RITA: Anisha and I agreed that we should roll this out in stages for the next few months. Last year, we gave everyone the whole set of Web Content Accessibility Guidelines (WCAG) all at once, and they just got overwhelmed. If we can get people to build the right habits and add to them over time, they'll be much more consistent.

JEONG: So do we have a defined outcome we are looking for?

ANISHA: I talked to Donald about it a bit more, and we agreed that the goal of the initiative is two things. First, we want to make sure my design team is creating consumer-facing materials that meet the top level of industry-standard practices for accessibility. I think we are already doing an okay job, and we're using an excellent consulting service, but I think we need to better define our standards and improve our internal practices.

Second, we can do better with our nonclient materials. A lot of the content we create in the company, like presentations, social media posts, and blogs for our own materials, doesn't go through anywhere near the same level of scrutiny, and I think our practices are hit or miss there.

RITA: And we don't have anyone in the company who has expressed a specific access need, but if we improve our overall practices for digital materials, it's better for everyone.

JEONG: So to frame our goal, we are defining a standard for client materials, a plan to achieve it, a related standard for internal materials, and a plan for that as well. What's next?

RITA: So we want to prioritize the most crucial behaviors and decide on a plan for how to address them.

JEONG: Ooo, time for sticky notes on the whiteboard? You know how happy that makes me. Almost as happy as tacos.

ANISHA: If we can get this all sorted, the tacos are on me.

BRAINSTORMING

After combing through several resources, they narrow down to a set of likely starting behaviors:

Brainstorm Behaviors

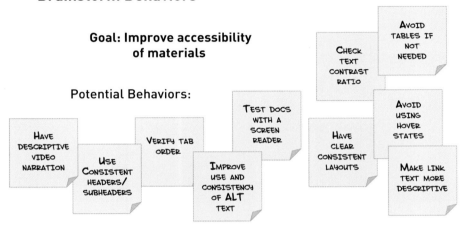

PRIORITIZING

JEONG: How do we prioritize?

RITA: We rate each behavior according to acceptability, practicability, effectiveness, affordability, spill-over effects, and equity.

JEONG: Huh. Practicability must be the fancy British way of saying "is it practical?"

ANISHA: I think you're right. What's the scale?

RITA: We can pick, but let's do 0 to 10 to keep it simple. We should probably research these to score them, but I know we are going to get to all of them, so I think we can go ahead. It's really just about picking the first one to start with.

Behavior	Acceptability (0 to 10)	Practicability (0 to 10)	Effectiveness (0 to 10)	Affordability (0 to 10)	Spill-Over Effects (−5 to +5)	Equity (−5 to +5)
Verify tab order	7	7	8	10	2	4

JEONG: What does this one mean?

RITA: If you are navigating using the tab key on a keyboard, you want the tabbing order to be logical. Usually it's starting at the top left and going down to the bottom right, depending on the content.

ANISHA: This one isn't a bad choice. It could be an option. The web developers check this before they load anything to the site, but we probably could do better in things like the reading order in presentations or digital documents. It's not hard to check, though fixing tab order is finicky depending on what tool you are using to create content.

Behavior	Acceptability	Practicability	Effectiveness	Affordability	Spill-Over Effects	Equity
Avoid using hover states	8	6	2	10	1	3

RITA: What does that even mean?

ANISHA: It's things like rollovers on a web page. Honestly, we aren't using very many of these, and it's not something that will occur by accident. I think I can manage this with my team. People would be fine with it, but it's just not going to have a big impact.

Behavior	Acceptability	Practicability	Effectiveness	Affordability	Spill-Over Effects	Equity
Have descriptive video narration	7	4	6	5	2	4

RITA: I thought we had a policy about closed-captioning all the videos? Are people not doing that?

JEONG: Is it the thing where they describe the other sounds, too? Because I always turn those on when I watch TV. My hearing aids don't always pick up those noises.

ANISHA: Captioning is for people with hearing access needs, but descriptive text is about describing the visuals where needed for people with vision access needs, not just transcribing the words. It's kind of like alt text for videos.

RITA: Would this apply only to people doing video production?

ANISHA: Pretty much. We could also put it into the scripting process, but visuals sometimes change after scripting. If we're willing to pay for it, the service that does our closed-captioning will add this. We can run that by Donald. Regardless, I think it only affects the small number of video production staff, so it's probably not the one we want to start with.

Behavior	Acceptability	Practicability	Effectiveness	Affordability	Spill-Over Effects	Equity
Improve use and consistency of alt text	7	10	10	6	3	5

JEONG: I thought we were already doing this one, too.

ANISHA: On our consumer-facing content, we are. Each image has an alternative text description associated with it to support things like using screen readers to read the description aloud. Though honestly, I'm not that happy with the quality of the alt text we're producing for that. It's pretty stilted and artificial and doesn't always focus on the important part of the image. And it's all over the place for our other content. Sometimes the application autogenerates alt text, and I think our folks think that's good enough. We could do a lot better.

Behavior	Acceptability	Practicability	Effectiveness	Affordability	Spill-Over Effects	Equity
Check text contrast ratio	8	8	8	10	2	4

ANISHA: That's the whole issue of there being enough visual contrast between the text and the background to be readable. We only have the graphics department creating visuals, so we can just focus on working with them on this.

JEONG: Did you see that presentation Marcus did a few weeks ago? It's a good thing he's a good lawyer, because he's never going to make a living doing design work. He picked some monochrome sports car presentation theme, and it had light gray on dark gray text. It looked cool, but was not at all readable. I wish it was just the visuals people doing visuals.

RITA: I thought people were supposed to use the company presentation template. We worked really hard to ensure it has the right contrast ratio. We'll have to remind everyone to use it.

JEONG: Get Donald to remind them. He's good at getting people to listen.

Behavior	Acceptability	Practicability	Effectiveness	Affordability	Spill-Over Effects	Equity
Have clear, consistent layouts	8	7	8	7	5	4

ANISHA: This is another one I would put with the visual design behaviors. This is a good one, but I think we should look at putting these together.

RITA: We probably need to separate the audiences for this. It's one conversation with all the graphics people, and a different conversation with all the "accidental" visual designers. All the rest of the staff need to recognize when they should deviate from the company templates and what they need to do then.

Behavior	Acceptability	Practicability	Effectiveness	Affordability	Spill-Over Effects	Equity
Make link text more descriptive	7	7	7	10	5	4

JEONG: What does this one mean? More adjectives in link text?

ANISHA: This means that if you put a link on a page, the link text says something like "Click to log in to your account" and not just "Click Here!" Also, pasting in plain links without link text can mean that the whole link gets read out to people using screen readers, with all the gibberish numbers and backslashes, so that's pretty unusable.

JEONG: Really? That sounds awful. I need to be way more careful about putting links in emails then.

ANISHA: The same issue applies to marking decorative images with an empty tag so screen readers can skip them. Otherwise, a slew of technical jargon gets read to people with screen readers. It's a horrible user experience. We need to make sure we include that in our revised standards.

RITA: So improve alt text, check contrast ratio, and make link text more descriptive are our top three, then?

Behavior	Acceptability (0 to 10)	Practicability (0 to 10)	Effectiveness (0 to 10)	Affordability (0 to 10)	Spill-Over Effects (−5 to +5)	Equity (−5 to +5)	Total
Improve use and consistency of alt text	7	10	10	6	3	5	41
Check text contrast ratio	8	8	8	10	2	4	40
Make link text more descriptive	7	7	7	10	5	4	40

JEONG: Which one should we start with?

ANISHA: I'd like a bit of time to define our style guide for link text and contrast ratio, so maybe start with the alt text question?

RITA: That sounds good. People have had alt text guidelines since the training last year, so I'd like to know a bit more about why it's not happening consistently. I'm going to talk to some of the staff.

JEONG: I can have somebody do a quick audit of a selection of documents on the main server. That can give us a baseline of where we are now.

ANISHA: I'm interested in the quality question. I'm still not totally happy with the alt text we're getting from the apps or the vendors. I think it's something we should have our own standards for, and I want to make sure we're being as clear as possible about what the expectation is.

DEFINING

To make sure the behavior was clear, Rita defined each part of the behavior:

WHO: Anyone who creates content using images in the organization.

WILL DO WHAT: Will verify images have usable alt tags by either checking the generated alt tag or by writing an alt tag.

TO WHAT EXTENT: On all images likely to be viewed outside the organization.

IN WHAT CONTEXT: Nonclient documents should have a functional alt tag. Client documents should have an alt tag that is verified by review.

FOR WHAT OUTCOME TO OCCUR: 100% of documents and materials that are likely to be viewed outside the organization will have alt tags for images.

JEONG: So we don't care about documents that are just used internally? That doesn't sound right.

RITA: I was talking to a colleague who has dealt with this and she advised us not to try to tackle everything at once. People get overwhelmed. Certainly, we can support people who want to do this with internal documents, and if we can build the habit of checking alt tags, it should spill over for internal documents, but that won't be an explicit goal for now. We can plan on expanding the practice down the road.

RESEARCH AND ANALYSIS

Key points from Rita's conversations:

JON, MEDIA ARTIST:

I've gotten pushback from clients when they don't think alt text should be necessary. I was working on images from a client who builds flight technology, and they flat out told me that a visually impaired person would never be flying the plane. I tried to explain that wasn't the point. You can have other people who need to access the materials for their jobs, even if they aren't pilots, but it would really help to have the account people setting some expectations, so it doesn't come as a surprise to clients.

MIRANDA, WEB DEVELOPER:

One problem I keep seeing is social media posts. People think there's no way to add an alt tag, and then they don't know what to do. Also, I've been asked about the "right" way to describe a picture, but I think it's not like that. The person who added the picture is the one who knows what they are trying to communicate with the image, so the description should communicate that. It's as much an art as it is a science.

ESTHER, COPYWRITER:

I'll admit that I worry about doing it well. I don't really know what "good" looks like. Also, it seems like it works differently in every piece of software. Once something is published, it's enormously difficult to get it updated. You have to figure out and track down the person who has access to updates. Anything we can do about that?

MARCUS, LEGAL:

Don't forget to look at the requirements in the government contracts.
My presentations? Do they really need alt text? Most of those just live on my laptop and never get shared. Except people do sometimes ask me for copies of my slides. Hmm…

WHERE ARE THEY GETTING STUCK?

Rita considers the steps someone might go through as they adopt a new behavior and considers which steps in the change ladder might be relevant for people in the company, though she recognizes that not everyone is going to go through every step.

Step	Rita's Assessment
Doesn't know about it (the behavior)	Everyone knows about the behavior, but they don't necessarily know how to do it well.
Knows about it, but doesn't really get it (doesn't understand why it's important)	I think they get the importance for external content but not for internal content.
Gets it but doesn't really believe it (they aren't convinced)	—
Believes it but has other priorities	This is definitely a factor, particularly if they don't think anyone will actually need the alt text.
Prioritizes it but doesn't know how	Some people need more guidance on how to get started.
Prioritizes it but thinks it's too hard	Often, people believe it's difficult in some of the software platforms.
Prioritizes it but isn't confident	A few people told me they weren't confident they were doing it right.
Is ready but needs help to start	—
Has started but isn't consistent	—
Has been consistent but is struggling to maintain	I didn't hear this from anyone, but I think it's something we should watch out for.

IS IT TRAINING?

Rita uses the checklist to judge if the behavior is not just a training problem. She determines the following issues are relevant:

- Lack of Feedback
- Unclear Goals
- Unlearning an Existing Behavior
- Unawareness of Consequences/Bigger Picture
- Lack of Environment or Process Support
- Social Proof
- Lack of Autonomy/Ownership
- Lack of Identity or Value Alignment

RITA: We definitely need to clarify goals and expectations and have better feedback mechanisms. The systems could be better or have better support references. There are habits to unlearn, and we need to model the right behaviors. I don't think people are resistant to taking ownership, and I'm sure they'd say that this is valuable, but I don't think it's on their radar enough to really think about it as a professional responsibility.

Rita determines the following are less relevant. Although they might apply, they aren't major issues:

- Anxiety/Fear/Discomfort
- Lack of Confidence/Belief About Capabilities
- Mistrust
- Learned Helplessness
- Misaligned Incentives
- Emotional Regulation
- Cognitive Overload

USING COM-B

Rita used the COM-B elements to consider the challenges for the behavior:

Question	Rita's Response
What physical capabilities do workers need to perform this behavior?	I don't think there's any issue with this.
What psychological capabilities do workers need to perform this behavior?	Everybody seems to understand the basics, but there is a lot of confusion about how to do this *well*.
How does the physical environment support the behavior?	Well, the fact that every system manages alt text differently is confusing.
	And with the autogenerated content, it can be pretty tempting to just accept what it says.
	For client or external-facing materials, we also think we may need to tighten up processes to ensure nothing gets released without alt text.
	Also, we aren't setting expectations for clients about how this works, and what information they will need to provide.
	And it will take some extra time to do it well. Not as much as people think, but some extra time.

How does the social environment support the behavior?	It's a problem that people usually can't see what other people are doing for alt text. They don't see what their coworkers are doing, and they should know what the standard is in the industry for high-profile content.
What is the reflective motivation of the workers? For example, do they have goals or beliefs about this?	The people creating client content get it. They are on board and just want to get it right. Internally, there's not nearly as much motivation right now. They just don't have goals, and they don't see this as part of their job competencies.
What automatic motivation (feeling, habits, biases) do you think influences the workers?	There are a lot of habits in play. I think it just doesn't occur to people when they post on social media, or create a presentation deck. I think there's some reluctance about putting out something that isn't right and discomfort about things being unclear sometimes.

INTERVENTION DOMAINS

Rita, Jeong, and Anisha meet up to share their results.

JEONG: I had my intern pull a random-ish sample of documents, and check all the images in each one. They found that client documents are quite compliant—a bit above 90%.

ANISHA: Ninety? I want it higher than that.

JEONG: Something to work on. I'll have them send you the ones that are missing alt text, so you can take a look. For nonclient documents, social media is only about 45%, and internal is more like 15%. That gives us a lot of room to improve, I guess.

RITA: I really think it's going to be an ongoing effort, but at least this gives a starting point to measure against. What did you figure out, Anisha?

ANISHA: We need to have two standards for evaluation. Client content is going to need more scrutiny. Since we are already including that most of the time, that's more about improving the quality. For nonclient documents, I think it can be a little less artful but needs to meet a functional standard. Not bad, but verification will be more about checking that it's there and that it meets functional requirements.

Rita, Anisha, and Jeong look at the list of invention domains and discuss which ones might be relevant:

- Education
- Training
- Persuasion

- Modelling
- Incentivization
- Coercion
- Restriction
- Environmental Restructuring
- Enablement

The team starts by looking at an item each from capability, opportunity, and motivation.

CAPABILITY ITEM: CONFUSION ON HOW TO DO IT WELL

JEONG: So we identified the capability issue that everyone knows the basics, but there is a lot of confusion about how to do this *well*. What types of interventions are relevant there?

RITA: We know that there will be an education and training component. I'm talking to that firm that does accessibility reviews and has a training curriculum we can customize for our own purposes.

ANISHA: I also think that modeling will come into play. We need to figure out how to make good examples visible to people. That also addresses the social opportunity issue we identified.

JEONG: Also, there should be a way that they could get quick feedback on their alt text if needed. I guess that would be enablement?

OPPORTUNITY ITEM: TIGHTENING THE PROCESS FOR CLIENT OR EXTERNAL-FACING MATERIALS.

ANISHA: I also want to look at how we can ensure nothing gets released externally without alt text.

JEONG: That's probably restriction. Can we talk about whether we want to restrict who can publish certain types of content? Right now, several different people can put up a blog post or a media post. I think those people should still be able to write that content, but if we limit who can actually publish things, then the person publishing can screen for good alt text before posting things.

ANISHA: I also think having a clear policy about how to do social media posts will help, too.

JEONG: And we want the technical environment to support the process. I'm actually looking forward to digging into the software issues. You know I take great joy in a well-optimized technology infrastructure.

RITA: This is why we love you. It's all yours, though I can help with some of the support materials.

MOTIVATION ITEM: CURRENT HABITS AROUND ALT TEXT

RITA: People have habits around how they do this now. We probably need to convince people to stop and consider things, rather than breezing through it.

ANISHA: Persuasion would likely be around the importance of this for internal documents. I don't really see us using rewards, but we likely need to have some consequences for not doing it. I would expect to give people time to get used to it, but then it would need to be a consistent behavior, or there would be some kind of consequence. That's the coercion domain, isn't it? That sounds kind of dire, but it's important for people to know we are serious about this.

The team then works through the remainder of the items in the COM-B analysis.

BCT SELECTION

Jeong, Anisha, and Rita sort through the Behavior Change Techniques (BCT) taxonomy techniques and identify ones that they feel are relevant.

CAPABILITY ITEM: CONFUSION ON HOW TO DO IT WELL

- Instruction on how to perform the behavior
- Demonstration of the behavior
- Social support (practical)
- Feedback on behavior
- Self-monitoring of behavior
- Social comparison

RITA: I'm planning to do a workshop on writing good alt text. We gave everybody the guidelines, but there's still a lot of confusion about what "good" looks like. We'll want to have a mechanism for checking and providing feedback. I'm thinking we'll do a buddy system for everyone after the workshop, so they have someone to run stuff by for the first few weeks. It'll provide some social accountability and give people a second set of eyes on things.

ANISHA: I'm also planning to do reviews of alt text with my team, so everybody can see what everybody else is doing and get help or examples for confusing situations.

OPPORTUNITY ITEM: TIGHTENING THE PROCESS FOR CLIENT OR EXTERNAL-FACING MATERIALS

- Goal setting
- Identity associated with change behavior
- Punishment
- Restructuring the environment

ANISHA: I think the most important things I see are establishing clear standards and helping the content writers and design folks to see this as part of their professional skill set. This should be something to take pride in as part of their professional identity—not a compliance requirement to be checked off.

My plan is to work with my design staff to all participate in the creation of standards for this, and in the process, make sure everyone can see what everyone else is doing. I think if it's a joint activity, they'll take more ownership. From that, we can establish standards, which will probably need updating over time.

"Punishment" sounds really harsh. I don't mean it that way, but there do have to be consequences for not doing it. I don't want to be an evil, mean boss, but it's not optional.

JEONG: Like I said, I'm going to work on the technology process, and Rita and I are going to make sure we've got good reference materials for all the different technology formats. There's a lot out in the world, so we should be able to leverage and curate existing resources for a lot of it.

MOTIVATION ITEM: CURRENT HABITS AROUND ALT TEXT

- Behavioral practice
- Habit formation
- Feedback on behavior
- Action planning

JEONG: I'm also going to look at a reminder strategy for refreshing their memories about it and to make sure they don't start strong and fade away. We can use some of the things my intern pulled to create small practice challenges. And we already talked about limiting who can hit the publish button on things, so there's an extra level of checking before things go live.

RITA: I want to have an activity in the training around identifying the cues that tell them they need to pay attention and have them think about their plan for taking action.

ANISHA: I'll reinforce it in team meetings, and we will want to spot-check documents and other materials for the next few months, so they know we are paying attention and following through.

LEARNING STRATEGY

Jeong, Anisha, and Rita talk through the learning strategies they want to use:

- Prelearning
- Learning activities
- Practice/experience
- Feedback, coaching, and mentoring
- Job aid, resources, and just-in-time learning
- Refreshing activities
- Further development

PRELEARNING

RITA: I'm thinking about a prelearning activity where participants find four of the last few things they did that had images. It could be social media posts, documents, presentations, whatever. They can post them to the training server. We do a check through all the materials and then have a total of which items have good alt text, which have any alt text, and which don't, and we'll use those totals at the beginning of the workshop.

LEARNING

ANISHA: I want the design staff to go through Rita's workshop, but then as a follow-up, I want them to do their own research into good alt text. Then we can have a brainstorming and design meeting where we create our shared set of standards.

RITA: That would be great. We will do some practice activities in the workshop. They can start out evaluating examples, and then create their own.

RITA: I'd also like to give them the experience of how poorly designed materials feel to people using assistive technology. I'm talking to that firm that does accessibility reviews and has a training curriculum we can customize for our own purposes. I'm hoping we can get or record some reviews of not-so-good examples, so our people can really understand the consequences.

PRACTICE/EXPERIENCE

JEONG: My intern has been building a nice pile of materials that need to be better. We can use them as practice activities during and after the training.

FEEDBACK, COACHING, AND MENTORING

RITA: So the plan is to have people paired in buddy system after the training program. Basically, they'll check in weekly for four to six weeks and review each other's work using alt text. If we see an issue, like someone not doing it, we can also pull in their buddy to see what happened.

RITA: I'll also be available as a resource, and Jeong's intern will periodically pull documents and materials that Jeong and I can spot-check to verify.

JOB AIDS, RESOURCES, AND JUST-IN-TIME LEARNING

RITA: The vendor has some good resources we can make available for just-in-time learning. Also, Jeong has the list of software products we need to support. His intern has also been saving all the help pages with instructions for each software product on how to add alt text to images. It's a bit of a mess, so it's on my list to clean it all up and make it more usable for our folks.

REFRESHING ACTIVITIES

JEONG: It turns out that our learning management platform has a reminder function! I vaguely remember that feature from the demos but had kind of forgotten about it. I thought I was just going to use email, but I can send out a monthly mini-challenge from the system as a reminder. I'm thinking I can send out the weirdest stock images I can find and ask people to submit their best alt text for them. That will be a little more fun than just describing boring regular stock art. Between that and updates on the spot-checks, we can keep it more top of mind for people. It's a process, not an event, right?

FURTHER DEVELOPMENT

ANISHA: I want the design group working together on this to just be the first part of developing our universal design practice as an agency. Rita,

I looked at the link you sent for the curriculum, and it looks like people can access a lot of that if they want to level up their skills. Also, we can lay out how we're going to address other behaviors and create a road map going forward.

FORMAT SELECTION

Rita went through each section of the learning strategy map and documented the formats for each part:

Section	Format
Prelearning	Email request
	Shared server location for files
Learning activities	In-person workshop
	Virtual workshop
	Design meetings (in person)
Practice/experience	Shared documents for examples and to track buddy assignments
Feedback, coaching, and mentoring	Tracking document for spot-checks
Job aid, resources, and just-in-time learning	Internal web pages with links to resources and reference materials
	Access to vendor materials
Refreshing activities	Reminder requests in learning management system sent via email/text
Further development	Access to vendor materials

IMPLEMENTATION PLANNING

Rita and Jeong work on a rollout plan for the effort.

RITA: We need a project plan for materials collection and creation, as well as an overall class schedule.

JEONG: We do need to have a pilot test to work out some of the bugs, too. Do you want to put together a list of six to eight people for that? I'll work on a plan for spot-checks and follow-ups. Do you want me to own that?

RITA: For the first six weeks, probably. After that, we can work with Anisha and her team.

JEONG: Do we have target criteria for success?

RITA: Anisha wants 100% for client-facing material and is going to evaluate against the rubric she and her team are going to devise. She's got her own timeline for that. I'm going to present the overall plan to Donald on Thursday and want to see what he says about the target for internal materials. I'm going to propose 80% as a target for the first three months, with a plan to reconvene at the three-month mark to look at how it's going. We can adjust and set additional goals from there.

EVALUATION

Jeong, Anisha, and Rita agree on the following measures:

- Quality of alt text based on spot-checks and design reviews, evaluated monthly for the first six months.
- Consistency of use, based on audits, spot-checks, and pair self-report.
- Attitude toward importance of alt text usage, measured with a pre/post attitudinal survey, and outcomes of design group discussions.

WRAP UP

JEONG: Well, it's a plan! Are you going to present it to Donald?

RITA: I am. I've been keeping him updated, and he's already approved contracting with the vendor for class materials. I'm ready to get started.

ANISHA: I think engaging the design staff on this will be really worthwhile. Good design should include making content work for everyone in the audience.

JEONG: You know what this means, right? It means that Anisha owes us tacos!

RESOURCES

Bailey, Eric. "The Importance of Manual Accessibility Testing," *Smashing Magazine*, September 12, 2018, https://www.smashingmagazine.com/2018/09/importance-manual-accessibility-testing/.

Pun, Karwai. "Dos and Don'ts on Designing for Accessibility," *Accessibility in Government* (blog), GOV.UK, September 2, 2016, https://accessibility.blog.gov.uk/2016/09/02/dos-and-donts-on-designing-for-accessibility/.

W3C Web Accessibility Initiative (WAI). "Images Tutorial," February 8, 2022, https://www.w3.org/WAI/tutorials/images/.

15

REAL-WORLD EXAMPLES

There are many, many design processes in the world, and—in my opinion—behavioral design is usually something to incorporate into your design process rather than an additional process to add to the mix. You should be able to leverage the behavioral design elements in this book regardless of what design process you are currently using.

That said, there are some parts of doing behavior design that are—also in my opinion—nonnegotiable if your goal is an effective behavioral solution.

An effective behavioral solution needs to have the following things:

- **Good problem definition, with outcomes and behaviors:** Make sure you understand what the underlying reasons are for stakeholders to be spending money or effort—what problem or challenge they are trying to address—and what actual behaviors will address that problem or challenge.
- **Analysis research with actual people in your audience:** Talking to the elephant only works if you really understand what the elephant cares about. YOU CANNOT ASSUME YOU KNOW THIS. Even the best and most aware stakeholders are filtering this through their own lens. Talk to actual people in your audience. Ideally, spend some time following them around in their own world to see what their hassles, joys, and frustrations look like.

- **Solution strategy:** Don't start with the strategy, start with the problem, and make sure you are asking the right questions to analyze it before you map to solutions.
- **Design prototyping and testing:** To test things, you need something you CAN test. This is where prototyping comes in. If you take a solution all the way through to final production without testing the design, it's likely going to be too costly and too complicated to undo if it doesn't work out well.
- **Implementation: User testing and piloting:** Try things out with actual users if you can. The case studies in this chapter have lots of different examples of how to test things with people in your audience. You can usability test a resource over video call, run a test pilot with time to make changes afterward, or use a combination of methods.
- **Evaluation: Measurement:** Try to figure out how to gather data on the efficacy of the solution. What measure will change if you are successful, and how do you access that? If you can't get data from the whole audience, look at small-scale testing or following a cohort subset of users about whom you can get data.

A friend of mine jokes that almost a decade in graduate school mostly qualifies her to get paid a lot to say, "It depends," with great authority, but behavior design challenges have so many variables that the right process for analysis, design, and implementation is very much an "it depends" situation.

I talked to Roberta Dombrowski (research advisor and coach at Learn Mindfully), who has a lot of expertise in both learning design and user research about how she determines a research approach:

> "The format of the analysis is going to depend on the questions that we're focused on. I think about the level of rigor and the level of risk related to the decision-making.
>
> "So if it's a high-risk decision, I'm going to want more data, and I might do multiple studies. I might do surveys and market analysis and multiple rounds of customer interviews with prototype testing. If it's a lower-risk decision, I might need less rigor and analysis but also the speed of learning is much quicker."

So given that the right solution to a behavioral-change challenge is usually "it depends," I wanted to talk to some of the people doing really interesting work in this space, so you can see some of the different ways they tackle their particular challenges. The rest of this chapter is those conversations.

PROJECT 1: BUILDING WOMEN'S ENTREPRENEURIAL SKILLS IN RWANDA

Who: Picture Impact is a user-centered social design studio that creates (among other things) learning experiences for diverse learners, including innovative materials for low-literacy audiences. I originally met the principals, Katrina Mitchell and Anna Martin, several years ago, and I've followed their work with interest.

What: In this interview, I talked to Katrina about a business skills/entrepreneurship curriculum they worked on for rural women in Rwanda. The curriculum was developed to be delivered by local facilitators.

Q: CAN YOU DESCRIBE THE PROJECT?

In 2022, we worked with Land O'Lakes Venture37 and a team of skilled facilitators to create and pilot a business training program with and for rural women who are members of agricultural cooperatives in Rwanda.

The learning content was geared to the identified needs and interests of these women, based on extensive discussions and intensive work over a period of three years with these cooperatives and women. The training aimed to increase women's confidence and capability not just in business through hands-on activities and identifying and practicing key competencies and was a part of understanding how gender plays a role in business and leadership.

Q: CAN YOU TELL ME HOW YOU FORMULATED GOALS FOR USER RESEARCH?

From the beginning, we developed some frameworks for understanding the impact that the women would have with these skills in their personal life, in their community life, in their cooperative life. We asked ourselves what will doing this curriculum give them—what would it afford them? What will they be able to do afterward that they couldn't do before?

So we might say that one of the impacts that we want to have in this curriculum is that a woman could have better relationships with their partner, their husband, or better relationships in their community, or more leadership at the cooperative. Then when we're designing the materials, we're integrating those things in an explicit way, asking things like, "OK, how would you share this lesson in the cooperative?"

We are asking how the learners use these ideas. Things like, "Oh, this is really great. How does this show up in your relationship with your husband?" or "Here's budgeting for business. How do you budget in your household? How do you both make decisions about that?"

These are things we want to know at the beginning, and we want to see if it changes at the end. For example, we asked the women about how confident they felt in speaking up in groups. That's a leadership thing that you can see now. It's a simple thing, but many of the women have never spoken up in a group, and then they got all this practice during the learning to do it.

Q: WHAT ARE YOU LISTENING FOR WHEN YOU TALK TO PEOPLE IN THE AUDIENCE?

We want to know where people are now. What's important to them? How can we understand their life better, their life today? What barriers do they face? What opportunities are there?

You also want to understand what they already know. Because you don't want to tell people something they already know. That's a great way to disengage people right away, and you also don't want to train at such a high level that the gap is too big for them to step into because that's also disengaging. So we want to get it as close as possible to where they're at now and just a tiny bit further—that doable step.

Q: WHAT ELSE DO YOU LOOK FOR?

We're listening for their capacity to take in information. We want to listen for how they take in information and how they learn in other contexts, and what are some of those modalities that they use? We're certainly listening for most of the parts of COM-B and are trying to understand what the cultural barriers are.

What are some of the cultural hooks? What are those motivations? Who are they influenced by in their community, and why those people? But ultimately, then we have to ask, "Where do we want people to be and what does that gap look like and how big, how wide is that gap?"

So, for example, what do they already know that we can reasonably take off the table? Do we have to teach them numeracy as part of budgeting? Because that could pretty much take up all 12 sessions. If they don't have numeracy, is there a way we teach budgeting without numeracy? Can we teach them the concept of budgeting? Enough that it's useful to them?

And then, really what are we working with in a very concrete sense? What is their literacy level? How familiar are they with reading and writing? How have they taken in information before? Have they ever been in a classroom before? Do they have positive feelings about a classroom? Or are we going to have to deal with some classroom trauma? We want to understand their prior learning experiences.

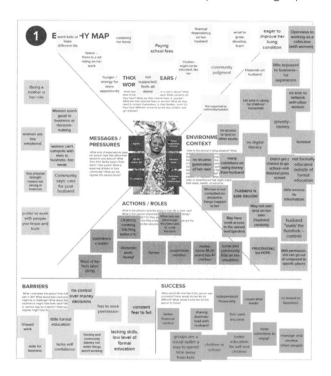

Q: HOW DO YOU DO INTERVIEWS?

Because it's about building a relationship, one-on-one interviews is often a go-to format for us, both for ethical reasons and for getting good information. We don't do what we call clipboard-style interviews, so we are not going to go in with a clipboard and formal notetaking. If we're in a relationship with the person, we want it to be a conversation.

We can't always manage it, but we like to develop interactive interviews. By interactive, I mean we'll create something to interact with in the interview. So it might be a set of characters. We'll have pictures of a set of characters, and we'll ask them to tell a story about those characters.

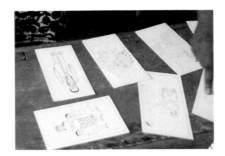

We'll set it up, "Here you see this new mom, and she's been told by the health provider that she should exclusively breastfeed, but here her mother-in-law comes in, and her mother-in-law says, 'Oh no. You need to give that baby water.' What does she do?" And then we ask them to tell us a story.

We might also ask them to tell us about their experience on a timeline. When we were talking to people about their experience with Wi-Fi use, we said "Tell me about your whole history with Wi-Fi. When's the first time you accessed Wi-Fi, and where were you sitting? And tell me about the next, and so on." You get a rich picture of people's history with something.

Or we might have sorting or trade-off games. It's really powerful to give people something to interact with that's not theoretical—not just in their mind—but is actually physical that they can interact with.

Q: YOU USE A LOT OF STORIES IN BOTH YOUR RESEARCH AND YOUR MATERIALS?

The way we talk about it, is that very few people—very few minds—work from abstract to concrete. Mostly our minds work from concrete to abstract, and so we use a story to get super concrete. So we might say, "Here's the abstract business concept of profit. Let's look at a story to get super concrete, and then we can go back to abstract."

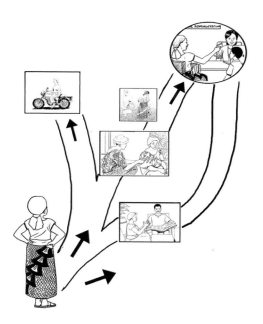

Q: YOU DON'T USE FOCUS GROUPS. WHY IS THAT?

We almost never do what people call focus groups. Mostly focus groups are a shorthand people use for a group interview. And a group interview is a waste of time for everybody. If what you really need is 10 people's opinion about something, you should have 10 interviews. Even if they're just 10-minute interviews, that's still a better use of those.

Otherwise, often 50 minutes of somebody's time is wasted while one person answers the question.

The only time to use a focus group—really a group dialogue—is when you're looking at interpersonal dynamics. For example, you could use it if you want to see how the group interacts with an idea, or how they build on or talk to each other about it.

Q: HOW DO YOU TEST CLASSROOM MATERIALS?

We actually do materials testing at three discreet times within a project.

One is within the initial user conversations: We pretest existing materials. What we do is we bring a wide variety of sample materials that are relevant to this project. For example, if we were going to do a curriculum for entrepreneurship, we bring worksheets and printouts, a module or two here and there from other kinds of materials; we'll also bring images, illustrations, and all kinds of things into that conversation to see how people react to them. Is this something they can fill out? We might create a false thing where we say, "Here's a worksheet, can you fill this out for me?" or, "Here's a thing; can you tell me what this story says?"

We want to see how they're interacting with materials right away because we know we're going to make materials for them. We want to know, how do they respond to them? Does it need to be in color? Does it need to be black and white? How much language are they actually going to fill in the materials?

Second, we test along the development process. We do some pretty specific testing with the actual users, and we usually test the images. When our work is really image heavy, we'll test the actual images, and we often anticipate that about 50% of the images they read super easily, and about another 30% they could understand if you told them what it was. And then there's 20% that they don't recognize, and with facilitation, they still are like, "I don't get it." So we will redo the 20% first, and then we might look at the other 30% if we have time.

And the third form of testing is really funny—we get pushback every single time this happens—we have facilitator training/train-the-trainer with draft materials, so we can still make changes after the train-the-trainer.

The facilitators thought it was just crazy. We don't have finished materials, and we have to deliver this in two weeks? And, of course, like five minutes into training, they're just like, this doesn't work quite the way that I thought it would work. And I was like, great, let's fix it before you deliver. And they're like, oh my gosh. Can you fix before we start with the women? Yes! Facilitator training is the best testing environment. If it doesn't work in train-the-trainer, then it won't work in the actual class. We encourage them to rip it up, and it's a great way to get bugs out and so on.

Q: TELL ME ABOUT SUPPORT MATERIALS FOR LOW-LITERACY LEARNERS.

Learners need great information. They need materials. And on this we sometimes feel like broken records, right? Just because we work often in a low-literacy context, they're like, "You can't give them a handout because that's written information."

We're like, why is it written? It could be pictures, couldn't it? What could we give them that will help them remember the material? Explicitly share the material with somebody in their household? What helps them reteach it? These people are so excited about the learning that they're doing, and they're so excited to teach it to others, right? We want to give them materials that support them sharing the information with others.

So we want to really be able to structure that and support that. You learn the thing in the class, but you've got to practice it next. You better give them some home-work—some things to do so that they can go and practice and build the actual skills.

We also ask, "Do you need a buddy?" Because a lot of people learn better when they have a buddy. And do you want to build that specifically into your program, so that people have that kind of learning support? These are all things we consider in the design of materials.

Q: CAN YOU GIVE US AN EXAMPLE OF HOW YOU DO DATA COLLECTION?

We did some quizzes, and some other things. We took pictures of their handbooks, for example. They didn't hand them in; they kept them, so we wanted to capture a record. They wrote in their own language, so we couldn't understand it without getting it translated, but what we could see was how much engagement there was across the different pages. If nobody wrote on a particular page, we knew that it probably needs to be changed next time, that kind of thing.

Q: WHAT WERE SOME OF THE OUTCOMES?

We have the results of the pilot. Almost all of the women reported an increase in confidence of both their business and decision-making and speaking within their household. Most of the women also reported an increase in leadership in their businesses and households. And most of the women reported an increase in behaviors like recording business transactions and separating their business and personal money.

We also found that gender impacts all aspects of business and leadership in this setting. There wasn't one issue that didn't have some gendered aspect to it—these barriers or challenges that women face every step of the way in seeking to provide a better life for their family, for themselves.

Q: IS THERE SOMEWHERE PEOPLE CAN LEARN MORE ABOUT THIS PROJECT?

Yes! This work was done in collaboration with Land O' Lakes Venture37 under the USAID-funded Cooperative Development Program. The Venture37 team is actively seeking partners for this work now and in the future. A full research report, a number of briefs, and information on this work are available from the Rwanda team. People can reach out through the Venture37 website at https://www.landolakesventure37.org/.   ∎

PROJECT 2: MINDGYM LEADERSHIP DEVELOPMENT

Who: Sebastian Bailey, PhD, is the cofounder and president of MindGym (https://themindgym.com/), a company that builds behavior-change programs based on behavioral science and research. I first encountered Sebastian's work several years ago at the ATD (Association for Talent Development) International Conference and Expo.

He was one of the few people I'd encountered in the field of learning and development at the time who was leveraging behavioral science as part of the design of learning programs. I particularly appreciated that he was able to explain the relevant research in a comprehensible way and show how that research informed the design of MindGym's offerings.

What: I interviewed Sebastian about how behavioral research and design models like COM-B influence the work MindGym does in leadership development.

Q: HOW SHOULD WE BE USING BEHAVIORAL SCIENCE TO INFORM LEARNING DESIGN?

I guess the place to start is the expression of the problem, which is how do you create sustained change to behavior, specifically in organizations? My PhD was on learning transfer, which I think is another way of saying behavior change. And when you look at quite a lot of the research (with the caveat that the methodologies behind the research are not always the strongest), you tend to find that the actual transfer rate, the likelihood of a sustained change to behavior, is pretty low.

When I did my PhD, I initially looked at a few questions. First, do they have full psychological engagement around the problem? Because actually, if people care about the problem, on the whole they'll look for ways to solve it. And then there's the question of whether they are actively participating in a community of practice to better understand or build their solution set. And then, finally, are they activating their prior learning appropriately?

I wanted to take a much more user-centric approach to describing behavior change because often the metaphor that learning and development professionals tend to use is one of "transporting knowledge." That's the idea that learning experiences are primarily about transporting knowledge from one place to the other. It's the knowledge that's moving, instead of being more oriented on the individual and asking, "Has the person recognized that this is an opportunity to activate their appropriate prior learning and use this behavior?"

We got so many issues where we've got the wrong metaphor being used, and that idea doesn't structure the learning experience around the person whose behavior needs to change. In my PhD, I addressed that, but then I came across COM-B, which I think is really good work. It has the systematic approach to mapping the issues, to talking about the kinds of interventions and the blockers (things that are blocking the behavior) and then applying different kinds of interventions. We've actually had quite a few people who trained with Dr. Susan Michie (main creator of the COM-B model) and they've done the behavioral science courses at UCL (University College London). They've brought those methods into the company.

We've used it in a number of different places and continue to use it because it's useful language. I also like the simplicity of the model. It's not too complicated at the surface level.

Q: CAN YOU SHARE A FEW EXAMPLES OF WHERE AND HOW COM-B WAS USEFUL?

We do specific research to identify what the blockers are to a behavior for a particular population, and we use the COM-B framework to analyze the behaviors.

So, for example, we were working with a client on management and leadership topics and looked specifically at the behaviors around giving and receiving feedback. With that client, there was quite a clear case of capability not being the issue. Actually, we discovered in the analysis that the real blockers were issues with motivation and social opportunity.

There were two components. One was low motivation. People believed that if I give this feedback, there's going to be a really negative long-term consequence on my relationship and on my career. And there was a social opportunity blocker because no one in leadership was modeling these particular behaviors. Once we identified those blockers, we designed and deployed our interventions, which we describe as behavior-change assets.

Q: WHAT IS A BEHAVIOR-CHANGE ASSET?

It's become a useful description of materials. So, for example, an asset can be anything from a poster to an email to a 5-minute how-to animated explainer all the way through to a 90-minute interactive training session on something like a three-step tool to express your feedback better, whatever it happens to be. Each asset could sit in a number of categories: communications or persuasion, education, enablement, environmental, or role-modeling.

We think about, first of all, what's the blocker of the behavior? And then we think about what kind of category or combination of categories of intervention are likely to work practically. And then we consider which assets should we deploy. Some of those are assets we have already designed, but often we have a series of them we design specifically for the client.

So for the client I mentioned, the intervention was first expressing to leaders that they needed to make small changes to their own behavior, like just changing parts of their conversation to support feedback.

For example, we had them try to develop a habit at the end of every meeting—have a quick review, invite self-reflection, invite some feedback, and then do some self-reflection. Don't do evaluative feedback; just do a couple of observations—e.g., this is what I observed. That was where we started with that client.

Q: SO IT'S IMPORTANT TO ADAPT YOUR APPROACH DEPENDING ON THE NEEDS OF THE CLIENT?

Yes. With a different client on the same topic of feedback, it was actually capability that was much lower. If capability is low, then the person is not confident about the fact they're going to be able to do it well, and they don't have a plan for it. Then they're unlikely to be motivated, and they're unlikely to recognize the opportunity. So with that client, it was much more about capability building to begin with. Because this was kind of a new muscle for them, we focused on aspects of the social opportunity as well. So, for example, we looked at questions like how do we build this into town halls? How do we do a small communications campaign around this? How do we get leaders to speak to some of these points?

So if I go back to COM-B, there was a capability issue, there was a motivation issue, and there was an opportunity issue. We started off with the component that leaders in particular need to role model. What we also found was that people would really respond to their peers' behavior. So we built a group of changemakers. And actually, with those changemakers, we train them in COM-B a little bit, so they could continue to develop their own behaviors in the organization.

Q: YOU MENTIONED THE IDEA OF HABIT LABS. WHAT IS THAT?

With some clients, we also said to them, can you help us become experimenters around behavior change? We then got them to come up with some of the behavior-change interventions to run as experiments within the organization and then report back on the results—whether or not the experiments worked. And then we work with them to generalize the interventions that started to work, and roll those interventions out to the rest of the organization.

Imagine if you put together behavioral science, user-centered design, and also grassroots change, then you would end up with what we call habit labs.

I really like it because you get this groundswell of positive experimentation and change, and people are really willing to just try stuff out. So they try it, and then you can ask, "Can you try measuring it in these ways?" And then they come back and they say, "Here's what worked, and here's what didn't work at all." That's brilliant because then we've done our field experiment on this behavioral change intervention. Then we can discard the ones that didn't work and put the resources into the ones that did work and look to scale and generalize. ■

PROJECT 3: SPORT INTEGRITY AUSTRALIA— ANTI-DOPING EDUCATION FOR ATHLETES

Who: Director of Education Alexis Cooper and Assistant Director–Resources Shelly Chard are from Sport Integrity Australia, the group that works to ensure sport in Australia is fair and clean, which includes anti-doping testing and education.

What: Alexis and Shelly and the rest of their team have been working on a series of innovative educational experiences and resources to support athletes, including materials to help prevent inadvertent doping through mistakenly taking a banned supplement or other substance.

Q: CAN YOU TELL ME ABOUT USING ATHLETES AS INSTRUCTORS?

The first thing we did to shake up our education program was to look at who was delivering our face-to-face sessions. Historically, our presenters were the same people who were conducting testing missions on the athletes, and although they knew the anti-doping testing process inside and out, very few had the experience of actually being the elite athlete on the other side of a test and some of the anxieties that can come from being an athlete bound by anti-doping rules.

So instead, we hired a new cohort of athletes to be our education presenters. These were either current or former athletes who had competed at a national level or above and had lived experience of things like having to check their medications, making decisions about supplements, managing injury recovery, or peeing in a cup in front of someone as part of the testing process.

It created a new connection between the athletes in the classes to know that the instructors really understood what their situations were like and could empathize with them. The presenters also role-modeled the positive behaviors we wanted other athletes to do.

Q: HOW DID YOU USE TECHNOLOGY TO SUPPORT ATHLETES?

In 2018, we developed a new app to help athletes make informed decisions about what supplement they should take. At this time, we were having between 10 and 17 athletes test positive from contaminated supplements each year.

One of the first people we reached out to get feedback on the app was an athlete who had received a nine-month ban from a supplement [that she hadn't known contained a banned substance].

Her feedback was, "I think this is an absolutely brilliant idea. Even though it won't guarantee a product is 100% safe, it will certainly assist athletes to make an informed decision in the minefield that is supplements…. It is great to see the lengths ASADA is going to assist athletes…. If I could prevent just one athlete from going through what I did, it would be worth it."

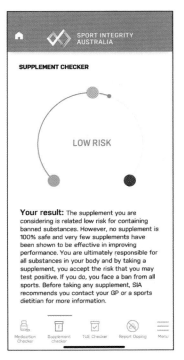

We launched the app at the 2018 Commonwealth Games on the Gold Coast and set up an outreach tent in the middle of the athlete village. There we could chat to athletes all day, walk them through the app and our other education products, and get their feedback. As a government organization whose reputation was seen as "catching athletes," we found athlete's expectations of us were pretty low. My favorite piece of feedback that we received from an athlete at the Games was, "This app is surprisingly not ****!"

When we first released the app, we had hoped it would be downloaded 1,000 times—essentially by our elite athletes representing Australia at the Olympics or Commonwealth Games. We had 8,000 downloads in the first year—eclipsing anything we ever hoped for, and now, more than 80,000 athletes have downloaded it, showing it has reached far more athletes than just the elite level.

Q: HOW DO YOU GET FEEDBACK FROM ATHLETES?
We now get athlete feedback in a range of different ways.

Because we use athletes to present our education sessions, they get to see the content before it is delivered. They will work with us to make it more relatable if we need. They also feed ideas into us on what we need to educate on, based on their own athlete experiences or what they are seeing in the community.

We have a formal Athlete Advisory Group who we run our new education products by before publishing for feedback. Again, we also seek ideas from them on what we need to be doing better.

We run education sessions with every athlete who has received a sanction, before they return to sport. These are great opportunities to hear from people who have broken the rules to find out what we could have done differently in our education programs to stop what happened to them. We also get to learn about their experiences through the legal system and understand what we can do better as an agency. I can't overstate how valuable it is speaking to people who have made poor decisions or gotten accidentally caught out before. Some of these athletes also work with us in an ongoing capacity in education.

Q: HOW DO YOU HELP ATHLETES PREPARE FOR THE STRESSFUL EXPERIENCE OF GETTING TESTED?

In many ways, a lot of our education products are designed to let people experience anti-doping in a safe environment before they come across it in real life, so we can try to reduce the risk of them making a mistake during the process or instill the behaviors that we want to see in more gray scenarios.

For example, we know that testing is an incredibly confronting experience. These athletes are required to stand with their pants around their knees and shirts up to their chest to provide a urine sample. Some athlete's first get tested as 16-year-olds—you can imagine how daunting this could be. There are also a bunch of rules around the testing process, and if an athlete breaks one (for example, leaving a test early, or trying to get out of a test), they could face a ban of four years. So the intent of our Doping Control VR is to let young athletes live through a test in a safe environment, where they learn everything that is going to happen in a test, without any anxiety or stress. It means when they get to doing their first test, they are a little less anxious, a lot more informed, and more likely to follow the process and avoid any mistakes.

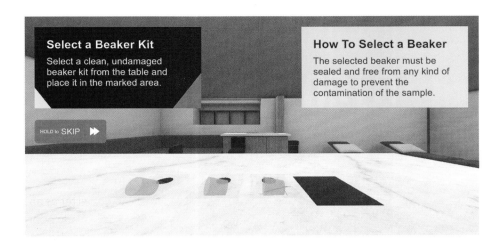

Likewise, our VR Ethical Decision Making experience and theatre sports sessions put athletes in confronting situations where they have to make difficult decisions based on their ethics and morals. In these experiences, they get to practice those decisions, as well as see what the consequences of those decisions are. We're giving them a training ground for decision-making.

Q: WHY IS IT IMPORTANT THAT ATHLETES HEAR FROM THEIR PEERS?

There's no doubt that athletes are more likely to listen to their peers than they are to a government organization. For that reason, we try to use the athlete voice in everything we do.

It starts with the athlete presenters, but then we also use stories from sanctioned athletes, which we use in our online and F2F sessions (athlete stories can be viewed on the Sports Integrity Australia YouTube channel).

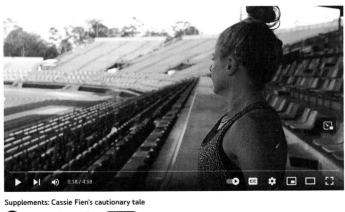

Supplements: Cassie Fien's cautionary tale

In our education, it's all well and good for us to tell athletes that they will face a four-year ban from sport. But sanctioned athletes have told us that reading those words on a page, or seeing them on a slide, is completely different to actually having to live through that experience.

Sanctioned athletes have the unique ability to bring to life what an anti-doping rule violation actually means for an athlete. They lose their identity, which is so wrapped up in being an athlete. They have to face the disappointment of their parents. Exclusion from their friends. They can't even play social golf or social netball on the weekend. It takes a huge toll.

Q: HOW DO YOU USE THEATRE SPORTS TO PRACTICE REAL SCENARIOS?

Of course, we can't use sanctioned athletes all the time, which is where the theatre sports program comes in. Here we work with an agency called Think About It (https://www.thinkaboutitgroup.com/), who use professional actors to create scenarios where participants can role-play confronting situations and then facilitate courageous conversations about why people respond in different ways.

For our audiences, we worked with Think About It to create real-life anti-doping scenarios that athletes might find themselves in. The actors then bring audience participants on stage and re-enact the scenario, driven by the responses of the participants.

In one scene, athletes are brought on stage to learn that one of their teammates (an actor) is possibly doping. The athletes then have to talk among themselves about whether they will report the doping or not. The actors serve as the opposite sides of the argument—challenging and stoking different viewpoints. At the end of the scene, we help talk to athletes about their obligations to report and what happens if they don't—for example, the whole team could lose their medals and sponsorship if the athlete is caught doping.

In another scene, athletes are brought on stage to find out they are about to appear on a national TV talk show to discuss one of their teammates who has just tested positive. The actors challenge their empathy (or lack of) and the team's reputation to highlight the consequences of doping going far beyond just an individual person.

One of the most powerful scenes doesn't involve participants at all—it is a monologue delivered by an actor, who is talking about their experience testing positive. It is incredibly powerful. I've seen audience members get teary, and I've seen other audience members not even believe it was an actor; they thought it was a real sanctioned athlete speaking to them! We built this scene with Think About It based on actual sanctioned athlete testimonials and interviews, so it is super realistic. It drives home how a poor decision can be made, how they might start with one small decision and then snowball, and the consequences not only for them but on their family, their sport, their teammates, and their day-to-day lives.

This technique lets athletes live real anti-doping scenarios, without the risk of real-life consequences. It's like a training ground to think ethically about how they might respond to certain situations and see the consequences play out in front of them.

The group (Think About It) specializes in this area of elite athlete training and also looks at other issues in sport and society more broadly—like gambling, sexual misconduct, racism, homophobia, and domestic violence—and works with other Australian sporting organizations, too.

One key point: We're not here to educate for the sake of it. We want Australian sport to be safe and fair, and we can only achieve that if people are behaving in ways that are safe and fair.

Q: WHAT ARE SOME OF THE OUTCOMES YOU'VE SEEN?

In 2016, we had 17 athletes test positive from supplements. In 2020–2021, we had zero. That's about $400,000 ASD saved every year in science, legal, and investigation costs. And we've seen a shift in the reputation of the agency from being here to punish athletes to now being here to help—to really focusing on helping athletes. ▪

PROJECT 4: A DIGITAL APP FOR BECOMEANEX.ORG (PART OF THE TRUTH INITIATIVE)

Who: Dustin DiTommaso is the Chief Design Officer and Head of Product at meQuilibrium and also the founder of the Behavior Change Practice Mad*Pow.

What: Creating a digital app for BecomeAnEx.org, which is part of the Truth Initiative (the largest non-profit public health organization dedicated to helping people quit tobacco).

Q: CAN YOU DESCRIBE THE PROJECT?

So the project was one I worked on at Mad*Pow, creating a digital app for BecomeAnEx.org, which is part of the Truth Initiative. The Truth Initiative does a lot of public health campaigns and looks to raise awareness and change beliefs around smoking, but they also have Become An Ex, which is a very specific and dedicated intervention for smoking cessation that they built in partnership with The Mayo Clinic Nicotine Dependence Center.

The project was to take what was a sort of 1990s-ish, older, very bare bones website with some tools and information on smoking and use their expertise and what had been learned from the researchers to create a state-of-the-art digital intervention for smoking cessation for both mobile and web. The project targeted adult smokers and was specifically about combustible tobacco cessation (e.g., cigarettes). Vaping was just kind of coming up, so vaping interventions followed afterward.

Q: HOW DID YOU DO RESEARCH FOR THE PROJECT?

There was already excellent research around how we can help people quit and stay quit, but not a ton [of research] at that time or trials on digital apps for smoking cessation. So there were lots of opportunities. From a research perspective, we are always going in and consuming the literature that's out there for smoking cessation. We go to the evidence, we go to the scientific journals, we do just a bit shy of systematic reviews. We dig in and do literature reviews to understand again, either in digital or in other kinds of treatments, what works [and] what doesn't work.

Then you think about where you want to ask more questions about the things you want to validate directly to your population. So in our case, the next step is also to understand smokers and get their firsthand experiences with trying to quit using any kind of quit aids, understanding what they've tried, what might have worked. We talked to both successful folks and folks who struggled and talked to people who may have used a digital program as well.

We also looked at how they use other kinds of digital products like step trackers or fitness apps. We asked when they use them, what they find helpful, what they find incredibly annoying.

We would do interviews and then code them back to the models we were working with, like COM-B or The Transtheoretical Model.

Coding Interviews

Dustin describes coding interviews. There are many ways to do this, but it can be as simple as reading through an interview transcript and highlighting or tagging items that relate to COM-B items or motivational elements. Then you can gather up comments related to different COM-B items and use that to help identify strategies and behavior-change techniques.

> For example:
>
> *I was doing really well for the first few weeks. I didn't even think about smoking. But then, one day,* **I was really stressed out at work** *(tag: physical environment, emotional cue).* **I went out for a break, and I saw a coworker smoking** *(tag: physical/social environment).* **I started to crave a cigarette** *really badly (tag: automatic motivation). I told myself that I could just have one cigarette, but I knew that if I did, I would start smoking again. I held out a few more days, but then* **the feeling just overwhelmed me** *(tag: automatic motivation, lack of agency) and I started again.*

Q: HOW WOULD YOU IDENTIFY USERS TO TALK TO?

Being a consultant, the folks who we're developing interventions for often, but not always, have a market or a population that they are dealing with that we usually tap into. Truth.org has a huge community of either smokers or successfully quit smokers that rally around, so we were able to talk to some of them. We also try to bolster sort of that direct response by getting our own population as well. We always try to get outside and talk to an audience that's not already familiar with The Truth Initiative. We do that by using third-party recruiters. There are a number of research recruiters from marketing all the way down to very specific niches like recruiters who very specifically focus on health or on digital products, websites, or technology. So we have a pool of recruiting agencies that that we work with. We then create a screener of the populations we want to talk to, and the agencies recruit those people.

Q: HOW DID THE DESIGN PROCESS WORK?

What we really wanted to do was get away from a very static didactic experience of an educational-based website and get to a more dynamic experience. We want to meet you where you are on what we think of as the quit journey, making that dynamic from deciding to quit, right: I've made a decision, I think I want to quit, or, I'm not sure I want to quit yet. If you are not ready yet, we can have information provision—inform them what the pros and cons to quitting can be, and so on. We want to help move you from there to deciding to quit, but if that's where you are, great.

Then, when you identify you are preparing to quit, we'll support that. Here's what you need to do to prepare to quit: set your day, get ready to crush your cigarettes, tell all your friends and family in advance that you are prepared to quit. Then, we want to keep that dynamic, and on your quit day, we double down on motivational support or helping you get access to quit aids.

Q: HOW DO YOU DO DESIGN AND PROTOTYPING?

First, we do usability testing of the intervention. If a person can't create an account or can't set the quit date or can't input how they're feeling or input what their triggers might be, then the intervention is never going to be successful. So we need to make sure that just from a design standpoint, that it is usable for each and every individual who wants to use it. We also want to make sure that the content is understandable—that the people can understand the terms, the instructions, the directions, and that the voice and tone feels right for our audience. We don't want it to feel like we're shouting at you or blaming you. It should feel supportive.

We get those in front of people in a wireframe form of black-and-white, low-fidelity, general layout, general functionality, with the buttons in the places that we want them and the language what we believe is the right language. We can test those low-fidelity designs and get them in front of a dozen or so folks—a small sample—make some changes; we can do that again a second time. And then continue that pattern: get a small sample, test some things, design a bigger chunk, and continue to test in either wireframe format or in a prototype.

Then they can in earnest try to use the app when maybe you've got 50 to 60% of your intervention working. Then you can see how they use it outside of the lab.

We understand that digital products are a series of two-way conversations: inputs and outputs. You can capture and measure sort of all the behavioral data, like did they respond to a notification? Did they set a quit date? Are they setting up triggers? Are they responding to the messages based on the triggers over that course of a week? You can also have them journal on the side as well—take a few minutes to give a bit more context around when they're using it, how they feel about it, is it working for them, and so on.

You pair that response with the digital data over the course of the study, and then you can also learn if people abandon it, and if they don't use it, or they're not using it, or they use it the first day, but they never came back, or they use it very here and there. We want to try to understand why, as well. What happened in between? And so you capture that data, learn from that data, and then you do follow-up interviews as well to understand their experience.

So it's test, learn, adapt, test, learn, adapt, iterate, iterate, iterate, each cycle, again, everything gets crisper, clearer, more confident, so on and so forth. But the intent is to increase confidence and reduce risk that we're building the right thing that people will use, and we believe is going to be effective.

Q: WHAT WERE SOME OF THE OUTCOMES?

Research is ongoing, but some of the data we collected included a 32% increase in the behavior of setting a quit date, a 43% increase in the behavior of reflecting on personal reasons for quitting and entering them into a user profile in order to strengthen motivational resources, and a 27% increase in tracking cigarette usage to identify triggers and patterns of use and engage in targeted strategies to counter those patterns increased. ▤

PROJECT 5: HARNESS HERO AND BEHAVIOR-CHANGE GAMES

Project: Behavior Change Games

Who: Brian Kaleida, CEO of Sigma Games, LLC

What: I first became familiar with Harness Hero during a construction safety project, but Simcoach Games has done well over 100 games across different industries like construction, safety, workforce development, education, and healthcare. In Harness Hero, the video game engages players in the key decisions of using a fall arrest system. At each step in the game, the player chooses where to anchor, what anchorage device to use, how to set up the harness, what connection device to use, and so on.

   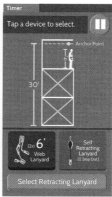

Q: CAN YOU TELL ME ABOUT SIMCOACH GAMES?

Simcoach Games designs and develops transformational and educational games that accelerate learning, improve decision-making, and positively change behaviors. Simcoach has developed hundreds of games that give players personal and safe places to assess skills, determine aptitudes, explore interests, and practice making decisions that lead to the best outcomes. We have developed games for sectors such as healthcare, behavioral and mental health, workforce development, and education/training.

Q: HOW DO YOU DO TESTING AND EVALUATION WITH YOUR GAMES?

Generally, we make sure to test our games in multiple ways, including internal testing, testing with the subject matter experts, and playtesting with the target audience.

Specific to Harness Hero, the team went to the training facility to test with the subject matter experts as part of the design and development process.

Our basic premise is to always incorporate play testing as quickly as we can into the process and with multiple constituents.

Using a different example, we are currently working on behavioral health games to support individuals with autism. We are working with a partner company that provides behavioral health services. We integrated their clinical director and clinicians into the design process from the start. The testing and evaluation process for those games included early clinician feedback, as early as the game prototypes. We also held "game nights," inviting parents and kids into their clinic to playtest early versions of the games. As we continued to develop the games, we expanded our testing into schools and special education departments. We conducted playtest sessions with the students, teachers, and support staff to get feedback on the games in the classroom environment.

It is important to us that the games be both engaging and effective. Evaluating the games for efficacy is challenging, especially over a longer time period. We have a number of different ways that we are exploring efficacy. Several of our games in healthcare have been included in clinical trials in partnership with academic institutions. While this is an effective way to explore the effectiveness of a game, it is a very involved process. We have also developed a data collection process, which we integrate into our games. This allows us to collect game-play data, including data critical to evaluating progress relevant to skills, behaviors, and learning objectives. We have a team that focuses on analyzing that data and working with other partners to help identify progress and outcomes.

Q: A LOT OF LEARNING GAMES HAVE LOOKED "GAMELIKE" WITHOUT BEING PARTICULARLY FUN OR ARE JUST TRIVIA GAMES. WHAT DO YOU DO IN YOUR DESIGN APPROACH TO PRODUCE ACTUAL BEHAVIORAL RESULTS?

As part of our process, Simcoach partners with subject matter experts and integrates them into our design approach. This integration is throughout the entire effort, including initial meetings, reviews of incremental builds, and playtesting. The team also spends a significant amount of time researching the subject matter, as well as spending time in the environment, whatever that may be for that particular game. This approach requires the team to invest a significant amount of time to understanding behaviors and outcomes, while also focusing on how to create a fun and engaging game to focus on the behaviors and results.

I feel that behavior-based games, or transformational games, are much more challenging to design and develop than games intended solely for entertainment. As you indicated, the games need to produce results, and also need to be engaging and fun to play, without reverting to puzzles or trivia games. To do so, the team focuses on environment, character design, art style, and the mechanics of the game that directly relate to the important behaviors. These include the decisions made within the game and the consequences of those decisions, as well as a number of other behavioral factors.

We also feel that designing for agency is essential, where the game provides a safe space for the player to discover, explore, and experiment, and where the game provides feedback on the decisions that the player has made.

Specific to Harness Hero, the team spent time at the training facilities where they teach harness safety and with the trainers. They spent time with the physical items that needed to be inspected to understand what to look for with each item. They reviewed the behaviors the game needed to teach: going through a checklist, making sure that you did not skip any of the steps, focusing on each item one at a time, eliminating distractions while you focused on that item, and making decisions based on what would keep you safe. And to understand the consequences of those decisions, which ultimately made the game fun to play.

Q: ISN'T IT ACTUALLY MUCH HARDER TO KEEP SOMETHING SIMPLE RATHER THAN LETTING IT GET OVERCOMPLICATED?

The team continually references this goal within the design process to ensure that they are focusing on the core objectives and not allowing the game to become overly complicated. Keeping things simple is a challenge. When you are in early design meetings, everybody gets excited, and you have a long list of learning objectives.

While one approach is to reduce the learning objectives to the three to five things that are most important, another way that we look at this is to ask if we should be considering multiple games. It may be that all of the learning objectives are important, but they should not all be included in the same game but rather be in a collection or series of games, each dedicated to a specific set of skills.

With Harness Hero, the team shared that they worked very hard to maintain the simplicity of this game. The flow of the game is an interactive instruction manual. The visuals in the game support the need to focus on the subject at hand. The mechanics in the game are very simple, so as to not distract the players as they consider their decisions. The team spent a lot of time with all of the physical items that are featured in the game, to ensure that the game was realistic. The result is a simple game, yes, and also one that is intuitive, reflects real-world decisions, and is fun to play.

Q: HERE'S ONE THING I'VE ALWAYS WANTED TO KNOW ABOUT HARNESS HERO. DID YOU EVER GET ANY PUSHBACK ABOUT ANYTHING, LIKE PUSHING THE CRASH TEST FIGURE TO DEATH OR INJURY OFF OF THE HARNESS SETUP?

I spoke with the team, and they shared that there was not any pushback on this; everyone loved this concept the first time they experienced it in the game. The team purposefully designed a character that was not realistic; a character patterned off of a crash-test dummy. Because the character was not realistic, they could include this action in the game to add an element of fun to a very serious topic. This is one of the benefits of a game, where the player is able to see the consequences of their choices in a way that you can't accomplish with traditional forms of training. And everyone remembers this about the game and comments on it, so it has left a lasting impression.

Q: THE GAME REALLY BALANCED THOSE THINGS WELL. ANYTHING ELSE?

Thank you for your comments and positive feedback on the game. I wanted to use this opportunity to recognize the team that designed and developed the game, who deserve the credit for all of the great results: Adam Chizmar, Garrett Kimball, Sara Will, and Anthony Zabiegalski. ■

PROJECT 6: PROJECT VALOR—SOCIAL MEDIA MARKETING TO PROMOTE VIRTUAL HIV CONSULTATION AND REFERRAL

Who: Manya Dotson, director, Demand Generation and Applied Design Thinking at Jhpiego (a nonprofit organization for international health affiliated with Johns Hopkins University)

What: VALOR Nigeria is a program that uses private-sector-style social media marketing to promote a virtual HIV consultation and referral service implemented through WhatsApp to increase men's participation in HIV screening and treatment.

NOTE: The VALOR activities described in this interview were made possible with support from the U.S. President's Emergency Plan for AIDS Relief, through the United States Agency for International Development–funded RISE program, under the terms of the cooperative agreement 7200AA19CA00003. The contents are the responsibility of the author and do not necessarily reflect the views of USAID or the United States Government.

Q: TELL ME ABOUT THE IMPETUS FOR THE PROJECT.

Getting adult men into health services—and specifically HIV testing—can be very difficult. These problems are well-documented and researched.

When we're looking at our [HIV] testing numbers, in many countries, there is a big gap between the number of men getting tested for the first time and the number of women. We get women in for healthcare services a lot more frequently than men. Men tend to use their female partner's test result as a proxy for their own status.

Q: WHAT ARE SOME OF THE BARRIERS TO MEN'S HEALTHCARE?

The basic thing is that norms of masculinity don't allow men to get vulnerable. And it doesn't help that many healthcare spaces feel like "women's spaces." Men think, "This just doesn't feel like it's for me. It feels like I walk in and there's a lot of women there. I'm going to be judged for sure for being there."

When we are trying to run efficient public health initiatives, we don't need *all men* to come in. We want those who are more likely to have acquired HIV. Unfortunately, men who do come for testing tend to be men who have been tested before and/or men who are pretty sure that they're not HIV positive. The men who are at risk—they know that they're at risk, and they're the very ones who are not getting tested because they are afraid. Even worse, they are lonely in their fear.

Through a series of human-centered design workshops in Malawi and Zambia, we realized that so much of the messaging that we create for men has shame hidden inside of it. People were telling us that "it takes courage to get tested" because HIV is often portrayed as a scary, catastrophic disease.

We know men experience fear of stigma, fear of discrimination, and fear of social consequences. Men look at that mountain of fear and conclude that they can't face an HIV test that might open the door to all of those scary things they anticipate. They weren't getting tested because they didn't feel like they had the courage to go down the entire path of managing a positive diagnosis.

So we started thinking about how to break down the journey of getting a test into tiny manageable steps. You don't have to find the courage to manage every aspect of an HIV diagnosis all at once; you just need to find the courage to do the next small thing.

Q: HOW DID THOSE WORKSHOPS INFORM DESIGN?

We aren't the only public health–implementing agency struggling with getting men connected with services. So, Jhpiego had insights that came out of HCD design sprints focused on men in Malawi and Zambia. And there were also great insights that came out of work done through the PMM project (the Prevention Market Manager—a comprehensive, collaborative project to accelerate the introduction of HIV prevention products funded by the Bill & Melinda Gates Foundation).

One of those insights was that we should think about approaching HIV prevention in a trauma-informed way. A lot of people in Southern Africa who lived in high-risk communities and situations remember HIV when it was a terrifying disease and have deep trauma associated with it. You hear, "Oh, all the old communication used to be about fear." And that's true, but it's not just that the communication was about fear, it was that people had a lived experience with beloved family members or friends dying of AIDS.

The second thing is that men have good reasons to think that HIV care and treatment is no picnic. They've heard that suddenly you're going to have to adopt a hyper-healthy lifestyle. And that those drugs—they remember their family members taking drugs all day long. And that those drugs caused yucky side effects and make you feel unwell. You may have to stop drinking, too. Basically, the fun stops here! That can be that undertone to public health communication. Just imagine if I said to you "You're going to lose everything about your life that's enjoyable. Your relationship is going to be compromised. Your partner's suddenly going to feel differently about you than they did before. You're not going to be able to enjoy yourself in the ways that are your favorite ways to hang out with friends. And you're going to be totally isolated."

People would rather be dead than be isolated. Ok, so you're telling me I could die? Isolation is worse than death, and it's worse having a life where I can no longer enjoy anything.

Q: HOW DID YOU DO RESEARCH AND DESIGN?

We did a series of very classic design exercises, including a client's journey map which was very revealing. The in-person work in Zambia and Malawi dovetailed into a bigger opportunity in Nigeria during COVID, which was tricky! Our team spent three months facilitating an all-virtual human-centered design process: holding consultations, mocking up social media posts, and organizing WhatsApp focus groups to have these conversations.

One thing we saw was that in our current system, we don't tell people considering HIV testing anything about positive living. We don't tell them that living with a positive diagnosis is not that big a deal. We don't tell them that the drugs are MUCH easier. You don't have to stop drinking. Nothing really changes. We don't talk about any of that until *after* you've gotten a positive test.

Well, considering the mountain of fear before the test, that reassurance is pretty late. Maybe we didn't want to waste those resources on everybody. You can see how the public health decision would be made about cost effectiveness. But if you're not telling anyone any of that until after they test positive, then they are going to be much more anxious about getting tested.

Q: WHAT MESSAGE WERE MEN HEARING?

Another thing that we realized is that a lot of advertising or persuasive messaging focusing on men is looking to shame them in some way. It was about competition, or what you needed to do to be a good man, or a good protector of your family, blah, blah, blah.

It's conditional, right? You'll be a really good man IF you get tested, you'll be a responsible partner WHEN you get tested. None of it was "you're a good man NOW." You're ALREADY doing your absolute best to be the best man that you know how to be. The empathetic mindset of human-centered design helped us to see how much men are craving affirmation for who they are now...and how they're really not getting it anywhere.

Q: WHAT THEMES EMERGED?

Fear and courage, that is what kept coming up. Fear and courage. Fear and courage. We knew from Malawi and Zambia that fear and courage were big.

We were talking about this in Malawi and listening to folks living with HIV talk about their journeys and bam we had a flash of insight: At the beginning of the testing process, people feel like they have to summon the courage for an entire lifetime journey with HIV. It's very hard to imagine how it's going to end up OK. There is no sense of pathway. It's like "I have to jump from here all the way over there." We wanted to change that inner narrative to: "I don't need the courage for the entire thing, I just need the courage for the next step."

That was a breakthrough. When we connected that insight with the insight about men craving affirmation and the notion of breaking down a big journey into tiny steps, we suddenly had a new creative direction to explore. A man doesn't have to manufacture new or different courage for HIV-testing. Every Nigerian man has been through tough things and has demonstrated incredible resiliency and courage and flexibility and resourcefulness. You just have to connect with the courageous man you ALREADY ARE. When you remember who you are, you definitely have the courage to take a very small next step. That step is to simply click here (in the Facebook ad) and open up a WhatsApp conversation. At the other end of that conversation is a compassionate, affirming, and nonjudging person who believes in you. Your guide is already impressed by the courage you displayed in reaching out. Your guide knows you have the courage to take the next small step.

Q: WHAT ELSE WAS CRITICAL?

We tell people, "You should just want this, if you're a good person," or "You should want to be healthy." But what we are absolutely failing to do is help people see clearly how their life will be BETTER. We fail to create a path where men are supported to create an achievable plan that feels doable. A path where success is celebrated all along the way.

Q: HOW DID YOU DESIGN THAT PATHWAY?

Our solution ends up being a journey where at every step we are reminding men of who they are, and we are using the last step as proof that they can do the next step. It's celebration along the way. You don't want people completely devastated or overwhelmed by how far there is to go.

So we focus on just the next step. It's only the next step. And then the next little step. And we worked on lowering the barriers to each of those next steps. (For example, your WhatsApp guide will help you find a convenient place to get tested.) And then at each step, we remind the person of who they are, how great they are, and celebrate how far they've already come.

You've already done the hardest thing, which was reaching out and saying the most courageous word in the English language, which is "help." You being here tells me the kind of man that you are.

Have you ever seen advertising like this for men? This is not how we usually advertise to men.

Q: HOW DID YOU PROTOTYPE AND GET FEEDBACK ON IDEAS?

This work in Nigeria was done during COVID, which was actually brilliant because COVID allowed for services outside of the health facility, and it forced us all to get more functional virtually.

We started with a set of prototypes. I used Canva Pro, which costs very little. You get access to all of the stock imagery you need, as well as attractive design templates.

We were not looking to validate those prototypes; we were prototyping to learn. We got men from all over Nigeria who would be potential clients, including some who are living with HIV, so that we could make sure that we weren't doing anything that was insensitive. We wanted to make sure that what we were doing was not ever creating tension between folks who are positive and folks who are not positive.

And then we used online WhatsApp groups as what I'd call, maybe, co-design advisory committees. They really weren't focus groups. We consented everyone in at the beginning and said, "Hey, this is the purpose of these conversations. This is how we're going to be using what we learn. Your information will never be shared. We may download these and run statistical analyses of these chats. If ever you're uncomfortable, just don't answer; opt out."

And then we gave people lots of different options on how they could interact with us. They could record their voice and send a voice text if it was too much to type. We did some discussions synchronously, where we asked people to get on WhatsApp at the same time to discuss things, and we would have a joint conversation.

We also asked men to respond asynchronously to one-off questions as they came up during the design process. We gave guys airtime (cellphone minutes or phone data bundles), more than they would need, as both an incentive and just to make sure that it was easy for them to participate. We didn't want it to cost them anything to participate.

I loved the WhatsApp advisory group format. There were lots of interesting things that happened using that medium. Everyone was anonymous on WhatsApp, which was great. They weren't having to say anything face to face with other men. It was side by side. They didn't know each other. Sometimes a man would reach out to one of our team members on the side to go deeper or get more vulnerable. That was always fascinating.

As we talked about courage, we asked, "what does it look like to be cared about? What does it feel like to be cared about? How do people signal that you're cared about? What makes you feel cared about? What makes you feel seen, courageous, encouraged, cared about?" It was very different from what they were used to hearing, and they really opened up.

Q: WHAT DID YOU LEARN FROM THE WHATSAPP GROUP?

Something that I've come to understand, and I've talked with about this with some of my male friends, is how men are constantly shamed and how impossible it feels to be a good man.

How do you even be a good man? You're getting these mixed messages that you should be like this, but don't be like this and don't be like that. And never be condescending, but don't be stupid, and don't mansplain. There are a million ways to come up short, and no way to thread the needle of being a good man. It feels impossible.

Men rarely get told they are already loved and worthy. Advertising around HIV is about standing up, being a man, protecting others. They see that, and then they shut down and feel ashamed. They're like, "I haven't gotten tested yet, so I'm not that guy. I'm not that guy who's a great protector or always does the right thing." And then they're also just so ashamed of being afraid. There's so much loneliness in the fear that they are feeling.

So one of my favorite moments on WhatsApp was when we showed them a picture. I was trying to translate stories that they were telling into images that illustrated these nuanced concepts of courage. One of the questions we asked our guys to explore was telling about a time that they felt valorous. They love the word *valor*, by the way.

We ended up naming the thing VALOR because it acknowledges that it's hard and it implies that you've already conquered. So we were trying to figure out images to represent the idea of valor. And they said maybe valor looks like a boxer winning his match. We tried an image of a coach holding up a boxer's arm in victory. Together they've overcome this really tough thing and it was a battle and so on.

But no, that was not it, they told us, for lots of reasons. Number one, this is reinforcing all of these gender stereotypes about having to be strong and tough. Number two, okay, this is victory. But victory isn't the same as valor. They guys said, "This is not what courage looks like." And we said, "Okay, what does courage look like?" And one of the guys says this is what courage looks like and...

....he sends a meme of two teddy bears hugging.

And, oh, that was insight right there. That was something. It was vulnerable to send it. And it was courageous vulnerability. Courage is somebody being with you. With you. Loving you. Seeing you. Courage is having someone admiring you and walking together with you and believing in you as you are.

Every image changed after that. And the tone changed. So it's still heroic, but the entire campaign is everyday guys being loved by their people. It's images of her saying yes to the engagement moment, or his people holding him, looking up at him with admiration and pride. Saying this is my man. My valorous man. Triangulating all of those nuggets of understanding changed everything and helped us to land a simple but beautiful and resonant concept.

And then the Nigerian creative agency we were working with got it, and then everyone got it. Something just shifted in our team. When they got it, they were like, we love him. We love our men. And our entire service is about communicating, "Bro, you're awesome. We love you. Get in here. You are worthy of a great, valorous life." I haven't seen anything quite like it in the U.S., but I think it would work here too, though it would need to be co-created for sure.

We rolled it out on Facebook and Instagram. It's called Valor Nigeria. And we've seen the gender balance has gone from it being about a third of new testers being men to just less than half.

Q: WHAT IS THE EXPERIENCE LIKE?

So now what we do is send Facebook ads out—paid Facebook advertisements—to people in and around the catchment areas where services are available.

And on the app, the call to action is, "Click here to talk to a VIP guide on WhatsApp, and just say hi."

When they're greeted by the guide, the message is "Hey! I'm so glad you're here. Welcome to Valor. You're the VIP. How can I be of service to you?" And the guy says "Ugh. I don't know. I have questions."

And the guide responds, "You know what, man, everyone has questions. Everyone feels the way that you're feeling. You are not alone. But the fact that you're here already tells me that you're one in a million." Affirmation, admiration, affirmation, admiration, affirmation. Zero judgment, zero judgment. Encouragement.

Our online coaches are case managers, so they actually really know what it means to be HIV positive. They're not lying to anyone about it. And they're credible, right? They say, "Hey, I am working right now with 50 guys who are all living their best life with HIV. And I'm here to tell you, man, it's one pill a day. It's not what it was before."

The HIV community is obsessed right now with the message U=U. They think that this is catchy. It stands for "undetectable means untransmissable." Which is okay and true. But that's three levels up from what it means, which is, "You don't have to worry about being a danger to anybody that you love. Your sex life doesn't really have to change. You're not going to lose your sex life. There's not a lot of side effects or drug interactions. You know what? You can still go to the bar—not a big deal. It's an easy-to-adhere-to regimen. One pill a day. One pill a day. No side effects or very few side effects. You don't have to change anything about your diet or what you're drinking or anything else. You get to keep what matters."

Q: WHAT RESULTS ARE YOU SEEING?

We encourage the really colloquial way of talking, to just connect. In the pilot, some guys agreed to get tested right from that first conversation. A lot of others, when we followed up with them, three months later, had gone and gotten tested, even though they weren't referred directly from us.

The ads are simple. Very matter of fact. They're not polished at all. And there's almost a DIY feel about them. Authenticity is at a premium right now, so it tracks. You can see the ads on the program Instagram feed at https://www.instagram.com/ValorNigeria/.

I had a feeling VALOR was going to work. The day we got the results of our pilot, we were on cloud nine. First, we had more men than ever before coming in for testing. Of all of the men who came in to get tested for the first time, about half had a Facebook account. Literally every man who had a Facebook account had seen a VALOR ad. And of those who had seen the ad, more than 85% said the ad was the reason they came in for testing.

At a much more intimate level, most of the guys in our WhatsApp group ended up getting tested too. One had the courage to reach out privately and tell me that his result was positive. When I thanked him for the courage it took to tell me, he said he wasn't afraid because he knew all he had to do was find the courage to take the next step. If that Isn't valor, I don't know what is. ■

CONCLUSION

(IN WHICH WE WRAP THIS UP SO YOU CAN GET STARTED)

I'm really glad the last significant piece of content in the last chapter is the story from Manya, because if there's any message I want to send you off with, it's this:

> To be effective, any behavior-change design must be grounded in compassion and empathy and connection with the people you are designing for (or with).

We've spent a lot of time in this book on models, processes, and categorizations. And I do believe those things are useful tools, and I hope they are helpful. But if I gave you the idea that behavior change is just a formula to implement, then I've failed you.

People are complex, and behavior is complex, so any tool or model should only be a starting place and should be part of an experiment where you gather data, talk to the people who are part of it, and adjust, adjust, adjust. If you are reading this book, it's likely because you care enough to want to make something better. Thank you for all that you do.

The title of this book is *Talk to the Elephant,* but please remember that doesn't mean that you should talk AT the elephant. The elephant isn't dumb and irrational; it's vital and valuable and recognizes what is most important in the world, including our connection to others.

We are all our elephants, and we need to take care of ourselves and each other.

Thank you,

Julie

NOTE: A portion of the proceeds from this book will go to support elephant preservation organizations.

INDEX

W–Z